Women and Work in Ru
1880–1930

KT-447-006

ook is to be returned on or before
e last date stamped below.

WOMEN AND MEN IN HISTORY

This series, published for students, scholars and interested general readers, will tackle themes in gender history from the early medieval period through to the present day. Gender issues are now an integral part of all history courses and yet many traditional text books do not reflect this change. Much exciting work is now being done to redress the gender imbalances of the past, and we hope that these books will make their own substantial contribution to that process. This is an open-ended series, which means that many new titles can be included. We hope that these will both synthesise and shape future developments in gender studies.

The General Editors of the series are *Patricia Skinner* (University of Southampton) for the medieval period; *Pamela Sharpe* (University of Bristol) for the early modern period; and *Margaret Walsh* (University of Nottingham) for the modern period.

Published books:

Gender, Church, and State in Early Modern Germany:
    Essays by Merry E. Wiesner
Merry E. Wiesner

Gender and Society in Renaissance Italy
Judith C. Brown and Robert C. Davis (eds)

Women and Work in Russia, 1880–1930:
    A Study in Continuity through Change
Jane McDermid and Anna Hillyar

Women and Work in Russia 1880–1930

A Study in Continuity through Change

JANE MCDERMID AND ANNA HILLYAR

Longman
London and New York

Addison Wesley Longman Limited
Edinburgh Gate,
Harlow, Essex CM20 2JE, United Kingdom
and Associated Companies throughout the world.

*Published in the United States of America
by Addison Wesley Longman, New York.*

© Addison Wesley Longman Limited 1998

First published 1998

ISBN 0–582–27987–9 CSD
ISBN 0–582–27986–0 PPR

British Library Cataloguing in Publication Data
A catalogue record for this title is
available from the British Library

Library of Congress Cataloging-in-Publication Data
A catalog entry for this book is
available from the Library of Congress

Set by 35 in 10/12pt Baskerville
Produced by Longman Singapore Publishers (Pte) Ltd.
Printed in Singapore

Contents

List of Tables

Acknowledgements

This book would not have been possible without the dedicated work of librarians in a number of institutions and countries, and in particular those who work in the inter-library loan service. Staff at the Bodleian library in Oxford, the library of the School of Slavonic and East European Studies at London University, the Russian State library in Moscow, the Saltykov-Shchedrin library in St. Petersburg, and Tomsk University library were generous with their time and expertise. Special thanks is owed to Dorothy Stratford of the Philip Lawrence library at LSU College, Southampton (now University of Southampton New College).

We are also grateful to those who read and commented on the manuscript: Hilary Shaw of Longman (whose patient encouragement and sympathetic understanding kept the book on track), Maggie Walsh of Nottingham University, Jan Rutter at LSU College, Frank Cogliano formerly of LSU now at Edinburgh University, and in particular James D. White at the Institute of Russian and East European Studies, Glasgow University. We have tried to incorporate all of their suggestions, from which the final draft has benefited substantially. Of course, this does not absolve the authors of responsibility for any remaining weaknesses.

This work is a collaborative effort, not simply because there are two authors, but also because, as the bibliography will show, we are indebted to the work of many American and British historians. Our intention was to build on their scholarship by shedding light on a specific area of the history of Russian women. We hope that our book will encourage newcomers to this field to turn to the work of those pioneers on whose shoulders we perch, such as Richard Stites, Barbara Alpern Engel and Linda Edmondson.

Finally, this work began when we were both employed at La Sainte Union College in Southampton. We feel tremendous gratitude to and affection for an institution whose staff and students throughout its existence (1904–1997) embraced a genuine community spirit. It is to them and to the religious order which established LSU that this book is dedicated.

'The best relief from sad thoughts is work' thought Vera Pavlovna, and she was quite right.

N.G. Chernyshevsky, *What is to be done?*, 1863

Introduction

Alexandra Kollontai (1872–1953) is generally accepted, at least in the West, as a, if not the, central figure in the movement for the liberation of women in Russia and in the development of Marxist theory on sexual relations. In particular, Kollontai insisted that work and not emotion should be the centre of women's lives, and further that it was productive work, by which she meant paid employment outside the home, which would make women independent and personally fulfilled. She wrote that 'woman's position, her rights, her recognition as an individual, her access to the storehouse of learning always follow from her role in the economy and in production'.[1]

In practice, before the revolution of 1917, although marriage was the destiny of the majority of Russian women, the stress was on the productive as well as reproductive value which they could contribute to the family economy. That economy changed dramatically with the abolition of serfdom in 1861, which made the peasant woman's ability to contribute to the household economy, whether by farming or through crafts, even more crucial for its survival, while it forced many upper-class women for the first time to support themselves. Thus the location of women's work after 1861 differed according to class, with the majority of peasant women tied to the home, and considerable numbers of gentry women pushed out of it. With the push for industrialisation from the 1880s, but especially from the 1890s, alongside growing impoverishment of the peasantry, more and more women were drawn to the towns in search of work. Often the type of employment which they found differed little from their village experience of work, especially domestic service, textiles, and cultivating kitchen gardens. However, as urbanisation developed and industry became more complex, women found a widening choice of jobs. Indeed, as the political opposition to the absolutist system of rule erupted into revolution in 1905, employers turned increasingly to women as replacements for

1. A.M. Kollontai, *Trud zhenshchin v evoliutsii khoziaistva* (Moscow, 1923), p. 45.

1

male workers, who were considered less reliable, not just politically but also because of their indiscipline, reflected most commonly in drunkenness.

Not surprisingly, the image of the Russian working woman in the nineteenth century is not a positive one in the eyes of Western feminists: she is essentially a beast of burden, passive in the face of often brutal patriarchy, epitomised two decades before the abolition of serfdom in the words of a Russian exile, Ivan Golovine:

> The Emperor abuses his courtiers, and they revenge themselves on their subordinates, who, not finding words sufficiently energetic, raise their hands against those who, in their turn, finding the hand too light, arm themselves with a stick, which further on is replaced with a whip. The peasant is beaten by everybody: by his master, when he condescends so far to demean himself; by the steward and *starosta* [headman], by the first passer-by, if he be not a peasant. The poor fellow on his part has no means to indemnify himself, except his wife and his horse; and accordingly, most women in Russia are beaten, and it excites one's pity to see how the horses are used.[2]

Such violence against women persisted despite the reforms of the next tsar, Alexander II, in the 1860s aimed at modernising the economy, which was essentially still based on feudalism. Indeed, as we shall see, women who entered factory employment faced sexual as well as physical abuse, not only from foremen but from male co-workers. Hence the image of passive drudges also persisted.

Upper-class women workers, however, tend to be seen in a different light, because of their access to a far superior education than the vast majority of lower-class women, and to openings in the professions, particularly health and education, by the late nineteenth century. Although men dominated the professions in terms of salaries and status, these gentry working women might be seen as paving the way for Kollontai's 'new woman'. Female professionals and social reformers did not see themselves as either individuals pursuing careers for self-fulfilment or champions of women's rights. Rather, they dedicated themselves to service to the people, judging it immoral that a few should prosper in the midst of such exploitation and suffering. Hence self-sacrifice, the other side of passivity, was added to the ideal of the Russian woman worker.

This image of the docile, submissive woman devoted to the interests of family and society above her own both exaggerates and

2. I. Golovine, *Russia under the Autocrat, Nicholas the First* (London, 1846), vol. 1, pp. 88–9.

oversimplifies the nature of women's work. It also assumes an unbroken continuity in their position. The focus here is social, within a context of economic and political changes. Our method is not to use documents, including statistics, to build up a general picture of working women. Valuable though such a representation might be, we feel that it often obscures as much as it reveals. What we have tried to do, through a mixture of primary and secondary sources, is to uncover women's lives by examining some individuals within the context of economic and political developments. In a situation of widespread female illiteracy, the existence of a woman worker's memoir or recorded reminiscences shows that she was exceptional. However, by placing her within the wider context of information about women workers, we can not only establish how typical her story was, but also throw light on the lives of the 'silent' majority.

Our aim, then, is to construct a cogent picture of the variety of female work in Russia, and of the working women themselves, over an extended period of political as well as economic upheaval. The revolution of 1917 was not a watershed in terms of the work women did. Profound changes came with Stalin's 'revolution from above', dating from the adoption of the first five-year plan for industry in 1928 and the collectivisation of agriculture set in motion at the end of 1929. The period covered here begins with the assassination in 1881 of the tsar, Alexander II, in which two female terrorists took part, and ends with the liquidation in 1930 of the Zhenotdel, the Communist party's women's organisation, on the grounds that it was no longer needed to achieve sexual equality. Throughout this half century, Russia remained a patriarchal society dominated by a peasant economy. Women's scope for public action and employment was indeed limited, yet it included farm labour, crafts, the service sector, some professions, philanthropy and politics.

In the first chapter we shall consider the general picture of the condition of the working woman in Russia, as conveyed in both Western and Russian literature. Few peasants, male or female, and few women workers (at least until after the 1917 revolution) left written records about their lives, so that most of the sources historians use have been produced by those who were unrepresentative, in the sense that they left written records at all, or 'outsiders', in the sense of being socially superior observers of rural and working-class life. There is a remarkable measure of agreement about their situation in the secondary sources and in the observation of upper-class contemporaries, resulting in admiration for the stoicism of Russian women mixed with frustration at their apparently willing

acceptance of a subordinate role. We believe that such an interpretation is one-dimensional. Women had a central role in pre-
industrial society and a strong sense of identity. As economic change
and increased demographic mobility diluted patriarchy, peasant
women manœuvred to strengthen their position even while they
struggled to retain their traditional way of life. Land hunger and
large families forced millions of men to move to the cities in search
of work, leaving wives and families behind to preserve what they
could of village culture and economy. Fewer and usually single
women also migrated in search of work. By the beginning of the
twentieth century, and especially with wars in 1904 and 1914, their
numbers greatly increased. Thus women's experiences of industrialisation and urbanisation differed in significant ways from men's.
The process of economic modernisation in this period did not
entail a complete break with the village. Hence, before going on to
a detailed examination of what work women did, we shall consider
the impact on gender roles of the continuation of the patriarchal
tradition.

The second chapter will elaborate in detail the impact on women
of the tsarist programme of economic modernisation, with its stress
on heavy industry and railways, seen as bastions of male workers,
and the continuing importance of the traditional textile industry,
which became a key employer of women. The developing economy
also led to growth in the professions. Given the autocratic nature
of the political system, most posts were under state control. The
state's determination to keep down costs opened up some of the
professions, notably teaching and medicine, to single gentry women.
By the later nineteenth century, deterioration in the economic situation of the landed gentry meant that increasing numbers of these
women had to find employment to support themselves which would
also maintain their social status. They were, however, still expected
to work for less than their male counterparts.

Such work brought gentry women into close contact with the
lives of their social inferiors. The experience at first hand of the
poverty and ignorance in which the latter, in both village and city,
were forced to live pushed a significant minority of upper-class
women into political activity. Most worked for reform within the
system, but a significant minority turned against it. Some wealthy
women developed careers in philanthropy and as lobbyists for higher
education for women, while a smaller number became full-time
revolutionaries. Thus the third chapter will consider the impact of
political developments on working women before the First World

War, including the professional and revolutionary work performed by women among both the peasantry and the factory workers from the 1880s, and the participation of women in the 1905 revolution. Yet revolution and working-class organisation were still considered to be male affairs, and after 1905 employers increasingly turned to women, whom they assumed to be ignorant of and uninterested in politics. This process of replacing male with female labour was evident not only in textiles, which women came to dominate, but in a wide variety of industries, as reported in 1909 by a factory inspector in the Moscow province. He identified employers adopting this strategy as including

> sugar, tobacco, watchmaking, rope-making, glass, cement and brick factories; the sphere to which it is spreading is continually widening, affecting branches of industry where formerly male labour was exclusively employed. The reasons for such a phenomenon have already been explained in previous reports: women are a more peaceful and moderate element in factories, and above all, they are a significantly cheaper labour force than men.[3]

Yet it was women who took the first steps in the revolution which resulted in the collapse of the tsarist system in 1917. The First World War had resulted in both agriculture and industry becoming heavily dependent on working women. Feminists hoped that the contribution women made to the war effort would bring sexual equality, while revolutionaries were forced to pay more attention to organising women workers. Still the image is of the majority of women, both rural and urban, as politically unconscious, capable of acting only in a spontaneous fashion. The fourth chapter will examine the involvement of women in the First World War and the 1917 revolution, and challenge this stereotype of women workers as an elemental force.

The final chapter will consider the position of working women under the Communist regime which was developing in the 1920s. Tsarism had been overthrown, and yet the patriarchal and peasant nature of the old order continued to shape the new. The Communist party had committed itself to sexual equality, believing that the way to achieve it was by drawing women into the workforce. This widened the scope of female employment without challenging the traditional gender roles. Thus women retained the double burden of domestic responsibilities, which were regarded as their natural

---

3. A.G. Rashin, *Formirovanie rabochego klassa Rossii: istoriko-ekonomicheskie ocherki* (Moscow, 1958), p. 226.

sphere, and paid employment. As under tsarism, women in the 1920s were considered more politically and culturally backward than men. Any equality between the sexes would have come from the actions of the state. Hence the general view among historians that in practice little had changed in the situation of women since the revolution, and that the vast majority of women were not actors on the historical stage, but the mute victims of a male-dominated state. Yet, as we shall see, working-class women clearly felt that there had been some improvements in their lives since the revolution, which suggests that what is called for is a more nuanced interpretation.

We cannot claim to present a fully comprehensive picture of Russian women at work in this period. Thus, for example, we discuss the numbers of women in the printing industry but not in translating, editing, publishing or journalism.[4] Indeed, as female literacy grew, popular newspapers and magazines increasingly hired women as writers (of fiction and poetry as well as news stories).[5] We write at length of peasant women's crafts, but only hint at the role of women in the applied arts.[6] We spend considerable time on women as seamstresses and in the textile industry generally, but not on those who designed dress.[7] We describe the lack of time the majority of working women had for leisure, but ignore those women who worked in, for example, the theatre, and who were patrons of the arts.[8]

We concentrate on women in employment but only glance at women as employers.[9] The latter nevertheless are interesting because they reveal how varied was the female contribution to the economy of late tsarist and early Communist Russia. Catriona Kelly has pointed to the tendency within women's history to focus on

4. See V.R. Leikina-Svirskaia, *Intelligentsiia v Rossii vo vtoroi polovine xix veka* (Moscow, 1971), ch. 6 for the late nineteenth century. See also Mark D. Steinberg, *Moral Communities: The Culture of Class Relations in the Russian Printing Industry 1867–1907* (Berkeley, Calif., 1992) for examples of individual women in the industry.
5. See for example *Zhenskii Kalendar'* (Petersburg, 1906), pp. 302–26.
6. See Alison Hilton, 'Domestic Crafts and Creative Freedom: Russian Women's Art', ch. 14 in Helena Goscilo and Beth Holmgren (eds), *Russia, Women and Culture* (Bloomington, Ind., 1996).
7. See John E. Bowlt, 'Constructivism and Early Soviet Fashion Design', pp. 203–19 in Abbott Gleason, Peter Kenez and Richard Stites (eds), *Bolshevik Culture: Experiment and Order in the Russian Revolution* (Bloomington, Ind., 1985).
8. See Catherine A. Schuler, *Women in Russian Theatre: The Actress in the Silver Age* (London, 1996).
9. See Jo Ann Ruckman, *The Moscow Business Elite: A Social and Cultural Portrait of Two Generations, 1840–1905* (De Kalb, Ill., 1984), pp. 85–6, 98, 105–6, 157–61 for a few examples of women in the roles not only of wives and mothers of businessmen, but also as businesswomen and patrons of the arts.

'the victims of capitalism (prostitutes, factory workers)' and ignore its beneficiaries, including those women who owned factories, who were merchants or traders. She also notes that the depiction of merchant women in the nineteenth century was similar to that of the female peasantry and working class: submissive to patriarchal authority, passive, apolitical, socially conservative and uncultured. The main difference seems to have been that merchant women had the wealth to enjoy and indulge themselves. Their indolence reflected not simply the grasping success of their men, but also the latter's exploitation of the customers. What Kelly further reveals is that however wealthy and cultured merchant families might become, they remained outsiders, patronised both by the aristocracy and the tsarist bureaucracy, and by the liberal and revolutionary intelligentsia. Moreover, she has calculated that throughout the last seventy years of the tsarist regime, there were hundreds of female merchants, while there was 'a "hidden" class of wives and daughters who helped the family business along'.[10]

However, these women were very much a minority even within their own class. Our focus is on employment which linked and highlighted differences not only between women and men, but also between women, such as domestic service, education and medicine. The general conditions of women's work, their attitudes towards their work and the obstacles they encountered are identified through detailed case studies. The picture which emerges is one which shows not only the burden of work weighing on women who had no choice but to sell their labour or themselves, no role outside the family; but also the strength, courage and initiative of Russian women at work. It is harder to reveal the satisfaction which women derived from their jobs and from their place in the household economy, but there are glimpses that even unremitting toil has its rewards. This helps explain why so many clung so fiercely to a traditional way of life which observers then and historians now perhaps dismiss too easily as one of patriarchal oppression. At the same time, women were not completely resistant to change. Rather, they did not simply accept what their social superiors or the state held as progress, but questioned what it held for them and their families. Certainly, few Russian women in the late nineteenth and early twentieth centuries embraced the Western individualistic ethic and put their personal interests above all else, a choice which was open only to the upper

10. Catriona Kelly, 'Teacups and Coffins: The Culture of Russian Merchant Women, 1850–1917', ch. 4 in *Women in Russia and the Ukraine*, edited by Rosalind Marsh (Cambridge, 1996), pp. 56–62 especially.

classes. However, peasant and working-class women were by no means simply the 'grey mass' which generalisations about their subordinate position imply. We do not underestimate the difficulties or the inequalities which they faced, but neither do we underestimate the women at work in Russia.

CHAPTER ONE

To Labour, to Bear and to Endure: The Lot of the Russian Woman Worker?

The Russian girl is not a woman in the European sense, not an individual: she is merely a would-be bride.[1]

This judgement, made by the literary critic Vissarion Belinsky in the early 1840s, was repeated in the late 1850s by another critic, Nikolai Dobroliubov, who commented that to give a woman a serious education would have meant recognising her right of personality, which would have gone against all the traditions upon which Russia, that 'realm of darkness', was based.[2] The enduring impression of Russian womanhood is one of abject passivity and selflessness within a patriarchal peasant system which survived urbanisation, industrialisation, war and revolution. It suggests not only continuity in female subordination between the tsarist autocracy and communist dictatorship, but a common female condition, despite vast social, cultural and economic differences between Russian women in the late nineteenth and early twentieth centuries. Their shared destiny was marriage, which entailed exchanging one male authority figure, the father, for another, the husband. Yet the majority of Russian women were also expected to contribute to the household economy through working both inside and outside the home, in the fields, in workshops, in other people's houses, and in factories. They had done so before the push for industrialisation in the late nineteenth century, indeed even before serfdom was abolished in 1861.

Most women continued to work after marriage. Indeed, what shocked British travellers to Russia in this period was the shared workload between female and male peasants, and that the latter looked for strength rather than beauty in a wife. Western visitors

1. V.G. Belinsky, *Selected Philosophical Works* (Moscow, 1956), p. 261.
2. N.A. Dobroliubov, *Selected Philosophical Essays* (Moscow, 1965), pp. 282, 305.

assumed that economic modernisation would improve the lot of Russian women, and bring them more into line with what was regarded as the superior situation of women in Britain. The isolation of the village was being eroded by improvements in transport and communications. There was also the development of a rural intelligentsia and the growth of a hereditary urban working class. Yet peasant women seemed reluctant to embrace 'progress', and village traditions proved remarkably resilient. Indeed, to foreign visitors the Russian town did not seem radically different, socially or culturally, from the countryside.[3]

Nineteenth-century Russia was an overwhelmingly peasant country. Until 1861 the political, social and economic structure had been based on serfdom, which had tied the peasants to the land. Such a feudal system weakened Russia's status as a great power in the context of the rapid industrialisation and urbanisation of its rivals. For Russia to keep up with the Western powers, serfdom had to be abolished. The economic changes which followed the abolition of serfdom in 1861 included the impoverishment of many peasant families left with insufficient land. This placed even more importance on the contribution women could make to the household economy. At the other end of the social scale, the loss of their serfs so impoverished many gentry families that by the end of the 1860s contemporaries observed that 'a female proletariat' had arrived on the scene: not the women from the peasantry who, at least until the end of the century, were needed even more on the farm, but the women from the gentry which had 'lost' its serfs, the spinster aunts and sisters, the divorcees and widows, no longer living in and supported by the extended patriarchal family, but forced to fend for themselves.[4] The situation had indeed changed since Dobroliubov's time. Publications from the 1860s to the end of the century identified education as a solution to the problems facing upper-class women. As a foreign observer noted:

> Every year the necessity of providing some kind of higher education for women became more and more pressing, as an ever-increasing number of women belonging to the gentry were driven by the effects

3. See P. Herlihy, 'Visitors' Perceptions of Urbanization: Travel Literature in Tsarist Russia', in D. Fraser, A. Sutcliffe (eds), *The Pursuit of Urban History* (London, 1983), pp. 125–37; H. Norman, *All the Russias* (London, 1902), pp. 381, 453.

4. See for example E. Karnovich, *O razvitii zhenskogo truda v Peterburge* (St. Petersburg, 1865), pp. 64–7; S.S. Shashkov, *Istoricheskie sud'by zhenshchiny* (St. Petersburg, 1871), pp. 312–13; V.V. Stasov, *Nadezhda Vasilevna Stasova: vospominaniia i ocherki* (St. Petersburg, 1899), p. 215.

of Emancipation [of the serfs] to seek education as providing a means of self-support.[5]

Hence work was a large part of the lives of the majority of Russian women, and the type of work was determined not simply by what was expected of their sex, but by the social, cultural and demographic impact of changes in the economy. Until the late nineteenth century, the urban population had expanded and contracted through the seasonal migration of mainly male peasants. The demands of industrialisation from the 1890s, however, called for a stable labour force and at least a minority of skilled workers, again predominantly male. Revolutionaries, who at least until the 1905 revolution had to operate illegally, concentrated their efforts on the latter. Through propaganda circles and a desire for self-improvement, a corps of politically conscious workers grew. It was a small and overwhelmingly male minority. Peasant women who went to work in the towns were more restricted than their male counterparts in terms both of jobs open to them, and opportunities for training and education. Yet the very move to the town indicated that the female migrant was exceptional among peasant women. The fact that she was more likely than men to loosen or cut her ties to the village also indicated that she was more urbanised than many of the unskilled male migrants. Hence, before going on to a detailed examination of what work women did, this chapter will consider the impact on gender roles of a process of economic modernisation which did not entail a complete break with the village.

Women, work and family

The recorded reminiscences of a 56-year-old female factory worker, A.D. Batova, published in 1934 were intended to encapsulate the process of industrialisation and political upheaval in the late nineteenth and early twentieth centuries as experienced by many lower-class women, culminating in the improvements brought about by Stalin's transformation of the economy.[6] Batova had worked in a particular textile factory in Moscow for nearly 40 years. Born into a poor peasant family of 12 children, all of whom were illiterate, Batova was a farm labourer from the age of 10; in the winter, she

5. T. Darlington, *Education in Russia. Special Reports on Education Subjects*, vol. 23 (London, 1909), p. 215.
6. I. Kor (ed.), *Kak my zhili pri tsare i kak zhivem teper'* (Moscow, 1934), p. 11.

made lace and knitted, payment for which was in kind (soap). At the age of 14, she went to a textile factory in a nearby village. By law, she should have been 16 to be hired, but her father had bribed the local priest with eggs and meat to change her birthdate. Within a few days, and without training, Batova was put to work at a conveyor belt, earning seven roubles a month. She lived outside the factory, sharing accommodation, in effect a space on the floor, with between 25 and 30 other workers, men and women.

The hours were long: Batova left for work at 3.30 a.m., and returned at 10 p.m. She went to the public baths, which were overcrowded, once a week; she had to wash her clothes outside, even in winter, because there was no running hot water and no laundries. Food was cooked by the landlady, and the staple diet was bread and kvass (a sour, fermented drink); tea was a rarity. When meat was available, each worker would buy a piece, wrapping it in a dirty cloth, which would be marked to distinguish it from the other portions. All would be placed in the same big pot, and once cooked the landlady would fish out the bag of meat from what was essentially cabbage soup and try to identify the owner: if the mark had worn off, there would be arguments. Like the other workers, Batova paid extra for the cooking of the meal: in her 'spare' time, she did some sewing or embroidery for the landlady. All had to eat out of the same pot as none of the workers possessed plates; indeed, all had to sleep with their spoon under the pillow, for fear of thieves, and when they went home they would give their spoon to the landlady for safekeeping.

When she was 17, Batova married a cabinet maker from Moscow. Instead of staying in the village as so many peasant wives did, Batova moved to Moscow, in the hope that life would be easier. At first, their accommodation was the space under her husband's worktable in his workshop, and it was only before the birth of her first child that they managed to rent a windowless room at four roubles a month.[7] By then, Batova was earning 15 roubles a month. She continued to work throughout her 13 pregnancies, leaving the factory only hours before each birth, giving birth at home with an old woman acting as midwife. Eight of her children survived into adulthood. Although a very religious person (and by implication

7. Barbara Engel implies that they lived separately at first, taking 'their pleasure' on the shavings under the husband's workbench, and that it was only Batova's pregnancy which forced his employer to assign them a room. See B.A. Engel, *Between the Fields and the City: Women, Work and Family in Russia, 1861–1914* (Cambridge, 1994), p. 214.

conservative), Batova had nevertheless been affected by the political developments of the period, and participated in the 1905 revolution, helping to build barricades. Indeed, she had lost a child who was born prematurely after Batova tried to defend a nephew from cossacks' whips. What, if any, action she took in 1917 is unrecorded, as is her experience of life in the 1920s, though the implication is that she continued in employment. Her religious faith survived the 1917 revolution, and was only shaken when she went to a meeting of the 'godless' campaign in 1920. In the early 1930s, Batova was still working at the same machinery in the Moscow factory as when she had first arrived, but she recognised that there had been changes. In her opinion, conditions were much better: she worked seven hours a day instead of 15; foremen had to treat the women with respect; there was a factory canteen, and the pay was good (140 roubles a month). Indeed, Batova had been given an added responsibility: she had been made a 'visitor' of those absent workers claiming illness. She reported that she had found one woman at a drinking session, who was then sent to court. In Stalin's Russia, Batova was helping to enforce work discipline, but she might also be seen in the traditional female role of moral guardian. It is tempting to portray women like Batova as downtrodden, ignorant and politically unconscious, potentially ideal subjects for a dictator such as Stalin. Indeed, the editor of the collection in which her memoir appeared argued that such women had only recently become politically aware.

Studies which consider lower-class women in the period from 1880 to 1930 tend to look at them *en masse*, with only occasional references to individuals. Even then, such individuals are generally politically active, so that they stand out from the crowd. Examples include the revolutionary workers Vera Karelina and Anna Boldyreva, who participated in the labour movement for around twenty years, setting up circles for women workers in the late 1880s, and continuing their political work into the 1905 revolution. Karelina organised women in Father Gapon's assembly of Russian Factory and Mill Workers. Both women were elected to the Petersburg soviet, though Karelina had to withdraw through ill health. Boldyreva was still active in 1917. Their stories are valuable for showing that the female working class was not an amorphous mass, not simply powerless and passive victims of a profoundly patriarchal system. A focus only on the lives of politically active women such as Karelina and Boldyreva, however, tends to highlight their uniqueness.

Indeed, it could be argued that Batova's experience was more typical. Most lower-class women, whether urban or rural, were not politically conscious, and tended to accept their situation. That acceptance, however, entailed a great deal of action, of movement, and of courage, and was punctuated by episodes of sometimes violent protest, as the bare narrative of Batova's life reveals. Above all, it meant a lifetime of hard, ceaseless toil, interrupted only briefly (if frequently) by pregnancy. It was a life which was seen as a partnership with her husband, however unequal in terms of his patriarchal authority, of women's low and unequal pay, of the demeaning treatment in the factory to which women were subjected simply because of their gender and assumed inferiority to men. While she did not discuss her views of marriage, her reminiscences show that in practice it was based on the commitment she shared with her husband to work for the economic survival of their family. In Batova's memoir, it is a partnership portrayed in terms of what the wife contributed to the family, rather than the husband, who remains silent. Indeed the wife, however self-sacrificing and seemingly fatalistic in adversity, is central in her account.

Still, if Batova is 'more' representative of women workers' experiences, she too is relatively unusual in the fact that she left the village on marriage to move with her husband to his work in Moscow. The general pattern was for migrant male workers to marry early and leave their wives in the village, often for years, as described by the metal worker Kanatchikov:

> Among the pattern-makers there was one group whose appearance set them off from the rest – the pattern-maker peasants, whose ties with the village were still strong. They wore high boots, traditional cotton-print blouses girdled with a sash, had their hair cut 'under a pot', and wore beards that were rarely touched by a barber's hand. Every pay day without fail they would send part of their money back to the village. They lived in crowded, dirty conditions and behaved stingily, denying themselves everything in order to accumulate more money for the village. They were always looking for a free drink. On holidays they attended mass and visited their countrymen, and their conversations were mostly about grain, land, the harvest, and livestock. When they weren't able to return to their village on visits, the 'missus', that is, their wives, would come to the town to visit them: these were fat, big-bosomed women in woolen skirts, in bright red calico sarafans, with whom the men would go to the taverns on holidays to be entertained and listen to the music 'machine'.[8]

8. *A Radical Worker in Tsarist Russia: The Autobiography of Semen Ivanovich Kanatchikov*, translated and edited by Reginald E. Zelnick (Stanford, Calif., 1986), p. 21.

Kanatchikov, himself born of a peasant family in 1879 and moving to Moscow at about the same age as Batova (at 16, he was a year younger), had become urbanised, and saw himself as part of the politically conscious proletariat, in revolt against peasant patriarchy. Kanatchikov's condescension to the 'peasant-workers' and their wives is obvious. The general portrayal in histories of the Russian working class in the late nineteenth and early twentieth centuries is of a backward, conservative, volatile mass, whose ties to the village and whose even more superstitious wives left a huge gulf between them and the minority of urbanised, skilled, and overwhelmingly male workers, like Kanatchikov. Indeed, within the cities the cultural chasm between the skilled and the unskilled was highlighted by the perceived abyss between male metal workers and female textile workers, described by one of the former:

> Metal workers felt themselves to be the aristocrats among the rest of the working class. Their profession demanded more training so that they looked down on weavers and such like, as though they were inferior country bumpkins, at the mill today, back to ploughing tomorrow. . . . I was struck by the oddness of the textile workers. Many of them still wore peasant clothes, looking as if they had wandered into the town by mistake, and as if tomorrow they would find their way back to their native village. Women predominated among them, and we never lost an opportunity to pour scorn on them.[9]

Textile workers like Batova, then, were looked down on with contempt by the politically conscious skilled male workers; indeed, the still religious Batova, as a wife and mother, would have been seen as a drag on the development of the labour movement. Yet like Kanatchikov, Batova, as well as the politically active working-class women Karelina and Boldyreva, had become a city person, so that there was more to this dismissal of women as superstitious peasant-workers. Kanatchikov records that ordinary uneducated and politically apathetic male workers would 'frequently chase after the girl stocking-knitters', whereas the politically conscious worker 'would look upon every contact with girls either as an attack on their personal freedom or as the loss of a comrade for the revolutionary cause'.[10] In practice, only a minority of skilled men maintained such an attitude towards marriage. Some, like Vera Karelina's husband, formed political partnerships with their wives; the majority

---

9. A. Buzinov, *Za nevskoi zastavoi: zapiski rabochego* (Moscow, 1930), pp. 20–1.
10. *A Radical Worker*, p. 103.

established traditional marriages in which politics remained the male sphere.

Many politically active women agreed with this assessment of the backwardness of female workers. Often cited as evidence of this attitude is the testimony of Cecilia Bobrovskaia, a Social Democrat: 'It never occurred to us to carry on work among them; the job seemed somehow a thankless one. Besides, there was so much other work which we could barely cope with that agitation among the women was left for more favourable times.'[11] No wonder Batova remained politically unaware. Barbara Engel's study of women, work and the family in Russia between 1861 and 1914, *Between the Fields and the City*, records the Bolshevik Anna Boldyreva accusing male metal workers in 1905 of standing back from the struggle, yet blaming their wives: 'You accustom your wives to eat and sleep well, and it's therefore frightening for you to be without wages.'[12] Such caution is surely understandable if we consider that even families of skilled workers such as Batova's husband could not survive on his wage alone. Yet even as the quotation from Boldyreva supports the stereotype of the woman as a drag on the politically conscious male worker, it also implies that however patriarchal the society men's decisions were influenced by their wives.

Moreover, the politically unconscious Batova was active in the 1905 revolution, suffering a miscarriage as a result, while women such as Karelina clearly felt it was both a necessary and a worthwhile task to organise female workers. It is a mistake simply to quote from workers' memoirs as if what was written or said about one point in their lives is a constant. Kanatchikov in fact acknowledged that his views changed, that his prejudices about women were challenged. Just after he remarked on the general attitude of contempt, which he shared, toward women workers, he pointed out that 'here and there some conscious women were beginning to stand out among the female workers', such as the two women who had joined his study circle:

> Until this time, as was customary in a workers' milieu like ours, we had looked upon the woman worker as a creature of a lower order. She had no interest in any higher matters, was incapable of struggling for ideals, and was always a mere hindrance, an encumbrance in the life of a conscious worker. How great, then, was my surprise and admiration when for the first time, I made the acquaintance

11. C. Bobrovskaia, *Twenty Years in Underground Russia* (London, 1934), p. 109.
12. Engel, *Between the Fields and the City*, p. 235.

of two conscious women workers, women who argued logically and debated just like the rest of us.[13]

The focus of such memoirs is politics and the women workers' relation to the labour movement, rather than the working experiences of women; the focus is the city and the factory, with the village seen as an anachronism, though one with a continuing, even baleful, influence on city dwellers. Peasants of both sexes, and male workers who retained their links with the village, are portrayed by Kanatchikov as backward. To state the obvious, memoirs were written either by those who had been educated above basic literacy, or those like Batova who had someone to record them. We must, therefore, bear in mind that the sources on which historians base their reconstructions of the lives of the majority of women workers in this period were written either by members of their own class who were not typical, or by their social superiors who assumed that their observations reflected the general picture. Hence much has been concluded on the basis of theory and of what was written about the lives of lower-class women who rarely surface as individuals, in marked contrast to the female intellectuals.

Service to the people

Until the 1970s, studies of Russian women concentrated on the intelligentsia, which may be explained by the rich body of literature which they have left behind.[14] In addition, it is their political rather than their work experiences which are examined. When the census was compiled in 1897, professional women made up 4 per cent of the female labour force, while many wealthy women were engaged in charitable work.[15] An example of the latter is a society, established in the city of Kharkov in 1869, to encourage the schooling of the poor, especially girls. Its work was carried on both in and out of school. By 1909, the society was supporting 40 mixed primary schools, three girls' schools with workshops attached, a number of

13. *A Radical Worker*, p. 93.

14. See for example Barbara Alpern Engel and Clifford N. Rosenthal, editors and translators, *Five Sisters: Women Against the Tsar* (New York, 1975); Cathy Porter, *Fathers and Daughters: Russian Women in Revolution* (London, 1979).

15. See for example N.V. Kechedzhi-Shapovalov, *Zhenskoe dvizhenie v Rossii i zagranitsei* (St. Petersburg, 1902). For a memoir of a professional woman (a doctor) see M.T. Pokrovskaia, *Kak byla gorodskim vrachem dlia bednykh* (St. Petersburg, 1903).

artisan schools for boys, and Sunday schools, offering basic literacy skills, which were also open to adults.[16]

At first, the overwhelming number of this society's active members were men, and women simply gave charitable donations. However, the society realised that girls were not being sent to the mixed schools, and turned to female artisan schools in 1877, giving scope for the increasing involvement of women. The most popular trade chosen by poor parents for their daughters was seamstress, and as the girls were often sent at an early age to a workshop, they were deprived of literacy. Hence these artisan schools were to fill that gap. In the first year, 50 girls acquired basic literacy skills; then they went on to job skills. The head of the first school was a woman, F.P. Maksimovich, but at first almost all the teaching was unpaid. Each society member was assigned a personal tutee from the poor girls, for whom the member was financially responsible. There were no service personnel, and all the cooking and cleaning was done by the students themselves. Physicians gave their services free of charge.

By 1880, the number of students had risen to 180. There was a fee, but those who could not afford it received free tuition. At first, the school had no premises of its own, but operated from private flats. It relied on private donations, on membership dues, on those who could afford to pay a fee, and a small city grant. Finally, enough was saved to erect a school building on land granted by a private individual. Parents of past pupils helped with the construction, and some teachers opted for their salaries to be put towards the cost of the building, which opened in September 1889.

There were attempts to widen the trades taught in the school. In 1884 a cobbler's workshop was set up, but within two years it had closed due to lack of interest. Girls proved reluctant to learn this trade, explaining that they did not want to laughed at, or to be left without a job. The school regretted their attitude, since cobbling offered better pay and, it was believed, was less damaging to health than working as a seamstress. Even if such attitudes about what was fit work for women were not changed, there were still some successes in improving the girls' education. Gradually, teaching was extended to a period of five years, and girls were only allowed into the workshops if they had had primary education. Lessons in the workshop lasted from the end of August until June. There were two

16. *Istoricheskii obzor deiatel'nosti Khar'kovskogo obshchestva rasprostraneniia v narode grammotnosti 1862–1909* (Moscow, 1911).

departments: one for dressmakers, and the other for seamstresses. Girls studied in both, and had to sit examinations. This school was the first in Kharkov to provide primary education and job training to girls from poor families. In 1893 there were 156 girls in the school, and 73 in the workshops; in 1908 there were 146 at school, 151 in the workshops. By 1908, the total number of graduates from the school was 525, and from the workshops 149. Most girls' Sunday schools were led by women. In 1908, there were 319 men and boys in the society's Sunday schools, and 167 women and girls.

The society also set up summer camps where children with poor health were given treatment. Other services included public libraries and publishing (educational material as well as fiction). There was also entertainment, generally on special occasions, and lectures. In all spheres, women were active participants. Indeed, most of the educational material was written by female members of the society. Both men and women, but more of the latter, taught in the school, which may be explained by the fact that most teachers were poorly paid. Still, however few it reached, this charitable society successfully operated within the autocratic system; indeed it made a profit. It also provided some upper-class women with an opportunity not simply to serve the people, but to gain organisational and political experience (since official permission had to be obtained and retained). Finally, however low the salaries, it provided a few women at least with respectable professional employment.

This society had been established in the wake of the abolition of serfdom to help poor peasant youth, but it also offered a few needy female gentry an opportunity both to serve society and to support themselves. There were, however, opportunities outside philanthropy for women both to pursue a personally fulfilling career and to be socially useful, as represented in the memoirs of two female physicians practising in Russia in the late nineteenth and early twentieth centuries. The memoirs were published together in 1937, after the death of one of the women. They provide examples of the upper-class desire to serve the people, as well as the obstacles in the path of a professional woman. In addition, whereas such memoirs generally focus on the job and give little information about personal life, this joint memoir (in two parts) gives a strong indication that there was a long-standing lesbian relationship between the authors.[17] Whether or not that was the case, their reminiscences serve to

---

17. *Vospominaniia vrachei Yulia A. Kviatkovskaia i Mariia Pavlovna Rashkovich* (Paris, 1937).

illustrate the lives of self-supporting women workers who were wealthy enough to remain single and independent of men.

Yulia A. Kviatkovskaia (1859–1936) was born in Tomsk into an aristocratic family. Yulia was her mother's fifteenth child. Because they were rich, the family had many servants, nannies and governesses, and the majority of the children had a good education. A number of family members were involved in the medical profession: two of Yulia's brothers were doctors; a sister-in-law worked as a physician treating venereal disease, mainly among prostitutes. Two of her brothers were non-Marxist revolutionaries, one of whom was arrested and exiled to Siberia. The other devoted his life to political work, and was executed in 1880. Yulia brought up one of this brother's daughters, who came to stay with her as a 3-year-old, travelling with her across Russia, wherever Yulia's work took them.

Yulia qualified as a doctor in January 1886. There were no restrictions on her medical practice, but Yulia complained that all the women who worked in zemstvo (local government) hospitals were limited to women's wards. They had great difficulty in winning the respect of their male colleagues, whom she regarded as the enemy. Physicians such as Yulia were pioneers who helped establish women doctors, and opened up new areas for them to practise. Yulia and her friend Mariia Pavlovna Rashkovich (the other memoirist) decided to work as both feldshers (medical orderlies or paramedics) and physicians to give them more independence. They took up posts in a hospital run by another woman, Aleksandra Gavrilovna Archangelskaia. Mariia and Yulia performed much heavy, dirty work as feldshers, and took the opportunity to study the economics of running a hospital. From 1887, they began specialising in eye problems. Together they moved to the Poltava region, where Yulia managed a smallpox isolation ward, Mariia an orphanage. In 1893 they moved again, this time to Kishinev, where Yulia continued the work she had done in Poltava and Mariia at first took a job in public hygiene, and a year later started a private eye clinic. In 1896, with another woman doctor, Yulia toured Central Asia, treating people with eye problems.

Yulia became a respected eye surgeon. In 1899, with Mariia assisting, she opened an eye-hospital with ten beds. Their work was partly funded by private donation. Within ten years, the hospital was extended and another woman doctor was employed. In 1916, Yulia went as a doctor to serve at the front. The fall of tsarism in 1917 brought her into politics. She was elected a member of Kishinev's city council, on which she was the only woman, and was made responsible for medical services and, for a short time, for schools. She was not, however, a Communist and left public life in 1919. In 1936 she was awarded a pension in recognition of her service to the citizens of Kishinev.

Yulia spent most of her adult life with Mariia Rashkovich, whom she met in St. Petersburg in 1880. Mariia was also born in 1859, in Odessa. Her father was a wholesale manager. Mariia was the seventh of her mother's eight children. Her father died when she was 6 years old, and three older brothers supported the family financially. Mariia was educated in a gymnasium (grammar school), and participated in a non-political study circle. Nevertheless, she was friendly with many revolutionaries in Odessa in the 1870s. In 1878 she studied for a year at the medical courses for women in St. Petersburg. After a year she dropped out, partly because of poor health, partly because of her involvement with revolutionaries. She went abroad (to Berlin and Bern), both for her health and to study, but missed Russia and returned in 1880 to St. Petersburg. She met Yulia as soon as she arrived. Mariia regarded this meeting as the most important event in her life. Their relationship deepened when Mariia supported Yulia through the death sentence and execution of the latter's revolutionary brother. They set up home together, and became life partners until Yulia died in 1936.

In Petersburg, they sometimes shared a flat with other students. Although most medical students were from the upper classes, they made friends with a remarkable woman, who had been a peasant at birth, and illiterate until she was 16. Now she was studying medicine. In 1886, Mariia and Yulia moved to Moscow because of the latter's illness. They decided to devote themselves to working for the zemstvo, as a means of sacrificing themselves to help the people. Mariia's memoir shows that one reason for the frequent moves was the poor state of Yulia's health. Yulia's interests lay in practising medicine, whereas Mariia turned to public hygiene, particularly in schools. She was especially interested in the fight against contagious diseases. The impact of famine in the early 1890s not only exacerbated the latter, but resulted in a serious problem of orphaned and abandoned children. Mariia was particularly concerned with the high death rate among this group.

They seem to have spent most of their private lives in the company of women. Their family consisted of Mariia's sister and Yulia's niece, with occasional visits from each of their mothers. In their work and studies, they co-operated with men, forming a circle which carried out educational work, and setting up a Jewish technical college for women (Mariia was Jewish). Some members of the circle taught in a male Sunday school. The circle opened a free public library in 1897, and organised a summer camp for about 60 children. In 1914, they set up a society to care for children, opening canteens, kindergartens and clubs. Despite her early interest in revolutionary thought, Mariia did not take part in the movement. She expressed a dislike for practical work, which is reflected in her interest in the more intellectual aspects of medicine. Yulia was more practical and active.

In their memoirs, neither Yulia nor Mariia discussed their personal relations, which they described, without elaborating, as intimate. Yulia mentioned one platonic relationship with a man, before she went to study in St. Petersburg. He married someone else. Mariia wrote that she had the chance to marry five times, but that she had not been attracted to any of the suitors. She felt that it was shared idealism which accounted for the 56 years she and Yulia shared so happily. It was not an exclusive relationship, nor one which was solely devoted to work. Indeed, Mariia recounted the story of another woman, Elena Petrovna Dzunkovskaia, with whom she developed a close friendship. Born in 1855 to a very wealthy family, Elena had avoided an arranged marriage into the nobility because her mother died before finalising it. Once her father had died, she inherited a large landed estate, half of which she sold at considerably below the market price to the peasants, the other half of which she managed as a model estate, establishing a school for the peasants, agrarian courses, a library and a clinic. Mariia, who occasionally practised private medicine, was asked to treat Elena when she became ill. In her memoir, Mariia wrote that an intimate friendship soon developed. In 1903, the three women travelled abroad, Yulia to Italy to visit a nephew, Mariia and Elena to Paris. Mariia and Yulia met in Berlin on their return home. There was another tour of Europe in 1908. Elena died in 1910.

Whatever the nature of their relationship, the memoirs of Mariia and Yulia reveal that being committed to the service of the people or indeed to each other did not mean a life of unremitting self-sacrifice and submersion of individual identity. They also show that, whatever the restrictions caused by gender expectations and a political system which sought to smother individual initiative, professional women could find outlets to develop their careers, justifying the feminist strategy of working for reforms within the established order. Not all such women, however, were prepared to accept either the limitations placed on them by a patriarchal society and an autocratic political system, or the meagre results of their hard work when compared to the enormity of popular needs. More often referred to in studies of upper-class Russian women are the words of Vera Figner, who like Yulia came from a wealthy family, yearned to be socially useful and trained for medicine so that she could work among the people, but who, in contrast to Yulia, became a full-time revolutionary because she judged her actions to be a sticking plaster on a festering, gangrenous wound, 'a small patch on a dress which should never be mended, but rather should be discarded and replaced with a new one'.[18] Figner recorded that those women who developed a revolutionary consciousness turned away from 'individual' concerns for education and a profession, from the hope of changing society gradually, towards dedication to social revolution through renunciation of personal ambitions, and indeed of a personal life, for the cause of the masses.

It is easy to see why women such as Figner were so interesting both to contemporaries and to historians. Our period effectively opens with the execution in 1881 of Vera's comrade, Sofia Perovskaia, for the assassination of Alexander II, and Vera's own arrest in 1883. Although a tiny minority of upper-class women, their bravery acted as a catalyst to relatively large numbers of others to devote themselves to the *narod* (the common people) by working within the system to 'patch up' the lot of the people. They trained for the only available professions open to women, in medicine (as doctors, paramedics/feldshers, midwives) and teaching, and worked either in the villages or in the growing working-class areas in the cities. While their dedication to 'the people' possibly retarded and weakened the development of a feminist movement, by the time tsarism was overthrown in 1917, there was a tradition of female radicalism which could be traced back to the mid nineteenth century.

Yet their contribution to the social transformation of the period, especially after 1880, was at worst not recognised, at best seen as the work of a few heroines who were indeed exceptional, and not representative of Russian womanhood. Moreover, their heroism was of an inspirational rather than a practical nature, in terms of their relations with the masses, particularly the female masses.

18. Vera Figner, *Zapechatlennyi trud* (Moscow, 1964), vol. 1, p. 122; or see her abridged *Memoirs of a Revolutionist* (New York, 1927), p. 43.

The deep social gulf between these upper-class exemplars and women peasants and proletarians is reflected in the life of Galina Fedorovna Cherniavskaia-Bokhanovskaia. She was born in 1854 into a landowning family which moved to Kiev because of financial difficulties, perhaps stemming from the 1861 abolition of serfdom. Galina had dreamed of becoming a village doctor, but her family's straitened circumstances pushed her into teaching. By 1875, she had become an active revolutionary. She took a job in a confectionery factory, but after only a winter's work came to the conclusion that propaganda among the women workers was impossible. In 1876, she attempted with another women, P.S. Ivanovskaia, to participate in Jewish unrest as a form of 'going to the people', but again found that she could not carry out propaganda. Galina's brief experiences of the masses showed that the female intelligentsia were not taken seriously by the men, while the women did not believe them. Galina abandoned her efforts even before the season was over. By the end of the 1870s, she had become a terrorist; by 1883, she was living abroad, first in Paris then Geneva, publishing revolutionary material.[19]

Such a trajectory into becoming a professional revolutionary after failing to make inroads into the people through direct contact is highlighted by the anthology *Five Sisters*, published in 1975. Like Cherniavskaia-Bokhanovskaia, some – inluding Vera Figner's sister, Lydia – tried to take their propaganda to the people by working in factories. They soon found, however, that the female workers were unresponsive, due to their sheer physical exhaustion and low cultural level. Hence the female radicals turned to agitation among the male workers, though the harsh regulations governing the social life as well as the labour of factory workers made this very difficult. Nevertheless, they managed to read to the men in their barracks, readings which included information on workers in the West. Such propaganda, however, did not escape the notice of the tsarist secret police, and there were mass arrests, culminating in the 'Trial of the Fifty' in 1877. There, one of these women, Sofia Bardina, then aged 23, made a rousing speech which was widely reported and is considered to have had an enormous impact, impressing people with the integrity, independence, bravery and dedication of these female revolutionaries. She saw the employment of women and children in factories as socially and morally degrading:

19. *Entsiklopedicheskii slovar' 'Granat'* (Moscow, 1926), vol. 40, p. 586.

As far as the family is concerned, is it not really being undermined by that social system which forces a woman to leave her family and go to work in a factory for a miserable pittance, a subsistence wage, to be debauched there, along with her children?[20]

Yet in practice women such as Bardina were unable to make much of an impact on the workers with whom they came into contact because of their too brief stay, of two or three months only, in the factories. It was not simply a case of the ignorance of the women workers making them virtually inaccessible to revolutionary propaganda, in contrast to the men. Apart from the crushing of their efforts by the police, the conditions of life proved too difficult and depressing for the female intelligentsia to continue working there. They were also demoralised by the fact that, of necessity, the wretched problems of everyday life took precedence, particularly for women who earned such low and unequal wages. Moreover, the male workers did not see women as capable of rational thought and action, reflecting the general patriarchy which held women in low esteem. These factors are illustrated by the experience of three revolutionary women of the 1870s, Bardina, Kaminskaia and Lydia Figner, who had left factory employment much too soon to have made an impact:

It proved impossible for elegant young 'ladies' dressed up as peasant girls not to attract attention in the miserable surroundings of the factory. Everything they did set them apart; their small, tender hands were unaccustomed to working, and ten or 12 hours of labour in an unsanitary workshop ... exhausted them beyond endurance. They couldn't even conduct propaganda, because the consciousness of their female co-workers was too low, and so, disguised in their worker's clothing, defying custom as well as the outright prohibition of the factory administration, they went to the barracks of the male workers to try to get them interested in books. They offered the material to everyone, but since few workers were literate, they eventually resorted to reading aloud. The sight of a solitary young woman, reading in the filthy, ill-lit, stinking barracks to a circle of those workers who hadn't yet tumbled into bed, was extraordinary to behold. Since the women would permit no 'fooling around', the workers couldn't figure out why they were there.[21]

20. For Bardina's speech, see V. Burtsev, *Za sto let* (London, 1897), pp. 124–7. For its influence, see Richard Stites, *The Women's Liberation Movement in Russia: Feminism, Nihilism and Bolshevism, 1860–1930* (Princeton, 1978; 2nd edn 1990), p. 142.

21. Engel and Rosenthal, *Five Sisters*, p. 29.

Their inability to 'stay the course' meant that the gulf between the upper-class female revolutionaries and the women workers remained extremely wide, while the fact that the former gave up on the latter so quickly and turned instead to the male workers might even have widened the basic lack of understanding between the two classes of women. It mirrored the distrust and indeed outright hostility between the intelligentsia and the minority of radical skilled workers which dated from the 1870s and persisted until 1917, and indeed into the 1920s. The politically unaware factory women may well have shared the opinion of the politically conscious male worker, Pavel Tochisskii, that the intelligentsia were 'accidental' or temporary guests in the labour movement.[22] However much the female intelligentsia sympathised with their lower-class sisters, they were seen as culturally and socially, as well as economically, a world apart. Thus the female physician E.V. Aptekman, who lived and practised among peasants for three years in the early 1880s, recorded that however hard she worked and however warm was the gratitude from the peasants, she remained very much an outsider. She keenly felt her cultural isolation in particular, and found it very difficult to come to terms with what she experienced as the vulgarity of everyday village life.[23]

Gender and the development of the working class

From the 1880s, but especially from the 1890s, Russia experienced intensive industrialisation and urbanisation, yet remained a society and economy dominated by peasant agriculture. In a collection of essays published in 1977, Dorothy Atkinson argued that there had been a general continuity of subordination in the lives of Russian women from the beginning of the tenth to the beginning of the twentieth centuries.[24] She pointed to two crucial factors which affect gender roles: social stratification and economic development. Neither Atkinson nor the other contributors to *Women in Russia* were arguing that there had been no change. Among them, Richard Stites first attempted a wide-ranging study of the lives of Russian

22. A. Breitfus, 'Tochisskii i ego kruzhok', *Krasnaia letopis'* (1923), no. vii, p. 326.
23. E.V. Aptekman, 'Iz zapisok zemskogo vracha', *Russkaia mysl'* (Dec. 1884), vol. 5, part 12, pp. 48–82: 77.
24. Dorothy Atkinson, Alexander Dallin, Gail W. Lapidus (eds), *Women in Russia* (Stanford, Calif., 1977), p. 35.

women over a sustained period of time: *The Women's Liberation Movement in Russia: Feminism, Nihilism and Bolshevism, 1860–1930* (1978). Although there was considerable detail on the lives of working women, the individual portraits he drew tended to be of leading women and men in their various political movements. A pioneering work, *The Women's Liberation Movement in Russia* encouraged others to follow up some of the many themes covered by Stites in more depth.[25] The fascination still lay with the individual revolutionary, especially where it was possible to identify with her, as with Alexandra Kollontai, whom one biographer dubbed the 'Bolshevik Feminist'.[26]

An exception was the work of Rose Glickman, another contributor to *Women in Russia*. In *Russian Factory Women: Workplace and Society, 1880–1914* (1984), Glickman revealed the significance of gender in the development of the Russian working class, highlighting the peasant legacy of female subordination to men, which she argued convincingly was perpetuated in the sexual division of labour at the factory. Though its focus was relatively narrow, Glickman's 1984 study of factory women broke new ground, both in terms of their conditions of work and life, and the obstacles encountered by revolutionaries who tried to organise them and who were too ready to dismiss them as backward.

Although not solely concerned with women, *The Russian Worker*, edited by Victoria Bonnell and published a year before Glickman's study, contained some additional useful information on certain categories of female paid employment not covered by the latter, such as sales and clerical assistants, garment as well as textile workers. Indeed, Glickman's focus on factory workers among the female proletariat can be challenged as unrepresentative. In Russia as a whole before 1917, domestic service ranked second among major women's occupations. Domestic service covered a variety of jobs, including, for example, general maid, chamber maid, cook, scullery maid, laundress, wet-nurse, nanny, governess, housekeeper. Although women constituted 29 per cent of St. Petersburg's labour force (with women constituting as much as 68 per cent of the textile workforce, 47 per cent in food and tobacco, and 42 per cent in

25. See for example Barbara Alpern Engel, *Mothers and Daughters: Women of the Intelligentsia in Nineteenth-Century Russia* (Cambridge, 1983); Christine Johanson, *Women's Struggle for Higher Education in Russia, 1865–1900* (Montreal, 1987).

26. B.E. Clements, *Bolshevik Feminist: The Life of Aleksandra Kollontai* (Bloomington, Ind., 1979). See also B. Farnsworth, *Aleksandra Kollontai: Socialism, Feminism, and the Bolshevik Revolution* (Stanford, Calif., 1980); Cathy Porter, *Alexandra Kollontai: A Biography* (London, 1979).

chemicals), numerically domestic service undoubtedly remained the largest single source of female employment in the capital. Nor was domestic service confined to a private home, for women might also be employed by workmen living in artels (co-operatives), by laundry owners, and by brothel keepers. Moreover, some forms of domestic service, such as floor washing, might be hired by the day. In addition and as was the case throughout Europe at the time, being employed in industry did not necessarily mean working in a factory. For example, in 1897 the Russian occupational census showed that only a third of women listed in textile production worked in factories; the majority worked at home or in small shops, as was typical of most industries. Indeed, more Russians, men as well as women, were employed as day-labourers, servants, shop assistants, in restaurants and taverns, as artisans and in trade than in factories.[27]

Diane Koenker's study of the Moscow working class reveals that in 1912 domestic service accounted for almost 100,000 wage earners, of whom 93 per cent were women, and she argues that they had little family life of their own in the city, and were among the most isolated and vulnerable of women workers.[28] Robert Johnson has painted a similar picture for the late nineteenth century, pointing out that whereas factory women, contrary to expectations, were responsible for a disproportionately low share of babies left at foundling homes, women who worked as domestic servants, day-labourers or seamstresses accounted for a disproportionately high share. Yet domestic service and sewing at least were considered appropriate jobs for women, whereas the factory was seen as a masculine environment and was believed to lead to promiscuity. Johnson is not implying that factory women were any less likely to become pregnant, but rather that

> the evidence of factory life suggests that sexual abuse and also voluntary liaisons were not uncommon. Unlike servants or artisans, however, factory women were part of a community that maintained many of the traditions and sanctions of village life. In such a setting, a father may have found it harder to shirk his obligations, and a pregnant girl less likely to be left to her own devices.[29]

27. A.G. Rashin, *Naselenie Rossii za sto let* (Moscow, 1956), p. 323. See also Robert B. McKean, *St. Petersburg Between the Revolutions: Workers and Revolutionaries June 1907–February 1917* (New Haven and London, 1990), p. 19.

28. Diane Koenker, *Moscow Workers and the 1917 Revolution* (Princeton, 1981), p. 41.

29. Robert E. Johnson, *Peasant and Proletarian: The Working Class of Moscow in the Late Nineteenth Century* (Leicester, 1979), p. 96.

The community to which Johnson is referring is of peasant origin. Peasants from the same locality sought each other's company and help when in the city, often living together and working in the same factories, as Kanatchikov's account of the pattern-makers has shown. Rooted in peasant life and regional solidarity, this form of association was known as *zemliachestvo* and it seems to have eased the transition into the urban environment. Indeed, many students practised a form of *zemliachestvo* when they set up communes based on their previous place of residence. It is difficult to assess the extent of its impact on women workers, since much of the information on *zemliachestvo* comes from the memoirs of skilled male workers such as Kanatchikov. There is some evidence, however, provided by that same collection of women workers' memoirs published in 1934. P. Sleptsova's migration to Moscow at the age of 16 was eased by a cousin who not only travelled with her, but found her a job in the same textile factory where the cousin was employed. It was not an entirely altruistic act, however, since Sleptsova had to pay the cousin three roubles a month for training.

A.F. Golubeva had a less positive experience of kin sponsorship. Both Golubeva's parents worked in different factories, and when her father had died she had been sent to a grandmother in the village. The village's main industry was textiles, especially silk, at which Golubeva was set to work as soon as she arrived. In summer she worked on the land. Before she was the legal age for hiring, her mother took her to the factory and got her to stand on her tiptoes in a successful effort to convince the employer to take her on, where she worked as her mother's apprentice. Within a year, however, Golubeva had to return to the village for want of accommodation at the factory. When she returned in 1905, she could only find a job as a servant in the factory manager's house, where in her view the work was even more exhausting and time-consuming than factory labour. On falling pregnant, she was summarily dismissed. Her mother was so ashamed that she beat her and refused to help her. Left to her own devices, Golubeva took the infant to another village where there was an orphanage. For her, the *zemliachestvo* had been of limited help, although certainly she fits Johnson's pattern by being impregnated as a domestic servant, rather than as a factory worker where her kinswoman's presence may have afforded her some recourse. Indeed, her mother's shame may partly have been prompted by her inability to protect her daughter. It was ten years before Golubeva was able to return to that orphanage, only to discover that the child had survived for less than three months.[30]

It was not only in the factory that a man might be shamed into regularising his behaviour towards a woman. The feminist physician Mariia Pokrovskaia recounted the tale of two sisters who rented accommodation along with both single male workers and married couples. The sisters saved money by sharing a bed and looking after their own domestic chores. On a particular occasion, after Dasha, one of the sisters, had come home earlier than the other and gone to bed, one of the single men asked if she would go out with him at the weekend. She replied that she would, on condition that her sister accompany them. By midnight, when the sister had not come home, having decided instead to stay with her godmother, this man tried to get into Dasha's bed, and when he refused to leave despite her protestations, she shouted for assistance. In the event, help came not from the other men in the flat, who simply laughed and turned back to sleep, but from the women, who berated the man. In his defence, he claimed that he thought Dasha had been agreeable, but he went off muttering, 'You think you are a princess, but I can find a better girl than you.' Some time later, however, the young man told Dasha that he hoped she was not still angry with him, and that if she was not prepared to sleep with him, then he wanted to marry her. She agreed. Of course, Dasha, with family members living in the city and her sister as first line of defence, or supervision, may also have been acting according to traditional collective morality, by holding out for a legal rather than a common-law marriage.[31]

Whatever the situation with unwanted pregnancies such as that of Golubeva, the Russian urban working class did not reproduce itself, even into the twentieth century. It grew overwhelmingly through migration from the countryside, and the migrants, especially men who had left their wives behind, maintained links with the villages. Given the high cost of living and low level of wages in the cities, and the fact that, with the exception of prostitution, women earned considerably less than men, it made sense economically for the wife, and indeed marriageable girls as future wives, to remain on the land.

A man, however, had the right to summon his wife to his side. In that same study published in 1903, Mariia Pokrovskaia related

30. Kor, *Kak my zhili*, pp. 28–34 for Sleptsova, pp. 21–7 for Golubeva.
31. M.I. Pokrovskaia, *Po podvalam, cherdakam i uglovym kvartiram Peterburga* (St. Petersburg, 1903), pp. 96–7.

the story of a young peasant wife, Olga, who was summoned by her husband, Andrei, to join him in the city. Andrei was considerably older than Olga, and Pokrovskaia described him as a traditional despot. He demanded wifely obedience, and viewed Olga simply as a possession. He had sent her money for the journey, and ordered her to leave their son behind in the village, which had upset her. Yet she would not have dreamt of refusing. Olga went to the flat in Petersburg where her husband rented a bed. When she arrived, he was at work. The landlady had recently been widowed. She had two young children, and was supporting them with the rent, which provided enough to pay for the flat and leave six or seven roubles on which to live. She did not consider factory or laundry work because her children (a 2-year-old son and a 5-year-old daughter) were so young. Andrei shared a room with other lodgers, and there was no curtain around his bed, as was expected if a married couple lived together. Two single workers sharing a bed paid four roubles a month, whereas a married couple paid 50 kopecks less. Andrei had in addition paid 50 kopecks a month to the landlady to do his cooking and washing. Hence Andrei sent for Olga to save a few kopecks, and to have her perform unpaid domestic service for him.

Olga had been completely overcome by St. Petersburg: the sheer size of the buildings, the crowds of people, the speed of city life where horses ran so much faster than in the countryside. Her husband was one of the last to return home. He did not express any joy at her arrival; his greeting was quite indifferent. He said that he did not have money to give her for a meal. The landlady, however, offered the soup which she had cooked for the single workers, saying that there was enough for all. Andrei gave Olga three roubles to buy some crockery and food so that she could cook for him, a little table, and material for a curtain to put round the bed. Having purchased the first two, she had only 30 kopecks left, which was only half of what curtain-material would cost.

Pokrovskaia claimed that the husband spent his money on wine, women and cards. He had lived in St. Petersburg for three years and not sent any money back to the village. Andrei frequently came home drunk and beat Olga. He had little money left after spending it on drink and friends, and would send her to the shops to get vodka on credit. Yet he would accuse Olga of being good for nothing, and he was a jealous man, even of another male lodger who offered Olga a slice of bread. One night Andrei woke up to discover that he had lost some money, and beat Olga so badly she could not rise in the morning. That evening the doctor was called, and diagnosed TB. Olga was taken to the hospital. As usual, Andrei spent his wages on drink, and had to borrow 20 kopecks to visit his wife. She died two weeks later. Andrei buried his wife, and arranged a wake.

Pokrovskaia's story portrays the feminist stereotypes of the brutal and drunken patriarch and the passive, stoical wife. What is not clear is how representative Andrei and Olga were. Certainly Olga's story contrasts sharply with Batova's, and, as we shall see below, peasant men who moved to the city did so to provide for the family farm and sent money home. They could, of course, have sent more had they imbibed less, but alcohol was an integral part of the old-fashioned masculinity of which Pokrovskaia so disapproved.[32] Olga and Batova had both migrated to the city as wives, but for different reasons, the former to cook and clean for her husband, the latter to find a job and establish a home with hers. Both men had migrated for work, but Olga's husband had left his child to be raised in the village whereas Batova and her husband established a city-bred family. Generally, however, men made up the majority of labour migrants, leaving wives behind in the village.

Patterns of migration differed by region: for example, peasants who went to Petersburg in search of work travelled considerable distances, whereas Moscow's migrants came from surrounding villages. In general, however, the same demographic pattern can be traced: more men than women migrated, the majority of both were single and there was a tendency for children to be brought up in the countryside.[33] Once again, we see how Batova was, in practice, not a typical case.

Barbara Anderson's study of late nineteenth-century migration led her to the conclusion that, although migrating in fewer numbers, women may have been responding to the same kind of motivations and inducements for migration as men, and suggests that women may have exercised more independent decision-making in migrating than has generally been supposed.[34] Yet a move to the city may have signified that the female migrant was either single or widowed and childless, categories which predominated within the urban female labour force, and so had no role within the village household other than contributing to the family income.

---

32. Ibid., pp. 64–5.   33. See for example Rashin, *Naselenie Rossii.*
34. Barbara Anderson, *Internal Migration During Modernisation in Late Nineteenth-Century Russia* (Princeton, 1980), p. 78.

The speculations of both Johnson and Anderson are difficult to prove. However, it can at least be asserted that the assumption which they challenge, an assumption reflected in Glickman's portrait of peasant patriarchy in which the female peasantry, and by implication the majority of women workers, are rendered 'mute and powerless', is too sweeping and generalised.[35] It is a widely held view, however, and appears soundly based on the sources. Yet, as pointed out above, there is a dearth of written records from peasants themselves for the nineteenth century. Our information comes from a range of material collected by various government commissions and by local organs of self-government (or, to be more accurate, self-administration), and the published studies of contemporary ethnographers. The evidence yielded by these sources comes from educated Russians who brought their own preoccupations, attitudes and assumptions to bear not only on their descriptions of peasant life but on the questions which they asked and on their decisions concerning what to record and what to omit, which in turn was affected by tsarist censorship.

Others have followed Glickman. In 1985 in *Mothers and Daughters* (which focuses on the female intelligentsia), Barbara Engel claimed that while peasant wives were valued according to 'their capacity to labour, to bear children and to endure', the peasants regarded women's work, even in the fields, as 'unproductive'.[36] In his study of the peasantry before serfdom was abolished in 1861, Steven Hoch claimed that 'according to numerous observers, discord within peasant households was commonplace, wife-beating was usual'.[37] In her examination into women's roles in rural development in the Soviet Union, Susan Bridger repeated the generalisation that contemporary observers of the extended peasant family invariably described it as hierarchical, patriarchal and authoritarian.[38] Yet this apparently static picture of female passivity and submission has been modified to a degree. In a later publication (1994), *Between the Fields and the City: Women, Work and Family in Russia, 1861–1914*, Barbara Engel softened this image, while she also acknowledged the attractions of patriarchy for women. Engel's study of the significance and consequences of peasant women's migration for work draws on

35. Rose L. Glickman, *Russian Factory Women: Workplace and Society 1880–1914* (Berkeley, Calif., 1984).
36. Engel, *Mothers and Daughters*, p. 8.
37. Steven L. Hoch, *Serfdom and Social Control in Russia* (Chicago and London, 1986), pp. 131, 161.
38. Susan Bridger, *Women in the Contemporary Soviet Countryside* (Cambridge, 1987), p. 7.

first-person accounts which allow us to see these women as individuals. However, Engel also confirms Glickman's pessimistic conclusion that Russia's urbanisation and industrialisation favoured men
more than women.

What is clear is that the working class in late nineteenth-century
Russia developed through a peculiar interlacing of village customs
and institutions with industrial change. The village's influence on
factory life was subtle and complex, with the women in the villages
maintaining peasant culture. Moreover, women workers were seen
as living apart from urban society at large, their lives contained
within the narrow orbit of home and mill:

> exhausted, ill from unhealthy, unrelenting mill work, having no peace
> at home from morning to night, day in and day out, month after
> month, the worker-mother drudges and experiences only need, grief
> and worry.[39]

Male workers continued to see women above all in their traditional,
'natural' role of housekeeper and childrearer, and associated women
with peasant culture. The patterns of migration reinforced the town–
village nexus so that even where peasants became year-round factory workers, their ties with the village persisted, and the industrial
system in Russia was permeated with the institutions, habits and
customs of a recently enserfed peasantry whose communal tradition retained its vitality. There was thus no sharp division between
town and village, peasant and worker.[40] The peasant hierarchies,
including those of gender, were now supplemented by urban hierarchies in which women generally remained at the bottom. Given
the stark contrast between the minority of skilled workers and the
mass of unskilled, the hierarchy of labour assumed particular importance. Most women were and remained unskilled. As the memoirs
of skilled workers such as Kanatchikov and Buzinov have shown,
there was condescension and even scorn for the unskilled peasant-
worker, and especially for the women. Buzinov recalled that as an
apprentice, he had been painfully aware of the inequalities among
workers, whereas once he was established in his trade of metal work,
it seemed a minor matter, an acceptable fact of working life.[41] Still,
by the early twentieth century such a craft hierarchy was being

39. *Rabotnitsa* (19 Apr. 1914), p. 12.
40. See for example M.N. Nechkina, *Iz istorii rabochego klassa i revoliutsionnogo dvizheniia* (Moscow, 1958), p. 282; I.I. Ianzhul, *Fabrichnyi byt moskovskoi gubernii* (Moscow, 1966), p. 155.
41. Buzinov, *Za nevskoi zastavoi*, pp. 20–1.

diluted by the influx of female and male peasants into the growing number of semi-skilled jobs. Thus, as industry developed the balance of forces within the working class shifted, though the dominant position of the skilled male, and specifically skilled metal workers, was not significantly altered.

Nevertheless, memoirs of workers as well as urban studies, notably of Moscow and St. Petersburg, have revealed that the working class was highly diversified: between skilled and unskilled; between urbanised and recent migrant workers; between those working in huge plants and those employed in small workshops; between women and men.[42] What most historians point to is the influence of peasant patriarchy on urban gender relations. Yet in terms of work, the peasant women toiled in the fields as well as in the home, so that the division of labour was not completely rigid, at least as far as women were concerned. Peasant notions of gender thus did not confine women to the home, though they were always held primarily responsible for the housework and childcare. Likewise in the cities, as Batova's case shows, women's participation in the workforce was continuous, so that they combined childbearing and childrearing with wage labour. Indeed, in the city as well as in the village, a woman's capacity to contribute to the family upkeep by her labour was, in a sense, her dowry.

Between the 1880s and the First World War, there was a gradual increase both in the numbers of women in the urban labour force, and in the percentage of the whole. By the end of the 1880s, there were around 200,000 female factory workers, accounting for 25 per cent of the industrial labour force, and 40 per cent of textile workers. By the eve of the First World War, women constituted 58.6 per cent of the textile labour force, and one in three factory workers was a woman.[43] Table 1.1 reveals that, despite differences between industries, women always earned less than men.

The general argument is that mechanisation and low skill requirements led to the growth in women workers, and that there was a tendency to increase the use of female labour wherever great physical strength was not required. Nonetheless, women's work remained physically demanding. Thus women who worked as cleaners

---

42. See for example Johnson, *Peasant and Proletarian*; Koenker, *Moscow Workers*; Joseph Bradley, *Muzhik and Muscovite: Urbanization in Late Imperial Russia* (Berkeley, Calif., 1988); Daniel R. Brower, *The Russian City Between Tradition and Modernity, 1850–1900* (Berkeley, Calif., 1990).

43. Rashin, *Formirovanie rabochego klassa v Rossii*, pp. 185–95, 214–17. See also A. Riazanova, *Zhenskii trud* (Moscow, 1923), pp. 33, 68.

TABLE 1.1   *Female textile workers in Russia in 1913*

Industry	% of women workers	Women's wages as % of the average wage
Ribbon & lace	55.5	23.8
Cotton	61.5	49.4
Wool	56.7	43.3
Stocking-making	74.6	59.3
Silk	68.7	56.2

Source: 'Zhenskii trud v fabrichno-zavodskoi promyshlennosti Rossii za poslednie 13 let (1901–1913)', *Obshchestvennyi vrach* (1915), nos. 9–10, p. 595.

in factories performed heavy, sometimes dangerous jobs. For example, in one of the more modern Petersburg factories manufacturing office paper, a vertical pipe, used for transporting the raw paper, ran throughout the three floors. It was cleaned by women who, having taken off all their clothes, got into sacks and crawled down that pipe, cleaning off what had stuck to it with their shoulders and sides. Their bodies (naked under the sacks) were covered in scratches, rashes and scabs. The very method of work in many cases endangered the lives of the women.[44] Moreover, although textiles was above all a female domain, women were to be found in considerable numbers in the following industries: chemical, tobacco, lime, brick, glass, sugar-refining, distilling, food and rubber-processing.

Russian industry had a huge, impoverished and rapidly growing population to draw upon; indeed, because government policy in the 1880s and 1890s concentrated on developing heavy industry and railways, and neglected agriculture, the situation of the peasantry did not improve. Despite the facts that more land was brought under cultivation, that there were some limited improvements in productivity, and that there was the growth of an urban market for farm produce, the position of the peasantry deteriorated. The last two decades of the nineteenth century saw a fall in grain prices which, added to rising land rents and indirect taxation, hurt peasant income. More and more of their produce had to be sold simply to subsist, which meant that peasants had little in reserve and simply could not cope with famine, which was devastating in 1891, in 1901 and again in 1921. To survive, peasants, and increasingly women as well as men, had to find work outside farming.

44. E.S. Vostokova (ed.), *Istoriia rabochego klassa Leningrada: iz istorii rabochego klassa Peterburga-Petrograda* (2nd edn Leningrad, 1963), p. 34.

Migration to the cities was not the only alternative, however. There were rural craft industries, while agriculture remained important for female labour. Even at the end of the nineteenth century, around 25 per cent of all women wage earners were hired field hands. There were regional differences, but women always earned considerably less than men. Although on average, in field work as in urban employment, women earned a third to a half of men's wages, in places the gulf was immense: in early twentieth-century Saratov, women field hands earned a sixth of men's wages, in Odessa, a fifth.[45] In his study of the hiring market and migrant farm workers in European Russia, Timothy Mixter has found that from 1890 to the eve of the First World War, women made up between 18 and 40 per cent of the workforce. These figures suggest that there was considerable labour turnover among female field hands, the majority of whom were single and under 30 years of age, trying to accumulate enough money for a dowry. However, the turn of the century, Mixter believes, saw migrant farm workers in a difficult position, because of competition for jobs and the growing use of machinery, which depressed wages. In Yaroslavl' Province, male farm-hands earned between 44 and 55 roubles per season, females 25 to 30.[46] By then, the rates of male migration to the cities had stabilised, while those for women grew. Nor was it still only marginal single women who migrated to the city. Engel records that by 1900, a third of peasant women in St. Petersburg were, like Batova, married; and another 17.6 per cent were marriageable women aged between 16 and 25. Yet by 1900, compared to the industrialised powers Russia had the lowest percentage (only 8.4) of women living independently of men, whereas 41.6 per cent of men lived independently, which reflected the low level of industrial and urban development.[47]

Thus, it was still the case that more men than women went to the cities for work. At least in the provinces around Moscow, the putting-out system provided an opportunity to remain in the village. Thousands of women and men worked in various trades in small factories and workshops in the countryside, though they may have had to migrate to another village. In her study of women's

45. Rashin, *Naselenie Rossii*, p. 158; *Zhenskii vestnik* (1907), part 2, pp. 48–49.

46. Timothy Mixter, ch. 9 in E. Kingston-Mann and T. Mixter (eds), *Peasant Economy, Culture, and Politics of European Russia, 1800–1921* (Princeton, 1991), pp. 297, 312. For the wage rates for Yaroslavl' province, see *Otkhozhie promysly krestianskogo naseleniia Yaroslavskoi gubernii* (Yaroslavl', 1907), pp. 22–3.

47. Engel, *Between the Fields and the City*, p. 66; K.N. Kovalev, *Istoricheskoe razvitie byta zhenshchiny, braka i sem'i* (Moscow, 1931), p. 2.

domestic industries in Moscow province in the last two decades of the nineteenth century, Judith Pallott argues that women were more likely to remain in their own villages, which would indicate that they had household and childcare responsibilities; and when women moved away, they still stayed closer to home than men.[48] Single women who had gone to work in the city, however, were more likely to marry outside their home village. In some cases, particularly among the poorest, where both parents worked in the city, the child might be brought up in the village by grandparents, as had happened to Golubeva. In 1884 it was reported that women made up 35 per cent of factory workers within the Moscow district (7,606 women to 21,848 men), whereas in the city of Moscow the percentage of female factory workers was 21.4 (that is, there were 2,576 women workers to 12,008 men).[49] Batova's experience, of going to a neighbouring village to work in a textile factory when she was 14 years old, suggests that such migrants would have been young, single and childless. Indeed, that small move at such a young age may have encouraged the greater migration to Moscow when she was 17 and newly married. Again, however, Batova may not have been typical. Indeed, Barbara Engel believes that if a woman came from a province which had longstanding patterns of migration to either Moscow or St. Petersburg, then she was unlikely to have taken an intermediary step by working first in a smaller town before coming to the city.[50]

Gender, industrialisation and urbanisation

What did such migrants find when they arrived in the cities? Uprooted from the villages in the late 1890s, pushed out by peasant poverty and pulled by the industrial boom, the migrants came up against the problems of housing and sanitation (or the lack of both). By the end of the nineteenth century, the urban working class was crowded into inadequate accommodation, located in areas which lacked basic amenities, with such poor public hygiene that there were frequent cholera outbreaks (for example, in 1908–9), and very high death rates. Again, Batova's initial experience of housing

48. Judith Pallot, 'Women's Domestic Industries in Moscow Province, 1880–1900', in Barbara Evans Clements, Barbara Alpern Engel, Christine D. Worobec (eds), *Russia's Women: Accommodation, Resistance, Transformation* (Berkeley, Calif., 1991).

49. E. Mikhailova, 'Polozhenie fabrichnykh rabotnits na moskovskikh fabrikakh i uezdnykh', *Drug Zhenshchin* (1884), vol. 5, pp. 108–25: 109.

50. Engel, *Between the Fields and the City*, p. 131.

in Moscow (living at her husband's workplace) and the fact that only eight of her thirteen children survived infancy gives some indication of the hardships of urban life. Married to a skilled worker, she was better off than most, yet in order to rent a flat Batova had to remain in continuous employment, despite having a large family. A flat was certainly an improvement on sleeping under a workbench, but still often entailed sharing limited space with others. Dr. Mariia Pokrovskaia calculated that, by the early twentieth century, each room of a flat in the working-class districts of Petersburg housed up to 20 people. She described one flat which had a kitchen and three rooms. One of the rooms housed three children under 10 years of age and four adults: the two families were separated simply by a curtain. Another of the rooms was really a windowless hall used as living space.[51]

Batova's story shows that, even if in a minority among migrants, families did move as a unit. In the 1890s, Fedor Pavlovich Pavlov, an engineer, spent six years employed in the textile industry. He found factory villages in which entire families worked in the mills, with wives and daughters in relatively low-skilled occupations such as spinning and carding, while male workers were employed as machinists and fabric printers.[52] In his history of the working class in Russia between 1861 and 1917, L.M. Ivanov supported his argument that a hereditary working class was developing by pointing out that at the turn of the century there was a significant increase in the incidence of 'factory families' in cities.[53] Batova's family, with the children born and brought up in the city and both parents working in factories, would seem to provide support for Ivanov's thesis. Yet though there were some changes, there was no great urge for the transformation of the traditional peasant structure. The existence of a second generation at the factory was not in itself proof that its members had severed ties with the village. Parents could force a son or daughter migrant worker to send money to them by threatening to withdraw their internal passport. Issued by the village assembly, migrant workers needed such passports to reside legally in the towns. In return, they were expected to help the families they left behind meet certain responsibilities, including payment of taxes.

51. Pokrovskaia, *Po podvalam*, pp. 4–5.
52. For Pavlov, see Victoria E. Bonnell (ed.), *The Russian Worker: Life and Labour under the Tsarist Regime* (Berkeley, Calif., 1983), p. 18.
53. L.M. Ivanov, *Rabochii klass i rabochee dvizhenie v Rossii 1861–1917* (Moscow, 1960), pp. 99–100.

It was not only the male elder who could compel a migrant to contribute to the village household. An illiterate wife would find it difficult to correspond directly with her migrant husband, but she was not powerless, since he needed a passport from the village elder as proof of permission to leave the village. As Jeffrey Burds has shown in his study of the social control of peasant labour, the village and the family left behind had a considerable hold over the migrant, revealed in this exchange of letters between a peasant-worker in St. Petersburg and his illiterate wife in a village in north-west Kostroma province:

> You did not write, my dear Anna Zinov'evna, whether you received the money. I sent 15 roubles on 21 August. You wrote [asking whether I would be returning] to the village, but I don't think so because money is so short and it is bad to be without money in the village, but I thank you for the intention. If there is not great hardship, then write and I will come to the village. I remain alive and well. I inform you my dear wife Anna Zinov'evna, I beg you: would it be impossible to send an annual passport, because I don't have much time left. My brother had to pay 4 roubles for an expired passport. And if you send an annual passport so that I won't need to get one in the spring then I will come to the village. I will winter [here] reluctantly, as I would rather [come back] to the village. Please, tell me everything in detail. How is the horse now, since she had the colt? I think my coming home would be impossible. I could move timber on the water for household expenses, but I don't think I could winter there. Send a passport because I don't have much time. An expired passport is too costly. A passport is not to be wasted even in spring. Please write about everything. Farewell. To your health. You never write. Send a letter soon.

The brief reply he received from his wife, with the help of a literate neighbour, revealed the difficult situation such families were in, since if the migrant did not pay commune taxes as well as support his family, he was liable to be arrested and returned to the village in disgrace:

> Dear husband Polien Petrovich, you have written that I should send you an annual passport. I will not send a passport [because] I have no money and the village elder won't issue a travel permit. He is asking about the taxes. If you send money I will send the passport.[54]

54. The letters are taken from D.N. Zhbankov, *Bab'ia storona: statistiko-ethnograficheskii ocherk* (Kostroma, 1891), pp. 114–15; quoted in Jeffrey Burds, 'The Social Control of Peasant Labour in Russia: The Response of Village Communities to Labour Migration in the Central Industrial Region, 1861–1905', ch. 2 in *Peasant Economy, Culture, and Politics of European Russia*, pp. 76–7.

Migration was not an easy solution to the hardships facing peasant households by the end of the nineteenth century, while it put great strains on the family as a whole. At best, male migrant workers could combine their earnings with their family's agricultural income to achieve a basic, though insecure, measure of economic well-being for the peasant household, a retreat for them in times of unemployment or ill health.

Hence the continuation of rural patterns of early marriage and large families. The patriarchal family system remained strong in the rural areas of European Russia, and the 1897 census showed that natality levels remained high.[55] In practice, the general trend seems to have been that female factory workers either remained single, or married and either returned to raise their children in the village, or sent their young children to be brought up there. However, it appears that the decline in the birth rate was already underway at the turn of the century in the urban areas of European Russia. One possible explanation was that the unhealthy conditions in the factories and workshops adversely affected fertility. There was also no provision for working mothers to look after their children.[56]

It could be argued, then, that the abandonment of village traditions would be most apparent among those female, and for the most part unskilled, migrants who cut their ties with the village, as well as among the skilled male workers. However, the impression of the lives of the former is of constant struggle to subsist, and little chance to enlarge their cultural horizons. Men could afford to spend money on entertainment, particularly in the taverns. Women workers, especially those with family reponsibilities, generally could not. How did they spend the little free time which they had? Even on such low wages, single women workers at least could enjoy the cheap entertainments offered by fairs and pleasure gardens. Many, however, clung to religion. The impression is that many more female than male workers turned to the church. An ethnographic study published in 1928 showed 85 per cent of women workers had attended church before the 1917 revolution. Yet it also revealed that a not inconsiderable proportion of male workers (70 per cent) did likewise.[57] Still, the general perception among contemporaries was that women were more religious, or superstitious, depending

55. Rashin, *Naselenie Rossii*, pp. 167–8.

56. Ibid.; M. Lyadov, 'Koe-chto o zhenshchine rabotnitse', *Literatura Moskovskogo Rabochego Soiuza* (Moscow, 1930), p. 168.

57. E.O. Kabo, *Ocherki rabochego byta: opyt monograficheskogo issledovaniia domashnego rabochego byta* (Moscow, 1928), vol. 1, p. 132.

on the viewpoint of the observer. Indeed, and in contrast to the general association of lax morals with female factory workers, a male worker likened the women's factory barracks not to the more common epithet of the 'mare's yard', or cattleyard, but rather to a monastery, because icons were everywhere. An old woman worker, Gorlova, explained the strong religious feeling by referring to the difficult working conditions:

> We used to work [that is before the 1917 revolution] really hard at the factory, ten to 12 hours a day, and still had housework. You would feel really bad inside. We didn't know anything about entertainment, clubs or theatres; so our entertainment was going to the church.[58]

In fact, the number of hours which women were expected to work each day in the late nineteenth and early twentieth centuries was closer to 14, and sometimes more.

Indeed, while men also worked long hours, the factory inspectorate was of the opinion that the burden of industrialisation fell especially heavily on women. Inspectors noted that the generally held belief in women as weaker beings than men failed to prevent the growth of the female labour force. They recorded that employers saw women as more industrious and abstemious than men. In fact, not all women were such paragons of virtuous subordination, though again female factory workers were less likely to drink alcohol than, for example, domestic servants and prostitutes. The harsh life of a woman worker drove not insignificant numbers to drink, especially widows, according to Lapitskaia, while Oliunina wrote that in the high-class workshops around 1910, female tailors experienced so much tension that they always had a 'tincture of valerian' with them.[59] However, perhaps because of their lower wages and household responsibilities, such women could not afford alcohol regularly, but would organise a drinking binge in their bedrooms each autumn.

In addition, unless a woman was a proprietor, waitress or prostitute, it was highly unlikely that she would visit a tavern, which was identified as masculine space. The fact that prostitutes frequented taverns confirmed the popular association of alcohol with female sexual promiscuity. In any case, as long as a man supported his

58. S. Lapitskaia, *Byt rabochikh Trekhgornoi manufactury* (Moscow, 1935), p. 71.
59. Ibid., pp. 72, 77; E.O. Oliunina, *Portnovskii promysel v Moskve i v derevniakh Moskovskoi i Riazanskoi gubernii* (Moscow, 1914), p. 184.

family, working-class and peasant women viewed alcohol imbibed in a tavern among workmates as a man's compensation for heavy labour, while for a man it confirmed his masculinity and his place in the collective.[60] Drinking was an integral part of a man's social as well as his self identity. Women too had special occasions which they celebrated with alcohol, but they were fewer than those which men enjoyed. For employers, such occasional lapses were more than made up for by the fact that, compared to men, women were much less likely to organise to defend themselves against the bosses. Hence, whenever possible, and especially after the 1905 revolution, women were used to displace men, because of the former's cheapness and assumed passivity.[61]

Indeed, the male inspectorate accepted women working in factories as a fact of economic life. At the same time, they sought to ameliorate conditions of work so that the female employees could still fulfil what was seen as their primary natural function, and indeed social duty, of maternity. Improvements were needed to ensure the health of future generations of workers.[62] Considering the mortality rate among Batova's children, the inspectorate did not seem to have much success. Still, there was protective legislation for female labour. The Russian factory laws of the late nineteenth century have even been described as more enlightened than similar legislation in western Europe and the USA.[63] While it may have been a reflection of tsarist paternalism, the legislation allowed employers to reduce the already low wages for women on the grounds that night work was more demanding. Protective legislation thus appeared to put women at a disadvantage in the labour force, and to strengthen the division of labour which favoured men. Such laws not only took account of women's biological role as childbearer, they served to reinforce their cultural role as childrearer. The authorities seemed increasingly uneasy, afraid that the family life of the masses was being undermined by the rapidity of industrial development. Contemporary observers were alarmed by what they

---

60. See for example David Christian, *Living Water: Vodka and Russian Society on the Eve of Emancipation* (Oxford, 1990).

61. See Riazanova, *Zhenskii trud*, p. 34; Rashin, *Formirovanie rabochego klassa v Rossii*, pp. 235–6.

62. See for example I.I. Yanzhul, *Ocherki i issledovaniia* (Moscow, 1884), vol. 1, pp. 381–93; M.I. Tugan-Baranovsky, *Russkaia fabrika v proshlom i nastoiashchem* (St. Petersburg, 1898), p. 380.

63. See Kechedzhi-Shapovalov, *Zhenskoe dvizhenie*; Frederick C. Giffen, 'Prohibition of Night Work for Women and Young Persons: The Russian Factory Law of June 3, 1885', *Canadian Slavic Studies* (Summer 1968), vol. 11, no. 2, pp. 208–18.

assumed to be side-effects of urbanisation: increasing prostitution, illicit sexual relations, illegitimacy, abandonment of children, use of wet-nursing, and the spread of venereal diseases.[64] Thus it seemed expedient to bolster the family, and protective legislation was part of that strategy. It restricted women to certain hours and specific occupations, in the process confirming and strengthening male superiority in the labour force.

The law of 1885 prohibiting night work for women and youths was, however, more than part of a strategy to strengthen the family. In showing some concern for abuses of the factory system, it was also a response to the widespread industrial unrest of the 1880s. In addition, this law was a reflection of the competition between St. Petersburg and Moscow industrialists. The latter made extensive use of female labour and night work in their textile factories, which the former believed had led to over-production, besides harming the women, both physically and morally. Thereafter, the Ministry of Finance gradually extended the scope of the law to cover other branches of industry in which women and youths were extensively employed, though, as Karelina noted in her memoir of 1905, such protective legislation for women workers was often ignored.[65]

Yet single women who moved to the city were more likely to remain unmarried. In the 1890s the Social Democrat M.N. Lyadov had asserted that the majority of working women were not in a position to marry. He believed that men at least could avoid the burdens of marriage and a family, and satisfy their sexual needs, through recourse to prostitutes and illicit relationships. Any resulting illegitimate children were left at foundling homes which, if the children survived them, were recruiting grounds for capitalism's wage slaves.[66] Twenty years earlier, the revolutionary student Sofia Bardina had commented at her trial in 1877 on the low and very unequal pay for women workers, as well as the sexual degradation to which they were subjected. Praskovia Ivanovskaia's experience in an Odessa rope factory in 1876 seemed typical:

64. See for example S.S. Shashkov, *Ocherk istorii russkoi zhenshchiny* (St. Petersburg, 1872), pp. 265–75; M.G. Kuznetsov, *Prostitutsiia i sifilis v Rossii: istoriko-statisticheskoe issledovanie* (St. Petersburg, 1871).

65. For Karelina see P.F. Kudelli (ed.), *Rabotnitsa v 1905g. v S-Peterburge: sbornik statei i vospominanii* (Leningrad, 1926), p. 57; see also J.D. White, 'Moscow, Petersburg and the Russian Industrialists', *Soviet Studies* (Jan. 1973), vol. xxiv, no. 3, pp. 414–420; Tugan-Baranovsky, *Russkaia fabrika*, pp. 385–6.

66. Lyadov, 'Koe-chto', p. 168.

The women got paid 25 kopecks a day; the men, as I recall, got 30 or 40. Most of the women workers were totally rootless: as many of them told me, they had nowhere else to go but the streets. Some had to work there so as not to burden their families. In short, women were driven to the rope factory by the most pressing need, by the cruellest misfortune. Only women in this situation would put up with the ubiquitous rudeness, the men's disrespectful treatment of them, the pinches and searches as they entered and left the factory.[67]

By the turn of the century, little had changed. Vera Karelina related that foremen forced female factory workers into prostitution. She also noted that the practice of searching workers at the end of their shifts, to ensure that they were not stealing from their employers, led to widespread sexual abuse of female workers, many of whom were as young as 13 years of age.[68] In 1905, a woman factory worker complained:

> The administration treats us women-workers most disgracefully. They refuse to see us as people, [treating us like] human cattle. Flirting, pinching, innuendo, abuse and bad language are in abundance; and if among us there are some who treat such behaviour with contempt, they have to be careful lest they be sacked. Take, for instance, one floor-manager (and there are many like him). If he 'likes' a woman worker but she doesn't respond, then he can give her substandard goods to work with, which wouldn't bring her more than 50 kopecks, while underproduction may lead to her dismissal.[69]

The Bolshevik paper aimed at women workers, *Rabotnitsa*, complained in 1914 about male workers' sexually coarse and even brutal treatment of women workers, and, writing in 1917, the Menshevik Eva Broido asserted that sexual harassment was still rife, and that the culprits were not only foremen, but fellow male workers.[70] Nor was it only factory workers who were at risk of sexual abuse or humiliation. Indeed, domestic servants were particularly vulnerable, as we have already seen; so too were shop assistants, whom employers often insisted be young, attractive and well dressed. A female assistant in a bakery wrote in 1908:

67. For Ivanovskaia see *Five Sisters*, p. 104. For Bardina, see Stites, *The Women's Liberation Movement in Russia*, pp. 136–7, 141–2.

68. For Karelina see Kudelli, *Rabotnitsa v 1905g.*, p. 18. See also E. Bochkareva, S. Liubimova, *Svetlyi put'* (Moscow, 1967), pp. 3–4.

69. Kudelli, *Rabotnitsa v 1905g.*, pp. 5–6.

70. *Rabotnitsa* (23 Feb. 1914), no. 1, p. 11; Eva Broido, *Zhenshchina-rabotnitsa* (Petrograd, 1917), p. 7.

Work in bakeries begins at five or six o'clock in the morning and ends at eight or nine at night. In pastry shops, work starts at seven or eight and ends at ten-thirty or 11 at night. Year-round, we have to work a 15 or 16-hour day. We don't get any time off for lunch. We have to eat behind the counter. The wage of a female bakery clerk ranges from six to 18 roubles a month; in pastry shops, it ranges from 12 to 25 roubles. Work this out for yourself – a 15 to 16 hour workday comes to about 450 to 480 hours a month. This means we earn from two and a half to four kopecks an hour.

These long hours and low wages force us to turn to the shameful trade. Our wages do not give us enough money to survive, but the bosses still demand that we dress fashionably. We can't fight this because Petersburg is full of girls who are willing to work 15 hours a day just to get a crust of bread. The bosses want only good-looking girls. Most shop girls are from 17 to 20 years old, and a girl over 30 can very seldom be encountered, and then never in shops on the main street.[71]

Nor was it only shop assistants who were in this position. Many female white-collar workers, including accountants, cashiers, office clerks, and stenographers, resorted to casual prostitution in order to boost their earnings above subsistence level. Women who worked in banks were also expected to be well dressed, and often could not obtain a post without a bribe 'in kind' to a male manager or director. There were certainly more shop assistants than white-collar workers, but the position of the latter group was almost as difficult.[72]

Was this mistreatment of urban women workers simply a reflection of peasant patriarchy? There was also the sexual imbalance in the cities. In 1882, males represented 57.4 per cent (432,447) of Moscow's population, females 42.6 per cent (321,022). The gap narrowed, but still women were outnumbered: in 1902, males were 56.1 per cent (612,149) of Moscow's population, females 43.9 per cent (478,567). Migration to Moscow was mostly over short distances. Joseph Bradley's study of Moscow reveals that it was still a city of immigrants by the turn of the century: around 75 per cent had been born elsewhere, and the majority were male. Whereas in 1871 Moscow had only 700 women per 1,000 men, by 1911 that gap had narrowed to 839 women per 1,000 men. Among the men, around 75 per cent had left their families behind in the villages.[73]

71. See Bonnell, *The Russian Worker*, p. 195.

72. A. Gudvan, *Ocherki po istorii dvizheniia sluzhashchikh v Rossii, chast' 1, 'Do revoliutsii 1905g'*. (Moscow, 1925), p. 139.

73. Joseph Bradley, 'Moscow: From Big Village to Metropolis', ch. 2 in Michael F. Hamm (ed.), *The City in Late Imperial Russia* (Bloomington, Ind., 1986), pp. 13–15.

Yet the increasing ratio of women migrants was not constant. Indeed, there were occasional deteriorations, perhaps due to an industrial downturn: in 1882, Bradley has calculated that there were only 625 migrant women for every 1,000 migrant men, while in 1902 the ratio was similar, with only 677 women for every 1,000 men.[74] According to James Bater, migrants to the capital had a similar profile to Moscow migrants: male peasants aged between 20 and 40. Bradley, however, has also shown that the rate of female migration to St. Petersburg grew faster than it did in Moscow, so that in 1897 there were 826 women for every 1,000 men in Petersburg, whereas in Moscow the ratio of women to men was 755 to 1,000. By 1910 the percentage of women in Petersburg's population had risen to 48.[75] The longer-distance migration to Petersburg meant that there were fewer opportunities for maintaining contact with the village so that female migrants tended to remain.

As Kanatchikov's autobiography reveals, male migrants often lived within a largely male community, in his case as an artel (co-operative) of about fifteen men. The men, however, did not cook for themselves, but hired a woman to look after them.[76] Batova's memoir shows that women also lived communally, but most studies of urban life in the late nineteenth and early twentieth centuries reveal that women were more likely to lead isolated lives, and to live in cot or corner 'apartments', able to rent only a corner of a room. Since women earned considerably less than men, taking care of their own housework was economical; however, since women were more likely to live alone, rents would take up more of their income. For example, in 1900 in St. Petersburg it was recorded that the average payment for a bed was 2 roubles, 77 kopecks, which accounted for a fifth of a woman worker's earnings.[77]

Why were women prepared to spend so much even on very basic accommodation? While they earned less than men, they generally had fewer obligations in the villages. The assumption was that a married man with a family in the village would send them a significant portion of his wages, whereas less was expected of a single girl, partly because her earnings were so much lower than a man's,

74. Bradley, *Muzhik and Muscovite*, p. 134.

75. James H. Bater, 'Between Old and New: St. Petersburg in the Late Imperial Era', ch. 3 in *The City in Late Imperial Russia*, p. 52; Bradley, *Muzhik and Muscovite*, p. 134.

76. Bonnell, *The Russian Worker*, p. 41.

77. M.I. Pokrovskaia, 'Peterburgskaia rabotnitsa', *Mir Bozhii* (1900), vol. 12, pp. 32–7.

and the cost of living in the city was so high.[78] Caring for their living quarters, and for themselves, may have added to their sense of self-worth and of belonging to the city. Thus contemporaries observed that women would try to create a homely atmosphere even in the meanest accommodation, whereas male workers were less settled. Writing in 1900, Dr. Mariia I. Pokrovskaia described a visit she had made to some single women workers' flat. In contrast to male workers, she discovered that the women were less willing to save on rent by sharing beds. She found that if just single women shared accommodation, it was not only much cleaner and tidier, but there was an attempt to achieve a degree of comfort. One group which she visited had white pillowcases, clean sheets and blankets, net curtains on the window, a clean tablecloth, a dresser with a mirror, and a bouquet of artificial flowers.[79]

Nevertheless, the very poor living conditions for women and men alike stimulated upper-class fears for the morals of their social inferiors. The fact of so many married men in the city without their families and so many vulnerable single women living in such over-crowded conditions was believed to make relations between the sexes difficult. According to Laura Engelstein, faced with what appeared to be an epidemic of syphilis, contemporary medical commentators identified migrants, but especially the prostitutes they frequented, as the main conduits of venereal diseases.[80] Certainly, Kanatchikov's memoirs show the tavern and the brothel to be ubiquitous, and reflect another predominantly female occupation, prostitution. This was not a new concern. Even in the 1870s, Bardina had alleged that prostitution was 'a legal and necessary element of every "civilised" state'.[81] It seems that prostitution was a major supplement, or altern-ative job to women on inadequate wages, or in seasonal employ-ment. In a pamphlet devoted to female factory workers and intended for study in the workers' circles of the early 1890s, the Social Demo-crat Lyadov described the harsh and difficult conditions of labour and life for these women, drawing links between the low and un-equal pay for women (about a third to a half of the average male wage), their semi-starvation diets, frequent periods of unemploy-ment, the complete lack of security, and such widespread social

78. M. Davidovich, *Peterburgskii tekstil'nyi rabochii* (Moscow, 1919), p. 27.

79. Pokrovskaia, 'Peterburgskaia rabotnitsa', pp. 32–7.

80. Laura Engelstein, 'Morality and the Wooden Spoon: Russian Doctors View Syphilis, Social Class and Sexual Behaviour, 1890–1905', *Representations* (Spring 1986), no. 14, pp. 169–208.

81. Burtsev, *Za sto let*, pp. 124–7.

problems as prostitution and venereal disease. In his view, the 'choice' of prostitution was not an unusual one.[82] Lyadov was writing of factory women, but in fact the greatest number of prostitutes in pre-revolutionary Russia came not from the factories but from domestic service, those who worked in trades which were low-paid and seasonal, and day-labourers. In the early twentieth century, the average wage for female clerical workers in banks and offices was between 35 and 40 roubles a month; in stores, it was considerably lower, at between 20 and 25 roubles. Hence:

> As a result of these low wages, long hours and the very high cost of living in large cities, many of the less determined girls begin to follow the same course as the salesgirls. The income from an evening stroll helps many a cashier or secretary make ends meet.
>
> To make matters worse, even the decent and well-paying jobs, for example, those in banks, are rarely available unless one first grants favours to the director, the manager, or some other individual. I could name dozens of women who have made brilliant careers in business thanks to their compliance in this area, but there's no point in doing that. It's a well-known fact anyway. The young girl, driven to such acts by need and hunger, is not to blame. The blame lies with those individuals who use their strength and power to enslave women, body and soul. This sad state of affairs has caused more than one woman to take her own life.[83]

In 1884, a woman from the intelligentsia asked why peasant women left the village and a hard but 'free' life in exchange for the 'dark barracks': the factory. She concluded that such female migrants were extra mouths to feed and surplus hands to employ on too small plots. She agreed that a few were attracted to the 'high life' associated with the city but believed that, as was the case for men, most peasant women who migrated to the city did so for basic economic reasons.[84] They were attracted by the variety of jobs which the city offered women, in the service sector, sweatshops, factories, and on the streets. Industrialisation, especially from the 1890s, and military conflicts in 1904 and 1914, and civil war in 1918, opened up new areas of work, both in war industries and in jobs vacated by millions of conscripted men. Yet across the board, from the floor washer hired by an individual on a daily basis to the professional employed by the state, women remained at the bottom of the labour hierarchy in status and pay, and were generally confined to

---

82. Lyadov, 'Koe-chto', pp. 163–70.   83. Bonnell, *The Russian Worker*, p. 197.
84. Mikhailova, 'Polozhenie fabrichnykh rabotnits', p. 108.

jobs considered as 'women's work'. Indeed, until the transformation of the economy by Stalin in the 1930s, the situation of working women seemed remarkable in its continuity. Yet, as this study will show, it was a modified continuity in which working women acted and were not simply acted upon by outside forces.

PART ONE

Society, Politics and the Economy, 1880–1914

CHAPTER TWO

Women in Society and Economy before the First World War

In a distant foreign region he has fallen in love with another,
And me, the sorrowful one, the unfortunate one, he has forgotten
    forever.
He left me, he, the thief, the bandit, to sit forever among the maidens,
Forever among the maidens to sit, suffering a bad reputation.
No one will take me for his wife, poor me, unfortunate me!
Neither an old man, nor a young man, nor a man of my own age
    who is a terrible drunkard.[1]

This lament reflects the pressures which were bearing down on peasant society, and particularly on women, in the later nineteenth century: the need for male migration in search of work; the belief that the cities had a different morality which would corrupt not only those peasants who went there but those they left behind; the difficulties faced by peasant girls who lost their virginity to a man who did not marry them; and the increasing problems of subsistence, indeed of a role, for those women who remained single if they continued to live in the village, where the economy revolved around the household and marriage was the norm. Perhaps, too, there is an implication that while the man would be expected to marry a peasant woman and leave her behind in the village, he would not marry a city girl and send her to his village. Given the serious shortage of urban accommodation, any infants might be sent to be brought up in the father's village, but a city girl would have found it hard to be accepted by, and adjust to, the village.

Migration for work was not in fact a new phenomenon brought on by industrialisation. Even before the abolition of serfdom in 1861, peasants had migrated for work so that family patterns had

1. Y.M. Sokolov, *Russian Folklore* (1938; Detroit, 1971), p. 596.

long been shaped by interaction with the city. This interaction gradually undermined the isolation of the village, eroding the patriarchal structure of the family and commune. Moreover, while the vast majority of workers remained in agriculture throughout our period, non-agricultural occupations became increasingly important for the peasant household economy. In most areas, some form of seasonal migration had long been a necessity. Travellers to Russia in the late nineteenth and early twentieth centuries observed the extra responsibilities taken over by the peasant women, including having to work like a man in the fields. William Walling, an American who published an account of his visit to Russia in 1909, noted that during the harvest

> Bread is baked once a week, and this is about all the cooking; occasionally, with a great effort and at a sacrifice of her already exhausted strength, a peasant woman will be able to cook a little potato or cabbage soup in the evening. Ordinarily she leaves a few pieces of bread at home for the children, takes some more with her to the fields and returns only after an absence of 12 to 15 hours ... It happens not only occasionally, but very commonly, that the women give birth to children in the fields, that they are carried home only in the evening, and that in three or four days they are back again at work, taking the child with them. The inevitable result is that nearly every peasant woman of middle age is sick in some way or another.[2]

It is not clear whether the husband was still working on the farm, or a visiting migrant worker. However, there was a high incidence of illegitimate births in those regions, such as the north, where the migration of peasant men to the towns coincided with military garrisons.[3] What is clear is that a peasant woman's work was never done. She had a necessary, indeed central role in the household economy: 'neither in the home nor in the commune can a man be a complete workman unless he is married and can place at the community's service, together with his own hands, those of his wife'.[4] This quotation suggests that the husband and wife were interdependent. Thus, while women were indeed in a subordinate position, the labour which they could contribute to the husband's household was valued. Being a wife, then, socially defined the peasant woman's place in the village, and it was a working role. Peasant

2. W.E. Walling, *Russia's Message* (London, 1909), p. 173.

3. V.V. Bervi-Flerovsky, *Izbrannye ekonomicheskie proizvedeniia v dvukh tomakh* (Moscow, 1958), vol. 1, pp. 515–25.

4. A. Leroy-Beaulieu, *The Empire of the Tsars and the Russians* (London, 1902), p. 495.

women were accorded specific tasks within the family, reflected in the proof each had to provide of her housekeeping abilities before marriage. The fertility rites which were integral to the marriage ceremony symbolised that it was the mother who ensured the continuity of family, and indeed village life, since agriculture was labour intensive. The corollary of this is that single women (whether as spinsters or childless widows) lacked status in the community, and were marginal to the village economy.

Life on the land and the peasant economy

A report from a town elder described the peasant household in the Orel Province in the late 1890s:

> The peasant family in our town consists of several kinsmen, their wives and children, from 15 to 20 persons in all, who live in the same house. The elder wields great authority over the family. He keeps the family in peace and order; all of its members are subordinate to him. He assigns the work to be done to each member, manages the farm and pays the taxes. After his death, his authority goes to his eldest son, and if none of his sons is of age, then to one of his brothers. If there are no men left of age in the family, the elder's widow assumes his duties. . . . All the belongings [are considered] the common property of the family, except for the women's clothes, linen, canvas. . . . The elder's wife supervises the work of all the women folk; however, if she is not fit for the task, a younger woman may be selected for it. All the work is distributed among the men and women according to the strength and health of each.[5]

At specific times, such as the harvest, women were called upon to perform predominantly 'male' jobs, so that there was some overlapping of tasks and territories; and whatever the division of labour, the household economy depended on co-operation between the sexes. The work which women performed during harvest time has been described in an ethnographic study of the village of Viriatino.[6] Only old people and small children were left behind, as all able-bodied youth and adults left for the fields at around three or four in the morning, returning only in the evening. Ploughing, harrowing and sowing were done generally by the men. The men cut and the

5. M.N. Kovalevsky, *Rodovoi byt* (St. Petersburg, 1905), 1, pp. 32–3 in G. Vernadsky, *A History of Russia* (London, 1973), vol. 2, p. 133.
6. *The Village of Viriatino* (New York, 1970), translated and edited by Sula Benet, pp. 17, 28, 95.

women bound the sheaves. Only the men worked with the scythe and hook, while the sickle was the woman's tool when she was required to help with the mowing. Women weeded, spread fertiliser, collected the dug-up potatoes, and pulled the hemp. Women were also responsible for harvesting, treating and weaving flax, a process which required months to fulfil. After harvest, women had the task of gleaning.

Thus, although women worked alongside men in the fields, so long as the husband remained on the land there was a sexual division of labour during harvest time. Directing the field work was the role of the male head of the household. Away from the fields, there was a winter allocation of tasks: men chopped wood for fuel, collected manure, fed the farm animals, repaired farm tools; women processed hemp and flax, combed wool, wove, spun, and made clothes for the family. The latter was time-consuming, indeed took up most of the year apart from harvest time. As soon as they were able, that is around seven or eight years of age, little girls would prepare thread for weaving. By the time they were 12, they would be proficient spinners, and by the age of 15 they would be bleaching linen. Weaving, however, required both strength and expertise, and was generally tackled by women between the ages of 20 and 40. The men's contribution was to make the bast shoes [i.e. made from bark], though in 1882 it was reported that there was no gender divide in bast-sandal making when it was for sale. Indeed, it was seen as one of the most lucrative crafts for women (in 1882, women could earn up to 37 roubles a year), certainly paying better than the more traditionally female craft of stocking-knitting.[7]

In 1900 a peasant described the work for which his daughter was being prepared:

> In the future she will be occupied from morning to evening with various heavy tasks equal to those of men, in the field, forest, and garden, and also at home, where her work will be no lighter. She ought to prepare the family breakfast, dinner and supper, tend the cow, look after the children, bathe the whole family, and keep them in clothes.[8]

In general, whatever the season, married women were also responsible for the bulk of the housework, including the preparation of food, cleaning, washing, caring for the children, drawing water,

7. *Zhenskie promysly Moskovskoi Gubernii* (Moscow, 1882), p. 259.
8. Quoted in Jeffrey Brooks, *When Russia Learned to Read: Literacy and Popular Literature, 1861–1917* (New Jersey, 1985), p. 45.

tending any cattle, sheep, pigs and fowl. Girls, especially of marriageable age, had many chores, especially spinning. Family members would contribute to a common purse for the needs of the
household, including not only contributions from any migrant
family members' wages, but also what women earned by selling farm
produce, such as berries and mushrooms, and especially eggs, which
were one of the principal sources of women's income. Men took
care of the horses, and helped care for livestock by cleaning the
barn, removing manure, changing straw bedding. It was the man's
job to bring in fuel and feed the livestock, whereas all work in the
gardens, except for the initial ploughing, was done by women and
children.

In terms of the housework, while it was a female responsibility,
there was a division of labour, and a hierarchy according to age
and status. Most observers pointed to the isolated position of the
daughter-in-law. Within the house, the role of supervisor and director of work went to the older women. A favourite motif of popular
poetry were the complaints of the young bride who found that her
mother-in-law put all the work on her shoulders: 'they are making
me marry a lout, with no small family'.[9] In 1895, an English traveller
recorded one of these songs:

> My father hath given me away,
> Not into a small family;
> Alas! for me,
> Not a small one and not a pleasant one.
> Father-in-law and mother-in-law,
> And four brothers-in-law,
> Two sisters-in-law,
> And two aunts.
> What does the father-in-law say?
> That they are bringing in a she-bear;
> But the mother-in-law says,
> 'A filthy snake'.
> Brothers-in-law say
> That they bring in a dirty slut;
> The two aunts call me a goose-foot;
> All abuse me, a young woman.[10]

9. W.R.S. Ralston, *The Songs of the Russian People* (London, 1872), p. 289. For a
fuller version of the song, see Christine D. Worobec, ch. 5 in B.E. Clements, B.A.
Engel, C.D. Worobec (eds), *Russia's Women: Accommodation, Resistance, Transformation*
(Berkeley, Calif., 1991), p. 177.

10. C.H. Pearson, *Russia by a Recent Traveller* (London 1895; new impression 1970,
with a preface by A.G. Cross), pp. 101–2.

All it seems, with the exception of her sisters-in-law. As told in songs, the bride-to-be's future appeared forbidding: 'who is going to bring the water? The daughter-in-law. Who is going to be beaten? The daughter-in-law. Why is she beaten? Because she is the daughter-in-law.'[11] Caution needs to be exercised, however, in interpreting such lamentations, since tradition demanded that the bride weep bitterly at the beginning of the wedding; this, together with the songs, was a demonstration of her respect and love for the family she was leaving.[12] In addition, the songs recognised the status, and indeed the power, of the mother-in-law, who could become head of the household if her husband was dead, absent, or incompetent in some way. One consequence of high rates of male migration was that the women would have assumed the 'male' farm duties, on top of their own. Donald Mackenzie Wallace, correspondent for *The Times* in the late nineteenth century, noted that in the northern provinces, where a considerable proportion of the male population was absent, working away from the home, the village assembly generally included a good many women as heads of households. As such, they had the unquestioned right to be part of the assembly, and to participate in its deliberations. He noted, however, that they rarely spoke on matters of the general welfare of the village. Rather they concentrated on their own household. He observed that if a woman spoke, she exposed herself to uncomplimentary remarks, but 'any which she happens to receive she is pretty sure to repay with interest'.[13]

While such songs continued to be sung, by the late nineteenth century there had been changes, reflected, for example, in the form of the dowry which a bride brought to her marriage. The dowry 'served as the first basis of the separate property of the wife', legally defining her position as the daughter-in-law and confirming her rights with regard to family property.[14] Previously, she distributed gifts which she herself had made to all members of her husband's family, as proof that she was a good worker.[15] Especially among poor peasants, the wife had to be a capable worker. Even though female work was valued less than male, it was recognised as essential. However, by the end of the century expectations had

11. L. Tikhomirov, *Russia, Political and Social* (London, 1888), vol. 1, pp. 185–6.
12. Sokolov, *Russian Folklore*, pp. 212–23.
13. D. Mackenzie Wallace, *Russia on the Eve of War and Revolution* (edited and abridged from the 1912 edition by C.E. Black, New York, 1961), pp. 278–9.
14. V.O. Klyuchevsky, *A History of Russia* (New York, 1960), vol. 1, pp. 48–9.
15. Sokolov, *Russian Folklore*, p. 207.

changed. The bride's dowry now consisted of ready-made objects of urban culture which she had bought, thus demonstrating her earning capacity. Moreover, concerns about her physical strength had begun to diminish, reflected in changing views of feminine beauty, with more stress being placed on the prospective wife's conduct and physical appearance.[16] Indeed, the young peasant woman was said to want to dress fashionably, like the aristocracy.[17]

She was also thought to be increasingly assertive. There was a growing trend for dividing up the extended family's property as a result of internal family quarrelling, in which young wives were believed to play a large part. In the traditional patriarchal community, their role had seemed almost invisible. Now they sought a more prominent, influential position in an independent household.[18] By this time, peasant songs were not only full of traditional complaints about the state of female subservience, but often pictured 'the implacable revolts of the women for the reconquest of their rights, now trodden underfoot'. In these new songs, the wife declares that she is no longer a submissive creature. She answers the insults of the old people by 'insults ten times as great', and stands up to her husband:

> The husband let out with his hand
> and boxed his wife upon the ear;
> the wife let out with her hand
> and hit him right across the face.[19]

It seems that the wife made such a hell of family life that the old people themselves were inclined to beg the young couple to leave and set up their own separate household. However, Elvira M. Wilbur's study of peasant poverty in Voronezh province reveals that in practice arguments among the women were rarely responsible for a couple breaking away from the household.[20] Given that land was allocated to a household according to the number of male members and that farming was labour intensive, a nuclear family was likely to be poorer. Yet a few women at least saw life outside the family household, whether it be extended or nuclear, as an option. It was recorded in the 1880s that women

16. Ibid., p. 208.
17. Bervi-Flerovsky, *Izbrannye ekonomicheskie proizvedeniia*, vol. 1, pp. 517–18.
18. M.N. Kovalevsky, *Tableau des origines et de l'evolution de la famille et de la propriété* (Stockholm, 1890), pp. 126–8, 139.
19. Tikhomirov, *Russia*, vol. 1, p. 90.
20. Ch. 3 in E. Kingston-Mann and T. Mixter (eds), *Peasant Economy, Culture, and Politics of European Russia, 1800–1921* (Princeton, 1991).

are beginning to make the fruits of their labour (spinning and so forth) their own personal property. Often again, the women demand plots of land for themselves; sometimes they get them. . . . It is not uninteresting that celibacy, with a view to keeping their independence, is not uncommon among the peasant women. . . .

Her instinct of independence can no longer adapt itself to the old fetters. Our village tribunals receive numbers of complaints from the women against the oppression of their husbands and of the older members of the family. When complaints and protests are unavailing, the wife acts.[21]

Striking out on one's own and remaining within the village would have been seen as deviant behaviour for a woman of childbearing age, while earning a living from the land and her crafts would have been extremely difficult for the single woman. For a small minority, an alternative was to enter a religious community. Here, the work of Brenda Meehan-Waters is invaluable.[22] She charts the development of women's religious communities, which flowered particularly throughout the nineteenth century until the 1917 revolution, revealing that it was an overwhelmingly rural phenomenon. They were self-supporting, from the agricultural and craft work of the sisters, most of whom were peasants; they were also supported by the local people, for whom they provided charitable services. Meehan-Waters has found that the women who entered a religious community could do so on a temporary basis (as some soldiers' wives apparently did) and were not expected to take a vow of celibacy (though they were expected to remain celibate while living within the community).

Such communities were founded by women of all social groups, but mostly by wealthy widows. Generally women and men, but especially the former, were regarded as having worldly duties, which included bringing children into the world, so that it was traditional for a woman to delay entry into a religious community until the death of her husband and the adulthood of her children. Besides the religious convictions of the women, the local priest might

21. Tikhomirov, *Russia*, vol. 1, pp. 120, 197–8. See also Aleksandra Efimenko, *Issledovaniia narodnoi zhizni* (Moscow, 1884), vol. 1, pp. 84, 89.

22. Brenda Meehan-Waters, 'To Save Oneself: Russian Peasant Women and the Development of Women's Religious Communities in Prerevolutionary Russia', ch. 7 in Beatrice Farnsworth and Lynne Viola (eds), *Russian Peasant Women* (Oxford, 1992); 'The Authority of Holiness: Women Ascetics and Spiritual Elders in Nineteenth-Century Russia', in Geoffrey A. Hosking (ed.), *God's Servants: Church, Nation and State in Russia and Ukraine* (London, 1990), pp. 38–51; 'Popular Piety: Local Initiative and the Founding of Women's Religious Communities in Russia, 1764–1907', *St. Vladimir's Theological Quarterly* (1986), vol. 30, no. 2, pp. 117–42.

encourage the establishment of a community which could provide much-needed spiritual as well as charitable services, such as elementary education, and the care of orphaned children and homeless women.

Why was the latter a particular problem? Village life was harsh, but the conditions of labour in the cities were such that the death rate among migrant workers was higher than that of those who remained on the farm. Barbara Engel's research into the impact of male outmigration on the family economy in Kostroma province, where the majority of men had left to work in St. Petersburg, reveals that, of 61 peasant households in four villages studied in 1891, there were 26 widows ranging in age from 22 to 100, and only two widowers; and in 1906, a participant at the Ninth Annual Congress of Kostroma Physicians reported that while one would normally expect 120 old women for every 100 old men, in certain areas of Kostroma there were 212 or even 286 old women.[23] Meehan-Waters concludes that women's religious communities may have been a response to the consequences of male labour migration and modernisation.[24]

Yet entering a community was for many of the sisters not simply a last resort. The community provided more than just security, it offered survival with dignity, reflected in the opportunities for women to improve themselves, not only spiritually but educationally. In order to be able to follow the religious teachings and participate in services, the women had to be able to read, and Meehan-Waters has found much higher rates of literacy within the religious communities than among peasant women generally.[25] Thus living within a religious community could allow a woman to 'save herself' in a number of ways, and indeed to put her personal salvation at the centre of her life.

Of course, such a route was open only to a few. Moreover, much of the work done by women within the religious communities differed little from that on the outside: farm work, housework, crafts. The last became increasingly important in the late nineteenth century, as it brought much-needed cash income to the village. Besides the putting-out work which village women got from factories in the late nineteenth century, there were the traditional handicrafts. The importance of these was stressed in *The Russian Year-Book* of 1912: whereas the numbers of factory workers (women and men) totalled

23. Engel, *Between the Fields and the City*, p. 53.
24. Meehan-Waters, 'Popular Piety', p. 142.
25. *Russian Peasant Women*, p. 128.

1,500,000, there were more than 8,000,000 peasants in European Russia who divided their time between agriculture and various forms of craft production for sale, while about 4,000,000 were solely engaged in handicrafts and small machine industries outside factories.[26]

A few crafts involved both women and men, such as the making of reins, and toy-making. The latter was an important cottage industry, and for some became a way of life:

> One of the senior masters [*sic*] of toymaking in Kargopol', Ul'iana Babkina, who was born in 1888 and lived to age 99, said that she could not imagine herself not making her small clay figures; they had always been part of her life from childhood. For Babkina, modelling the clay was like singing.[27]

Generally, however, women and men worked at different crafts. The Central Industrial Region around Moscow was a key area for crafts, partly because of the close relationship between the city and the countryside, partly because, in contrast to St. Petersburg, factories were not completely concentrated in the city. As in Petersburg, peasant women would sell garden and dairy produce in Moscow's markets. Some of the crafts which employed women in the Moscow region were described in a publication of 1882.[28] A traditional craft for which Moscow merchants supplied the material (gilded thread) was the production of gold lace. Demand was variable. In each village one woman, who had previously been a lace-maker herself, organised the others, who all worked from home. Each lace-maker would work for 161 days a year, earning approximately 21 roubles. The best paid were young unmarried women, but lace-makers ranged from young girls to old women. In one district, as many as a third of the working women were lace-makers, while of the total of 328, 11 were 'managers'.

At that time, around 33,000 women were engaged in lace-making. Thirty years later, it remained a significant female handicraft. However, the impact of the wholesale dealers who bought the work from the peasant women had been to undermine the artistic value of the lace by replacing the traditional designs with the commonplace. The women made the lace to the requirements of the

---

26. Howard P. Kennard (ed.), *The Russian Year-Book for 1912* (London, 1912), p. 707.

27. Alison Hilton, *Russian Folk Art* (Bloomington, Ind., 1995), pp. 129–30.

28. *Zhenskie Promysly Moskovskoi Gubernii.* Unless otherwise stated, the information on women's crafts comes from this publication.

dealers, on whom they depended for their market. Another consequence of this dependence was that, despite the growing demand, the wages commanded by the lace-makers were very low indeed.[29]

Of course a problem for such crafts was changing fashions, as well as the seasonal nature of demand. Fringe-makers, some as young as 5 years old, were suffering a severe downturn in demand in the 1880s. More dependable was the making of knitted goods, such as stockings, socks, mittens, gloves, vests. Girls started knitting by hand usually at the age of 8, occasionally at 6, and were expected to produce a pair of socks a day; by the time they were 10 to 12, they would be able to work by themselves. In 1882, in the Moscow province women knitted for sale on average 35 weeks each year, earning around 30 roubles if they sold to a dealer. Knitting took up the best part of the day, but while it provided cash income and some measure of independence to the knitter, she still had other duties, including housework and field labour.

Only well-off peasants could afford to buy a knitting-machine, which then cost between 110 and 140 roubles. In such cases, it was the wife who ran the workshop, but the husband was the legal owner of the enterprise. Only in a situation where the machine was bought for an unmarried daughter could a woman become an owner. Having such a machine would allow a woman to hire a servant to do her housework, and other women to do the knitting. The latter were paid between two and four roubles a month, for which they had to work extremely hard. A major difference between the handknitters and the women who ran a machine workshop was that the latter were literate. Indeed, unless a daughter was going to be employed in a mechanised trade, her parents saw little reason to send her to school. In villages in the Moscow region which specialised in tailoring, teachers told E.A. Oliunina, who investigated the trade in the early twentieth century, that in general the craft adversely affected the mental development of all the children who worked at it, but that parents paid least attention to girls' schooling.[30]

Another craft which could be done by hand or machine was glove-making. By hand, it was done from home, or with several girls gathering together in one house. The quality of hand-made gloves was higher than those which were produced by a machine. The average starting age was 10. In villages at some distance from Moscow, a middle-man or woman would obtain the leather and then market

29. *The Russian Year-Book for 1912*, p. 711.

30. E.A. Oliunina, *Portnovskii promysel v Moskve i v derevniakh Moskovskoi i Riazanskoi gubernii* (Moscow, 1914), p. 75.

the finished produce. On average, girls worked 14 hours a day for over nine months (from mid September to early July), earning up to 35 roubles. However, those who relied on the middle-man/woman generally earned below the average. In addition, the strain on the eyes was considerable, so that within 10 or 12 years the glove-maker would have to abandon her craft.

As in knitting, the machine for making gloves was expensive, costing in the early 1880s around 115 roubles, so that in very few cases was a machine bought by the makers of gloves themselves. Girls either hired out for a month (earning up to four roubles, with food), or worked a piece-rate system, earning up to five kopecks a pair. Those who could make up to 20 pairs of gloves a day would get a 'reasonable' wage. On piece-rate, girls were expected to provide their own food. The study of Moscow province in 1882 recorded that it was difficult to calculate an average wage, but suggested that women could earn up to 89 roubles a year, though that did not take into account such expenses as broken needles, for which they were held responsible.

Where women worked independently, and were highly proficient, their earnings could be considerable. Thus straw-hat making could bring in up to 70 roubles a year. In contrast, where women worked for others, through middle-men or women or for factory owners, their earnings were depressed: thus those who worked at cotton-winding might be paid only up to 20 roubles a year. Given that such work ultimately depended on demand for the finished goods, such women – and in 1882 there were as many as 10,000 of them in the Moscow province – might well engage in other crafts during a slow period.

Some handicrafts, such as belt-making and bootlace-making, brought in little extra income (only around 10 to 15 roubles per annum). Again, by the 1880s these crafts could be done by machinery, and, as in knitting and glove-making, few of the girls (some as young as five) and women who made the articles owned the machinery. Instead they worked for wealthy peasant women, earning, with food, about two roubles a month, some of which was in kind (such as dress material). Crafts which earned more depended on location. A non-textile craft which employed women and girls from the age of six in the Moscow region was bullet-making. It originated in villages which had good road connections with the city. Like the other crafts mentioned, bullet-makers worked up to fourteen hours a day for up to nine months of the year, earning up to 40 roubles.

Clearly, craft work which was intended for sale was to supplement agricultural income. Determination to remain on the land even when the soil was poor was so great that all the able-bodied men would go to Moscow to work while the women added the men's agricultural tasks to their own. Yet even that was not enough to maintain the farm in some villages, so that the entire female population, with the help of the children, worked at net-making. As for so many of these crafts, little was required in the way of equipment, skill or literacy. Net-making was in good, though seasonal, demand (better prices were paid in the spring and summer), yet, for working about a third of a year, the women could earn only between 11 and 15 roubles.

From the description of these crafts, it is clear that peasant families resorted to a variety of strategies to remain on the land. Labour migration was generally considered an option only for the husband, who as a man commanded higher wages, and the single girl or widowed woman. The average female wage was between 50 and 75 per cent of the average male wage. Most peasant women, however, would still be expected to contribute cash earnings to the household, as well as their unpaid labour. The crafts were fitted around the harvest, and generally took up a considerable portion of the year, though in most cases demand fluctuated, largely because of the vagaries of urban fashion. However, female artisans did not depend simply on the luxury trade, but made cheap shawls, scarves and kerchiefs for the mass market. Since in most cases craft work was in addition to the work a woman had to do on the farm and in the household, daughters were frequently involved in both housework and crafts from an early age, which helps explain the lower rates of literacy among women compared to men. In any case, for most of these female crafts literacy was considered unnecessary. Moreover, as for factory work, female crafts commanded less status as well as less financial reward than male crafts (such as working with skins, metal, stone, wood), which were considered to be more skilled.

A few, usually those with some experience in the craft, earned more by acting as middle-women or agents; some could become relatively wealthy through running a workshop, though generally ownership of the machine was in male hands. In villages which worked for factories within close proximity, the craft worker could dispense with the middle-man or woman. The relationship between factory and village workers, however, was very much one which favoured the former, as reflected in Rose Glickman's description of the manufacture of cardboard tubes for cigarettes. This began as a factory job, was then put out to village women in the 1880s to cut costs, but by the early twentieth century production was back in the factory, with only a few women engaged in finishing work.[31]

While some women worked together, the localised nature of craft work, the need to combine craft work with other duties in the home and the fields, and the dependence on middle-men and women meant that the craft workers could do little to improve their situation. Rose Glickman insists that, had the women been more willing to co-operate with each other, for example in marketing, they could have cut out the middle-man, though she acknowledges that given their illiteracy the women were vulnerable to cheating. Yet there was co-operation on a small scale, both within families and between women. Perhaps because, however much time a craft involved, it was nevertheless regarded as subsidiary to the farm, the women were unwilling to expend any more energy on it. Glickman's general assessment is bleak, seeing the work as monotonous as well as exhausting:

> Given the constraints of their lives, their poverty, illiteracy, and lack of skill, it is not surprising that as eagerly as peasant women seized new opportunities, they were rarely capable of creating them or ferreting them out. For the most part, peasant women were the passive beneficiaries of benevolent chance.[32]

Yet, as the quotation from the toy-maker reveals, some at least took pride in, and indeed derived enjoyment from, their work. Moreover, as Glickman accepts, the crafts were a means to an end, which was to stay on the land. While it could be argued that married women with children had little choice, it took a great deal of courage as well as fatalism to accept the responsibilities of running the home and the farm, and adding cash income to the household economy by means of craft work. However small the earnings, they contributed not only to the family's survival, but to the peasant woman's sense of self. Moreover, however hard they strove to stay on the land, however isolated a life they seemed to lead, peasant women did not, indeed could not, entirely close themselves off from city influences. Thus they responded to urban fashion, using factory-made cloth and trimmings. Those peasant wives of the pattern-makers, whose brightly coloured and embroidered clothes were described so vividly by Kanatchikov, had at their disposal yarn made and dyed in factories:

31. *Russian Peasant Women*, p. 61.   32. Ibid., p. 67.

The bright yellow, purple, green, and orange shapes outlined in white chain stitch were especially striking on red calico cloth. Early twentieth-century towel borders, valances, and hems of rubakhi [over-shirts] from Olonets in the north exhibit this type of embroidery in combination with strips of ribbon or lace; costumes from Kharkov and Voronezh provinces in the south combined pattern weaving with aniline dyes and strips of purchased trim.[33]

The fact that peasant women would put so much effort into decorating their clothes, their home, and even their craft tools, such as the distaff used in spinning, suggests that they gained satisfaction from their work, however 'unskilled'. Moreover, as Oliunina has shown, by the beginning of the twentieth century, they were more likely to buy cheap manufactured town garments for everyday wear, keeping their traditional costumes for special occasions, such as a visit to their husbands in the city. That had an impact on the tailoring trade by the early twentieth century. Village tailors had sewn coats, kaftans, shirts, undershirts and a variety of traditional clothing, often working independently for a certain circle of clients. By the turn of the century, however, Oliunina reported that traditional Russian dress was being replaced by ready-made clothes, often of foreign cut, while the tailors lost their independence and began to work for an entrepreneur. Indeed, the peasant youth of both sexes, but especially young girls, were paying a lot more attention to their clothes. An Englishwoman who had visited Russia in the early 1890s concluded that peasant women cared for their appearance from their interest in the dress of foreign female visitors.[34] To marry, the girls in the early twentieth century needed a dowry of cash (as much as 80 to 100 roubles), as well as clothing, which according to Oliunina included a minimum of six over-dresses. Hence, she claimed, the majority of peasant daughters and sisters worked simply in order to afford clothes, and the only entertainment for peasant tailors was an inn for the men and dresses for the women.[35]

The position of peasant women in the home may well have been strengthened, given that economic change gave many of them more responsibilities for the household in the absence, often prolonged, of their men, and provided others with non-agricultural job opportunities, both in the countryside and in the town. It seems from the accounts of nineteenth-century British visitors that Russian peasant

33. Hilton, *Russian Folk Art*, p. 96.
34. H. Peel, *Polar Gleams* (London, 1894), p. 46.
35. Oliunina, *Portnovskii promysel*, pp. 57, 94.

women saw their households as a source of power as well as security, more important to them than potential independence as an individual outside it.[36] What is clear, however, is that in the changing economic conditions of the later nineteenth century, a key factor limiting women's job opportunities was lack of skills and frequent pregnancies.

From descriptions of recently arrived unskilled peasant-workers in the towns, there seemed at first little to distinguish the women from the men in terms of education. A major difference gradually appeared, however, which was that, while women tended to stay in unskilled work, men moved into semi-skilled or skilled jobs. Besides the influence of an overarching gender division of labour, the persistent lack of skills among women workers can be related to their literacy levels. Illiteracy was more widespread among women than men in Russia. In 1897, 21.1 per cent of the population as a whole was literate, of whom only 13.4 per cent lived in towns and cities. It was estimated that only 13 per cent of women were literate. Whereas among peasant women less than 10 per cent were literate, the rate of literacy among urban women was nearly three times as high (at 35.6 per cent); urban male literacy (at 54 per cent) was just over double the rate of rural men. Among factory women the percentage was 21.3, while the corresponding figures for male peasants and factory workers were 29.3 and 56.5 per cent.[37] Again, there were regional as well as age differences, with literacy highest among women, as well as men, in the more industrialised provinces, and among the younger generation. By 1912, the situation had improved, but women still lagged considerably behind men: in European Russia, 326 in every 1,000 men were literate, compared to only 137 in every 1,000 women. Thus, for every 24 literate males in 1912, there were ten literate females.[38] Mass literacy, particularly writing, is a concomitant of industrialisation, whereas the peasant world depended more on ceremony than on the printed word. Industrialisation and urbanisation, however, made literacy and numeracy more valuable, as peasants realised. In the early twentieth century, there was a spread of elementary schooling in the countryside, but though more female peasants acquired literacy, it was seen as less essential for their lives than it was for male peasants, for whom

36. J. McDermid, 'Victorian Views of Peasant Patriarchy in Russia', *Coexistence* (1992), 29, pp. 187–97.

37. A.G. Rashin, *Naselenie Rossii za 100 let: 1811–1913* (Moscow, 1956), pp. 293, 305–6.

38. *The Russian Year-Book for 1912*, p. 88.

literacy would ease the passage into the outside world, be it the factory or the army.

Education and work

Sophie Satina, who was a pioneer in the movement for higher education for women in Russia before 1917, and who herself taught and researched in botany before leaving Russia in 1921, wrote of the struggle her parents had in Tambov province (about 55 kilometres south-east of Moscow), trying to persuade the peasants to send their children to school:

> They were more willing to send boys because, in order to win the cooperation of the parents, the government announced in 1874 that special privileges would be granted in military service to literate young men. There were no privileges whatever for literate girls, and the parents maintained that their daughters were needed at home for various duties, and that education was useful only for nuns in their nunneries, and they did not wish their daughters to become nuns.

Yet the peasants' attitude was not set in stone, as Satina explained:

> It was easier to persuade those parents who were employed on the estate, such as engineers, carpenters, gardeners and others. Though not willingly, but they did send their daughters to school. In the end, however, when the villagers noticed that the daughters of our employees liked the school, that they could read and write, and brought home from the school library story books, fairy tales, poetry and religious books, the attitude of the parents in the village began to change and gradually the number of girls attending the school increased.[39]

The peasants, according to Ben Eklof, had a complex attitude toward literacy and school attendance.[40] From the point of view of the household economy, literacy was valued in specific ways: for work outside farming, for keeping accounts, for the army, for entertainment, for communicating with an absent spouse. Perhaps for a few, literacy would bring social prestige, but for the most part literacy was not seen as a stepping stone up the social ladder, and out of the village: it was a strategy for survival, not advancement. In

39. Sophie Satina, *Education of Women in Pre-Revolutionary Russia* (New York, 1966), p. 24.

40. Ben Eklof, *Russian Peasant Schools: Officialdom, Village Culture, and Popular Pedagogy, 1861–1914* (Berkeley, Calif., 1986), pp. 255–79.

most of these situations, literacy would be a masculine accomplishment, though peasants were not opposed in principle to daughters learning to read. It was a question of priorities. A woman's main career was marriage, for which spinning and weaving were crucial skills, while literacy was a luxury. That was the general attitude until the end of the century, when economic and demographic pressures on peasant farming led more women to seek work outside the village. Hence literacy for girls was now seen as a necessary skill, though still less necessary than for male workers. For example, textiles was the major factory employer of women, the metal industry for men, and by the end of the nineteenth century the former was more willing than the latter to take on child labour, some as young as 12 years of age. In addition, literacy was not a prerequisite for domestic service, an even bigger employer of women than textiles in the late nineteenth and early twentieth centuries.

Yet still there was unease about formal schooling, and fear of children, especially daughters, becoming 'over-educated', in the sense of being made dissatisfied with village life. In other words, literacy to the peasantry was, like labour migration, simply another means of preserving the traditional way of life. There was a division of labour in this defensive strategy, in which, for the most part, the expectation was that the men would leave and the women remain. Eklof cites a quotation from peasants which reveals how crucial women were to the continuation of the household, and suggests how expensive it would be to lose their labour:

> Why should we teach our girls? They won't be taken as soldiers or as clerks in the stores. They're too busy to read books. On weekdays they work at heavy labour side by side with their men, either in the fields, the woods, or in the garden. They have an equal amount of work waiting at home, preparing meals, tending the cattle, taking care of the children, and sewing the clothing. On holidays they are busier than ever![41]

This quotation also reveals that girls had household responsibilities and began learning the skills necessary for their future lives at a younger age than boys, and so had less time for school. Even if a girl was sent to school, as they were in increasing numbers from the 1890s, her domestic duties came first. She was being prepared for the home, whereas her brothers were being schooled in the understanding that they might well be required to leave the home. In both cases, there was little need to acquire literacy, or indeed

41. Ibid., pp. 278–9.

numeracy, skills above the mininum. However, as opportunities for elementary education spread in the late nineteenth and early twentieth centuries, as population growth led to an over-supply of labour on farms, and as more daughters had to find work outside agriculture, and even away from the village, an increasing number of girls enrolled in schools.

The stress remained on the 'three Rs', however, since the peasants feared that any further education would 'corrupt' children with urban ways. Hence attendance was brief for both sexes, but especially for girls, and generally not more than two or three years and not past 12 years of age. In addition, boys would have more regular attendance since their farm tasks tended to be seasonal, whereas the domestic duties at least of older girls were constant. Thus, Eklof argues that, rather than outright opposition to female education, peasants gave it a lower priority than male education for a number of reasons: the continuing usefulness of daughters in the home, and the need for them to be educated in a variety of skills essential to maintain the household economy; the continuing importance placed on female chastity which co-education in distant, crowded schools seemed to threaten; poverty and the need to prioritise who should receive schooling; lack of confidence in the morality, authority, and competence of the teacher. Eklof suggests that 'as women teachers came to dominate the profession, much residual peasant hesitation about sending girls to school may have evaporated'.[42] Yet given the low esteem in which women, particularly 'outsiders', were held in the village, this must remain speculation.

Whatever the reason for the growing numbers of girls enrolling in village schools, the spread of elementary education certainly offered professional opportunities to urban, upper-class women. Traditionally, the only teaching career open to women had been that of governess, and the first recognition that training was necessary, in part to remedy the deficiencies in the would-be governess's own education, had been in the 1830s, though only in the 1850s were diplomas awarded as proof of expertise. In 1868, women who attended church schools could also become governesses, and in the 1870s students of girls' grammar schools attached to the Ministry of Public Education could become primary school teachers; if a girl achieved honours, she would be recognised as a governess, which was still seen as a position of higher status than an elementary school teacher. Indeed, the village teacher was on the lowest rung

42. Ibid., p. 313.

of this career 'ladder', since her teaching was the most basic. Work in a village school, it seems, was not first choice, and was often resorted to only after failing to achieve, or being dismissed from, an urban post. Those who worked in the former at least could expect food and lodging – 'a warm oven and a slice of bread'.[43]

While increasing numbers of single women sought paid employment out of necessity, many also went into teaching with the intention of dedicating themselves to the service of the people. Some women who later became full-time revolutionaries began their working lives in this way. Thus, in 1871 and 1872 in Stavropol' in southern Russia the future terrorist Sofia Perovskaia taught courses preparing teachers for village schools.[44] The aim of such courses was to improve the standards of teaching. Between 1872 and 1897, out of a total enrolment of 1,516 women, only 428 completed the training course in Samara. The high drop-out rate was assumed to be caused by the poverty of the students, many of whom were from the villages. Yet it was also the case that even those who graduated did not take a position as a village teacher, but with their improved education sought another, urban, job. Peasants, it would seem, were right in their fears that any education past the 'three Rs' would entice girls away from the village.

However, in practice few peasant girls came from families which could afford to keep daughters in school for the length of time it would take to train as a teacher. Village teachers, therefore, were predominantly men until the end of the nineteenth century. Moreover, male teachers in the village came from different social groups than schoolmistresses. Of the 1,032 students who graduated from the pedagogical institute in St. Petersburg between 1874 and 1897, 387 were men and 645 women. The majority worked as teachers in the Petersburg province. Of the men, 29 per cent were from a peasant, and generally clerical, background, whereas only 8.5 per cent of women were; 25 per cent of men were from lower-middle-class and artisanal backgrounds, compared to 21.1 per cent of women; and 18.6 per cent of the men were children of gentry and civil servants, in contrast to 43.9 per cent of the women. Of those few women who came from the villages, the highest percentage (44) came from priests' families.[45] By the early twentieth century, however,

43. V.R. Leikina-Svirskaia, *Intelligentsiia v Rossii vo vtoroi polovine xix veka* (Moscow, 1971), p. 58. Unless otherwise indicated, the following discussion of female teachers is based on information from ibid., ch. 6.

44. V.L. Perovskii, *Vospominaniia o sestre, Sof'e Perovskoi* (Moscow, 1927), p. 54.

45. Leikina-Svirskaia, *Intelligentsiia v Rossii,* p. 163.

women had come to predominate among village teachers. In the 43 zemstvo provinces Jeffrey Brooks studied, he found that in 1911, 62 per cent of the 62,913 teachers in 38,272 rural schools under the authority of the Ministry of Education were women; in zemstvo schools, the percentage (71) was even higher.[46] Thus, female village teachers generally came from a higher social class than their male counterparts. This may have disadvantaged the women, who were regarded as upper-class outsiders by the peasants and, as women, lacking in the necessary authority to discipline children.

The qualifications of female teachers improved towards the end of the century, by which time impoverishment was pushing increasing numbers of gentry women into the labour market. In the last two decades, there was an increase in pedagogical classes for girls in secondary schools. In 1880 there were 24,400 village teachers in European Russia, of whom 19,500 were men, and only 4,900 women. In that decade, 7.6 per cent of the female teachers had their training while they were still at school: 23 per cent in gymnasia; 11.7 per cent at pro-gymnasia (which offered only the first four years of a gymnasium education); 28.1 per cent at a church school. The rest (37 per cent) had only primary or home education. In 1899, in all primary schools under the Ministry of Public Education, there were 57,200 teachers, of whom 32,100 were men, and 25,100 women.[47] By then, increasing numbers of female teachers had completed secondary education. Satina pointed to the differences in curriculum in girls' secondary schools from boys': the classical languages of Greek and Latin were not compulsory, while there was extensive instruction in modern languages, and less time was allotted to mathematics and science. Satina explains the differences by the fact that boys in gymnasia were being prepared for university education, whereas girls were being prepared for a career in schoolteaching. So long as secondary school graduates had taken a pedagogical course for at least one year, they had the legal right to teach.[48] In practice, this education was more comprehensive than that on offer to men (who tended to come from a lower social class than the female gymnasia students) in special pedagogical institutes. Again, this may have led to considerable frustration among female village teachers since the curriculum which they were expected to follow was so limited. In addition, the peasants would not have appreciated

46. Jeffrey Brooks, in Terence Emmons and Wayne S. Vucinich (eds), *The Zemstvo in Russia: An Experiment in Local Self-Government* (Cambridge, 1982), p. 255.
47. Leikina-Svirskaia, *Intelligentsiia v Rossii*, pp. 164–6.
48. Satina, *Education of Women*, p. 43.

the higher learning of women teachers, given their pragmatic approach to the schooling of their children, while the fact that women came to dominate primary teaching did not improve the status of the profession, given the low esteem in which women were held by peasants.

How are we to account for the increasing employment of women teachers in primary schools? There are four obvious answers: one is the low status which teaching commanded in nineteenth-century Russia; another is that, in a poorly (and often irregularly) paid profession, which was especially true of village teaching, women were relatively 'cheap' to employ, since they were paid less – and, according to the annual *Women's Calendar* published in the early 1900s, considerably less – than men. Eklof cites average salaries for rural teachers in 1911: in local government schools, men earned 403 roubles, women 365, and in church schools, men earned 284 to women's 269 roubles; in contrast, in factory and municipal schools, the average salary for men was between 560 and 642 roubles, and for women between 488 and 497.[49] A third is that educated women had far fewer opportunities generally than men, although there were regional differences; and, finally, teaching young children was deemed particularly appropriate for women as it was seen as a nurturing, caring profession.

The growing educational opportunities for women in Russia since the 1870s reflected government recognition of the social utility of women. Yet there were limits to what the state was prepared to accept as suitable work for women. Thus in 1871 it restricted the employment of women to the lower levels of teaching, medicine and clerical work. The 1876 statute which provided for pedagogical courses at all girls' secondary schools also allowed the establishment of women's industrial and technical schools, and advocated higher education courses for women in all university towns. The most famous of the latter were the Bestuzhev courses in St. Petersburg, which lasted until 1918. While some of the Bestuzhev graduates continued their studies and research, becoming, for example, mathematicians (such as Sofia Kovalevskaia, who became a professor at Stockholm University in the 1880s) and agronomists, most utilised their learning by teaching in remote provinces of Russia.[50]

49. Eklof, *Russian Peasant Schools*, p. 218.

50. I. Brainin, 'Bestuzhevskie', *Novyi mir* (1974), no. 9, pp. 242–3. For Kovalevskaia, see *Sofya Kovalevskaya: A Russian Childhood*, translated, edited and introduced by Beatrice Stillman (New York, 1978); A.C. Leffler, *Sonia Kovalevsky: Biography and Autobiography* (London, 1895).

Ruth Dudgeon's study of female students from 1872 has shown that at least one half and probably more than two-thirds of graduates of the higher courses for women before 1917 (excluding medical faculties) became teachers, many not from choice.[51] At least by the 1900s there were more opportunities for women within teaching: graduates from the Higher Courses for Women, which had been established in the 1870s in University towns, could become teachers at all levels of grammar schools, whereas graduates from teacher-training institutes could take posts in such schools only up to the fourth form.[52] The 1906 edition of the *Women's Calendar* also shows that there was a career ladder, with women appearing in increasing numbers in girls' secondary schools, and a few women at least becoming deputy headmistresses (30 in St. Petersburg) and headmistresses (six) of girls' secondary schools. In that year, women were given permission to teach some classes in male secondary schools, and five years later, in all of the classes. There were other, ancillary posts open to women in schools, including those of Lady Supervisor (responsible for the girls' behaviour and morals), school inspector, doctor and janitor.

Village teachers were generally hired on the basis of one for each school. They were not expected to teach more than the basics so that the more highly educated experienced a distinct lack of intellectual stimulation. Those female teachers who were not natives of the village also felt socially isolated, remaining very much the outsider, however dedicated. Eklof argues that this was particularly the case for female teachers, since the majority of them remained single (with most provincial authorities either dismissing any who married, or expecting their resignation on marriage), and so were less likely than male teachers to put down roots in the village. He records that while 80.6 per cent of female teachers in rural areas of European Russia in 1911 were single, only 15.7 per cent were married (3.7 per cent were widows), compared to 53.7 per cent of male teachers who were single, 44.2 per cent who were married (and 1.6 per cent widowed).[53]

Indeed, as the educational standards of female teachers improved, fewer were satisfied with the low pay, social and cultural isolation, and poor conditions of village teaching (which included high-handed treatment by zemstvo officials, as Chekhov's short story

51. Ruth Dudgeon, 'The Forgotten Minority: Women Students in Imperial Russia, 1872–1917', in *Russian History/Histoire Russe* (1982), vol. 9, part 1, pp. 1–26: 11.
52. *Zhenskii Kalendar'* (St. Petersburg, 1906), p. 216.
53. Eklof, *Russian Peasant Schools*, p. 197.

'The Schoolmistress' reveals). One response was to change jobs frequently, which in itself disrupted the children's education and confirmed the peasants' suspicions of female teachers as out of touch with rural life. As far as the peasants were concerned, teachers were appointed, and therefore imposed on the village, by the authorities. Was the situation of urban teachers much better? As noted above, the salaries were generally considerably higher. In a city there would be more opportunities for cultural stimulation, interaction with colleagues and other professionals, further education, and career advancement. The *Women's Calendar* for 1905 gave the names of a few women who lectured on the St. Petersburg Higher Courses for Women, including Maksimova (psychology and linguistics) and Petrukhova (Latin). Other women were employed as tutors for practical classes in such subjects as modern languages, chemistry and physiology. Yet here too there were restrictions, particularly in terms of what was expected of women teachers simply because of their sex. In her discussion of the 1897 marriage ban which was applied to female teachers in St. Petersburg, Christine Ruane refers to them as 'vestal virgins'. The ban was imposed partly for financial reasons: young and inexperienced female teachers commanded less in terms of salaries than either older women or men generally, and if the former were forced to leave teaching on marriage then they would forfeit the right to a pension.

The *Women's Calendar* for 1900, however, revealed that professional women's rights to pensions were hedged around by restrictions: for example, the woman had to submit a certificate from an employer for whom she had worked for a considerable period of time, showing that she had an unblemished record, with proof that she had insufficient means to support herself without the pension.[54] As primary teachers, women were fulfilling their 'natural' maternal role in advance, or in lieu, of having children of their own. Once women gave birth, it was clear that they were sexual beings, which many considered inappropriate for the teaching of young children. Ruane argues that the marriage ban was closely related to the feminisation of the profession, and was intended to ensure a male monopoly of promoted posts which involved management and power.[55] Another reason might have been a surfeit of women seeking positions in the capital's schools, reflected in the waiting list, which was restricted to women between the ages of 18 and 30. The fact that

54. *Zhenskii Kalendar'* (1900), pp. 80–5.
55. Christine Ruane, 'The Vestal Virgins of St. Petersburg: Schoolteachers and the 1897 Marriage Ban', *Russian Review* (Apr. 1991), vol. 50, pp. 163–82: 170.

the names of women who reached the age of 35 before being placed in a St. Petersburg school were removed from the list is an indication of how fierce was the competition.[56] The ban was repealed only at the end of 1913, largely in response to a shortage of teachers.

Medicine and women

The attempt to prevent married women from teaching highlights another key factor limiting women's job opportunities: pregnancy. At least, it was deemed a limitation in the teaching profession. It was not considered a bar to work in the fields, factories or service sector. Though a woman might be sacked from the latter two categories while she was pregnant, childbirth was not considered a bar to future employment. Indeed, this biological condition also gave rise to a number of employment opportunities for women, including paramedic, midwife (both traditional and trained, and increasingly from the late nineteenth century a combination of the two, as feldsher-midwife), doctor, and wet-nurse. In 1884, a woman doctor wrote that one of the reasons for high rates of infant mortality in the countryside was the poor health of the peasant mother, whose inadequate diet often rendered her incapable of breastfeeding. In addition, a sick wife who could not work was a disaster for the family. This physician related the case of a mother of five who caught typhoid. Even when each of the children fell ill, the husband received no help from the other villagers, who feared contamination. How, the doctor asked, could she possibly criticise the husband when he married again, only a week after he buried his wife? There was, she wrote, no time for grief.[57]

Like teaching, medicine generally was not held in high esteem in nineteenth-century Russia. It was open to two groups deemed inferior, Jews and, by the later nineteenth century, women. Nancy Frieden's study of Russian physicians between 1856 and 1905 has shown that whether in the public sector or private practice, medicine was badly paid compared to other professions, such as law. She reveals that in 1910, outside military service, there were 20,157 male and 1,590 female physicians in the Russian empire.[58] By 1914,

56. *Zhenskii Kalendar'* (1906), p. 217.
57. E.V. Aptekman, 'Iz zapisok zemskogo vracha', in *Russkaia mysl'* (Dec. 1884), part 12, pp. 48–82: 76–7.
58. Nancy M. Frieden, *Russian Physicians in an Era of Reform and Revolution, 1856–1905* (New Jersey, 1981), p. 323.

over 1,000 women were graduating annually from Russian medical faculties.[59] Women were at least accepted into medicine. The practice of law, however, was exclusively male, even when women's law faculties were established in 1906. Those women who graduated could only work as legal consultants.

As with teachers, it was the need for more and cheap medical personnel in rural areas which allowed for the growth in the numbers of female physicians at the end of the nineteenth century. However, medicine seems to have been more of a career of choice than teaching, and above all to have been seen as a means of serving the people. Such was the case for the feldsher-midwife Anna A., who began work on a landed estate in August 1881.[60] Anna's wages were 300 roubles per annum, with accommodation and heating (though she complained that the latter was sorely inadequate in winter). She was assistant to a physician who had a flat in the same building that housed the surgery and pharmacy, as well as the accommodation for a male feldsher, and for Anna. Memoirs of women in the medical profession often complain that the male feldshers were local peasants with little education and basic training; but in this case the initial misgivings which Anna had about her colleague evaporated. Indeed, she found him more helpful, generous and willing to work with her as an equal than the male doctor, who had authority over both of them, and who put many obstacles in Anna's way, undermining her efforts to improve the provision of medicine.

Not all zemstvo physicians, then, were concerned with serving the people. Anna's boss would often make his patients wait for long periods of time, and even not turn up at either the surgery or the hospital, instead ordering the two feldshers to substitute for him. When Anna remarked on the poor hygiene at the hospital, where bedlinen was changed only every two or three weeks and floors were washed even less frequently (every two or three months), the doctor announced that it was now her responsibility. He warned her that there was a shortage of funds, but she felt that the issue was not in practice one of money. The doctor received enough to employ three servants, but because he retained the power to hire and fire them, they paid no attention to the female feldsher.

A female physician who also saw her career in terms of service to the people was Anna Ivanovna Veretennikova, one of the first

59. Dudgeon, 'The Forgotten Minority', p. 13.
60. Anna A., 'Na zemskoi sluzhbe: iz zapisok fel'dsheritsy', *Vestnik Evropy* (1890), vol. 25, part 12, pp. 549–93.

female doctors in Russia (and, incidentally, a cousin of Lenin).[61] On graduating from the St. Petersburg medical courses for women, Veretennikova elected to go to a small district on the Volga river. She worked so hard, travelling from village to village, that her health suffered, and within a few years she had to move to a city practice in Kazan. Once she had recovered she returned to the countryside to work in a district hospital, but she effectively worked herself to death in 1887 (from tuberculosis). Nevertheless, she was convinced that rural female physicians disproved the conventional notion of women being too delicate for taxing work:

> How could you use an argument like that when I was slight in stature, physically 'weak', and yet could withstand all sorts of bad weather, sleepless nights, and all manner of desperation? Other stronger women could have put up with much more. However, no proof and no facts will ever convince people of something which they refuse to believe.[62]

Veretennikova came up against obstacles facing all physicians working for the zemstvo: grossly inadequate funding, too few paramedics, too large a district with a scattered population, poor accommodation, constant epidemics, arrogant and self-aggrandising officials, and irregular payment of salaries. Like so many village teachers, rural physicians felt culturally and socially isolated. However, in contrast to the hostility peasants often displayed toward female teachers, Veretennikova found that women doctors were more acceptable. Indeed, any resentment tended to come from the female élite, that one of their own preferred to be employed by the zemstvo to tend to the needs of the peasants, than to practise privately among her peers. She also experienced professional hostility from a male physician, whom she considered incompetent. As we saw in the previous chapter, another woman who qualified in 1886, Yulia Kviatkovskaia, wrote that female physicians who worked in hospitals had great difficulty in winning the respect of their male colleagues, whom she described collectively as 'the enemy'.[63] That was certainly the experience of the feldsher-midwife Anna A. She complained that the physician she assisted behaved more like a landlord than a doctor. Her care and attention to the peasants in time won her both their respect and friendship, whereas his patients held him

61. The following discussion of Veretennikova is based on the article 'Zapiski zemskogo vracha', *Novyi mir* (1956), part 3, pp. 205–32.
62. Ibid., p. 226.
63. *Vospominaniia vrachei Yu. A. Kviatkovskaia i Mariia P. Rashkovich* (Paris, 1937), p. 82.

in low esteem because of his neglect. In retaliation, he made life as difficult as possible for Anna, who had to make an official complaint to the zemstvo.

In the 1880s, male physicians who practised private medicine earned an average of 800 to 900 roubles a year, with accommodation, females between 480 and 800.[64] Nancy Frieden claims that in 1889, the average income of a female physician in state service was 944 roubles (for a male, it was 1,315).[65] It was possible for a woman to earn more, depending on the responsibilities of the position. In the memoir of Veretennikova, it was recorded that she earned an annual salary of 1,500 roubles.[66] Yet she spent little on herself; instead she used her own money to try to make up for the inadequate equipment and supplies. She had the assistance of a male feldsher, whom she described as the litmus paper of the strength of her patience. A peasant, his training she regarded as inadequate, and his behaviour erratic, due to his fondness for alcohol. There was also a midwife, whom she disapproved of as sexually promiscuous, but whom she nevertheless found to be more able than the feldsher. Indeed, since the peasant women did not generally call in the midwife, and turned to the doctor only in a crisis, Veretennikova gave the midwife extra training in basic nursing techniques, so that she could run the surgery when Veretennikova was on her rounds. In common with most professional women, Veretennikova also employed a servant, to free her from any household tasks which she felt would only detract from her work.

Another early woman doctor, E.V. Aptekman, had a similar experience of rural practice.[67] Despite the isolation, she took a delight in her situation, deriving great satisfaction from being an active member of society. Like Veretennikova, she was welcomed by the peasants, especially the women, who were thankful that the authorities had at last sent 'one of our sisters', with whom they could discuss their illnesses without embarrassment. At the same time, the male peasants were not shy in consulting her. Again, Kviatkovskaia's experience was different from Aptekman's, perhaps because the former worked in a hospital in which it was easier to segregate female physicians, simply by restricting them to women's wards.

64. Leikina-Svirskaia, *Intelligentsiia v Rossii*, pp. 141–2.
65. Frieden, *Russian Physicians*, p. 214, table 9.8.
66. 'Zapiski zemskogo vracha', p. 212.
67. The following discussion is based on Aptekman's memoir, 'Iz zapisok zemskogo vracha', pp. 48–82.

Medicine opened careers other than that of physician to women, including pharmacy, dentistry, nursing and midwifery. Indeed, Satina noted that a school for midwives had been established in the eighteenth century, the Sisterhood of Nurses was founded in 1844, and women were allowed to train and practise as dentists by Nicholas I (1825–55).[68] However, the first proprietary dental school was not opened until 1881, when women comprised two-thirds of the students.[69] Although the feldsher Anna A. recorded that there was a well-equipped pharmacy where she worked in 1881, the physician Veretennikova noted the general scarcity of pharmacies in the countryside in the 1880s. Mary Schaeffer Conroy's study of the profession and industry confirms that this situation did not improve over the next three or four decades.[70] Conroy sees pharmacy as providing career opportunities from the 1880s for women and national minorities, especially Jews, in tsarist Russia, though their numbers remained considerably lower than those of female physicians, who, like Veretennikova, often resorted to buying and keeping their own supplies of drugs.

Conroy argues that women were accepted as pharmacists on fairly equal terms with men because it was a profession in transition. Interestingly, while female physicians outnumbered female pharmacists, the former were predominantly Russian, whereas the latter were predominantly minority women who sought assimilation and advancement, rather than the promotion of national interests. What pharmacy shared with medicine and teaching was low status among the professions. Moreover, in the countryside, pharmacists faced competition from peasant herbalists and healers. Rose Glickman portrays the female healer as landless and without male support, but with children to provide for, so that becoming a healer was a means of both subsistence and remaining in the village.[71]

Peasant healers often became midwives. Memoirs of zemstvo physicians agree that peasant women were reluctant to consult trained midwives, who were regarded as unproven outsiders, while

68. Satina, *Education of Women*, p. 83.
69. Mary Schaeffer Conroy, *In Health and Sickness: Pharmacy, Pharmacists, and the Pharmaceutical Industry in Late Imperial and Early Soviet Russia* (Boulder, Colo., 1994), p. 493, note 5.
70. Ibid., and see especially ch. 7 on women in pharmacy. See also Mary Schaeffer Conroy's chapter 'Women Pharmacists in Russia before World War I: Women's Emancipation, Feminism, Professionalization, Nationalism, and Class Conflict', in Linda Edmondson (ed.), *Women and Society in Russia and the Soviet Union* (Cambridge, 1992).
71. *Russia's Women*, pp. 148–162: 155.

the women would turn to a doctor only in emergencies, and often too late. The doctors were generally scathing in their criticism of the peasant midwives, whom they associated with the high infant mortality rate (even at the turn of the century, as many as one in two children did not survive past their fifth year). Yet the physicians also recognised that poverty, bad diet, frequent epidemics, the prevalence of syphilis, and the demands on peasant mothers for work in the fields were significant contributory factors. So too was wet-nursing, which provided considerable numbers of peasant women, particularly in villages in the Moscow region, with additional income. Some served in the city's foundling homes for abandoned children before taking the child allotted to them back to the village; others acted as middle-women, fetching the babies from the homes and taking them to the wet-nurses. Using a middle-woman meant that there was less supervision of the wet-nurse. Neither was well-paid, and of necessity the job was temporary. Physicians considered the practice contributed to the high death rate among babies from foundling homes, while the foster mother may have neglected her own child.[72]

In addition, there was a suspicion that syphilis, which most doctors viewed as an urban disease, was spread by the peasant practice of taking in children from a city foundling home. E.V. Aptekman had found in her rural practice in the early 1880s that syphilis was widespread, from a young baby to an 80-year-old man. She did not deny that one of the most common reasons was in fact visiting labour migrants and soldiers. However, in her view the main source was the widespread use of common crockery.[73] Peasants, Aptekman claimed, would try to hide the symptoms. One 18-year-old girl delayed going to hospital for a year, because her father was ashamed to declare openly that a daughter of marriageable age had such a problem. In the same period, however, the feldsher-midwife Anna A. had recorded that although syphilis was the most common disease in her area, the physician refused to treat it.

Thus not everything could be blamed on peasant ignorance and superstition, wet-nursing or the poor hygiene of the village midwife. Moreover, when there were no complications in delivery, then

72. See David Ransel, 'Abandonment and Fosterage of Unwanted Children: The Women of the Foundling System', in David L. Ransel (ed.), *The Family in Imperial Russia* (Urbana, Ill., 1978), pp. 189–217.

73. For a discussion of physicians' attitudes towards syphilis and the peasantry, see Laura Engelstein, 'Morality and the Wooden Spoon: Russian Doctors View Syphilis, Social Class and Sexual Behaviour, 1890–1905', *Representations* (Spring 1986), no. 14, pp. 169–208.

the peasant midwife was likely to be as successful as the trained outsider, perhaps more so given the former's experience, including that of her own pregnancies. There was an added attraction, according to Samuel Ramer: the peasant midwife was willing to do household chores during the mother's confinement.[74]

The government tried training young peasant women as midwives, but often the peasants regarded them as having taken on city ways while, once trained, the midwives generally preferred urban practices to returning to the village. At the turn of the century, as few as two per cent of rural births were attended by trained midwives.[75] As we have seen, even the experienced midwife in Veretennikova's practice was called on so infrequently that Veretennikova trained her to act as a general nurse in the surgery in the doctor's absence. This initiative presaged a wider government measure of the early twentieth century, which was to train feldsher-midwives, who could fulfill a number of functions, and hopefully thereby win the peasant women's trust.

From his study of rural childbirth, Samuel Ramer judges this practice as having considerable success, although the peasant midwife continued to play an important role in village life into the Soviet period.[76] However, not all women were happy to combine the two jobs. In the early 1880s Anna A., who had trained as a feldsher, recorded that she was upset and disappointed when she learned that her main task in the villages was to be a midwife. She had previously worked as a midwife and found it so unrewarding, and so often ending in tragedy, that she trained as a feldsher. She was aware that the peasants sought a midwife's help only in the most difficult of cases, when no assistance could help. Yet still she found the successful delivery of a baby could be tremendously fulfilling:

> It was a minute full of happiness and bliss which could make up for an entire year of various adversities and privation. Such moments make our work worthwhile. They reward we midwives – that is, of course, if you don't consider a complacent and quiet existence as the sole purpose and aim of your life.[77]

As in teaching and midwifery, increasing numbers of female physicians sought urban posts. Again, practising in a city was better paid (though salaries for those in public service were hardly generous)

74. *The Zemstvo in Russia*, p. 303.
75. *The Family in Imperial Russia*, pp. 218–235: 220.
76. *The Zemstvo in Russia*, p. 304.   77. Anna A., 'Na zemskoi sluzhbe', p. 577.

and less isolated, while the professional could still feel that she was devoting herself to the people. Similar problems to those in the village confronted the physician: poverty, poor hygiene, superstition, bad diets and resultant stomach complaints. People avoided hospitals, partly because of the cost, which meant that the general practitioner often had to deal with very serious illnesses. Indeed, hospitals had so few beds that they were reluctant to accept patients with long-term illnesses, such as TB, which fell to the local physician. Dr. Slanskaia practised in a working-class area of St. Petersburg in the 1890s.[78] The majority of her patients were women and children. Like her rural counterparts, she found that she doubled as a pharmacist. Slanskaia also came up against women having frequent pregnancies: indeed, she wrote that mothers often gave her the wrong name of a child, excusing themselves with 'I have so many, my dear'. Infant mortality was also high in the city. One woman with a baby called after surgery to collect a death certificate for another infant. Having many children, and especially an illegitimate child, could put such a strain on the mother that the child might be abandoned. Alternatively, an urban woman, like a female peasant, might take in a child as a means of earning some money. One of Slanskaia's patients looked after the daughter of a French governess who had not visited the child for a year, and whose payments for the child's upkeep were irregular.

Women workers in the city

It seems, then, that in times of financial emergency poor city women, like peasant women, would take in foundlings and serve as wet-nurses. The physician Mariia Pokrovskaia described the situation of one of her patients, who lived with and supported her illegitimate child by looking after a flat, for which she was charged no rent, though neither was she provided with a bed. The father of the child had refused even to visit the maternity hospital, admitting that he had many such children, but claiming that he was not the only man to have had sexual relations with the woman, so that this one might not be his. Before the birth, the woman had worked at a thread factory. Once obviously pregnant, she had been dismissed. She found work at a rope factory, earning only 16 kopecks for a

78. E. Slanskaia, 'Po vizitam: den' dumskogo zhenshchiny-vracha v S-Peterburge', *Vestnik Evropy* (1894), part 29, pp. 204–42.

twelve-hour day (4 a.m. until 8 p.m., with time for a quick lunch at
1 p.m.). The most experienced female women workers there could
earn up to 60 kopecks a day. Once she had given birth, the woman
hoped to go to the foundling hospital as a wet-nurse; but because
she had fallen ill, she was not accepted. Pokrovskaia believed that
those young mothers who could work as wet-nurses were in a better
position than her patient, especially if they were wet-nurse to their
own child. The money they earned (up to nine roubles a month)
made it easier for them later to find factory work and hire a nanny
(usually a young girl).[79]

Why had Slanskaia's patient taken in a foundling? The woman
had been a factory worker who had lost an arm in an industrial
accident. Given the lack of safety devices, such accidents were not
uncommon. Indeed, a popular song from the late nineteenth century complained not only of unsafe working conditions, but also of
the devastating effect these could have on the chances of a young
factory worker finding a husband:

> Glorious summer is passing,
> frosty winter is coming.
> Frosty winter is coming,
> hearts of factory workers are sinking.
>
> They get up at midnight,
> to be in time for work;
> they drop off at the workplace,
> and lose their right hand.
>
> They lost their right hand,
> they sent news to mum and dad.
> Mum and dad are coming,
> they are weeping in sorrow.
>
> And the people are talking,
> they are cursing the owner:
> 'You have built the factory,
> you have damaged the people.
>
> You have damaged, you have spoiled,
> nobody wants to marry them.'[80]

Ironically, it was the introduction of machinery which paved the way
for increasing numbers of women to enter the industrial labour

79. M.F. Pokrovskaia, *Po podvalam, cherdakam i uglovym kvartiram Peterburg* (St.
Petersburg, 1903), p. 47.
80. S. Lapitskaia, *Byt rabochikh Trekhgornoi manufactury* (Moscow 1935), p. 47.

force from the 1890s, so that by 1909 female labour played a significant part in Russian industry:

> Out of a total of 308,000 operatives in the factories in 1909 there were 117,000 women, of whom 101,500 were employed in the textile industries, and their numbers continue to increase. The proportion of women employed is greatest in the larger factories. They begin work between the ages of 15 and 17 (as a rule), and after the age of 30 are considered to be less efficient and are therefore to a large extent dispensed with. Of the hands employed in the silk industry in 1909, 62 per cent were women; in the cotton textile industry 48 per cent, and in the wool industry 41 per cent were women. Their wages may be said to average less than 14 r. [roubles] (about £1. 10s.) per month, as against 23r. (£2. 10s.) for a male operative. It will be seen that the pay is very low; it is highest between the ages of 25 and 30, before and after which it is considerably less. The maximum is 16r. 50c. [kopecks] (say £1. 15s.) per month, and it is calculated that a woman can only afford to spend 14c. (three and a half pennies) per day on her food, which consists mainly of black bread.[81]

Indeed, between 1901 and 1913, and particularly in the wake of the 1905 revolution, the number of women working in factories had grown by 59 per cent, whereas for men the increase was only 29 per cent: in 1901, there were 1,238,004 male factory workers, 453,352 female; in 1913, there were 1,595,664 men, and 723,913 women.[82] According to factory inspectors, employers viewed women as more diligent and sober and as less assertive than men. In addition to their assumed political passivity, women were cheaper to employ.[83] Thus women moved into box-making, wallpaper manufacturing, printing (as type-setters), machine-manufacturing, saw mills, brick manufacturing, the food and leather industries.[84] A breakdown for 1910 of the numbers of women working in factories, shown in Table 2.1, gives some idea of the variety of work open to them.

What of wages? Writing in 1900 about female factory workers in St. Petersburg, Pokrovskaia calculated an average of between 14 and 15 roubles a month, but that hid considerable differences. For example, someone starting out in the textile and paper industries might begin as low as seven roubles, while the top rate might even

81. *The Russian Year-Book for 1912*, p. 703.
82. 'Zhenskii trud v fabrichno-zavodskoi promyshlennosti Rossii za poslednie 13 let (1901–1913)', *Obshchestvennyi vrach* (1915), nos. 9–10, p. 592.
83. A. Riazanova, *Zhenskii trud* (Moscow, 1923), p. 34; A.G. Rashin, *Formirovanie rabochego klassa v Rossii: istoriko-ekonomicheskie ocherki* (Moscow, 1958), pp. 235–6.
84. Rashin, *Naselenie Rossii*, table 276.

TABLE 2.1   *Female factory workers in 1910*

Occupation	Total no. of workers	No. of women	% of women
Textile	23,154	14,491	64.9
Hygiene products	10,958	6,408	58.5
Clothes & shoes	55,400	26,484	47.8
Cotton	7,376	2,267	30.7
Food	17,032	4,868	28.6
Hides, hair & leather	11,635	3,033	26.1
Soap & resin	2,188	323	14.8
Chemical	4,204	592	14.1
Printing	18,269	2,548	13.9
Machine tool	27,152	892	3.3
Processing wood	17,127	364	2.1
Processing metals	35,288	485	1.4
Construction work	19,823	91	0.5

Source: A.G. Rashin, *Naselenie Rossii za 100 let: 1811–1913* (Moscow, 1956), table 276.

reach 25 roubles.[85] However, what women were paid seemed to depend on age: young girls and old women earned the least, and as a woman's health deteriorated she might have to give up factory work for cleaning, or serving as watchwoman in a public lavatory.[86] Women always earned less than men, even in the textile industry in which women predominated.[87] What a woman earned also depended on her status. Thus in the Petersburg textile industry in 1912, the younger, single woman still living with her family earned on average 153 roubles, 67 kopecks per annum, whereas the single woman with more experience of work, and living on her own, earned 286 roubles, 50 kopecks, which was very close to the average wage for the married woman (292 roubles, 20 kopecks). In contrast, the widow with children earned less than both of the latter: 214 roubles, 33 kopecks.[88]

A study of the 41 budgets of textile workers in St. Petersburg in 1912 revealed the persistent low wages earned by women, in comparison to men, as well as lower rates of literacy and of trade-union

85. M.I. Pokrovskaia, 'Peterburgskaia rabotnitsa', *Mir bozhii* (1900), vol. 12, pp. 32–7.
86. L. Katenina, 'K voprosy o polozhenii rabotnits v tekstil'noi promyshlennosti', *Obshchestvennyi vrach* (1914), no. 3, p. 447.
87. 'Zhenskii trud v fabrichno-zavodskoi promyshlennosti Rossii za poslednie 13 let (1901–1913)', p. 595.
88. M. Davidovich, *Peterburgskii tekstil' nyi rabochii v ego biudjetakh* (St. Petersburg, 1912), p. 6.

and party membership. Of the total of 57 workers covered by these budgets, 21 were women, nine of whom were literate, while only four were in a trade union, and only one belonged to a political party (the Russian Social Democratic Labour Party, RSDLP). Of the 36 men, 33 were literate, 24 were members of a trade union, and nine were members of the RSDLP. Of the 27 families (of which three were each supported by the mother only), the average annual wage for the male workers was 383 roubles, 46 kopecks; for the females, it was 260 roubles, 74 kopecks. This was close to the average for the city as a whole: in 1908, men earned on average 355 roubles per annum, women 273.[89] In those families in which the wife stayed at home, she still earned money by taking in lodgers, and saved on expenses by her unpaid labour in the home, and on the allotment if the family had one. Alternatively, if the married woman had a job, a female peasant might be employed on such urban kitchen gardens, usually between May and early August, digging and planting vegetables and fruit, weeding and harvesting.[90]

Clearly, in the city as in the countryside, a woman with children whom she had to support by herself was in the most precarious position. Pregnancy was given no concessions in the factory, and, as in the field, women worked up until time. Indeed, one woman recalled that her colleagues encouraged her to continue working her shift even when labour had started. A doctor at the same factory remembered women giving birth next to their machines, at the factory gates, in the guard's hut – anywhere but the maternity hospital; and, like their peasant counterparts, they looked to a traditional, rather than a trained, midwife. Many gave birth prematurely, had stillborn babies, suffered various gynaecological problems, and looked old before they were 40. Yet the women did not accept this situation passively. Under pressure, the owners of a particular factory in Moscow from 1886 paid five roubles for a baby's christening (though in practice the money came from the fines imposed on workers for such offences as lateness or absence due to a sick child); and in 1898 the owners built a maternity unit with six beds. In 1905, for the first time, a demand was made for maternity benefit and leave, which was finally achieved in 1912 (women in law, though not always in practice, were given two weeks' leave before, and four after the birth, while the bulk – 75 per cent – of the benefit would be deducted from workers' wages). The manager at this factory saw

89. Ibid., p. 5.

90. A.A. Bakhtiarov, *Bruikho Peterburga. Ocherki stolichnoi zhizni* (St. Petersburg, 1887; 1994), p. 150.

this as too much: 'Such a long leave would so please women workers, they would start having babies twice a year.'[91]

On the one hand, it was claimed that, in contrast to peasant women, female factory workers did not hesitate to 'answer the call of romance'. Since the conditions of factory life were not conducive to the establishment of families, one consequence was that the incidence of illegitimate children was much higher in urban areas.[92] On the other hand, in the 1890s, it was pointed out that the unhealthy conditions of factory work adversely affected fertility among women, while there was no provision for them to look after children at their workplace.[93] At the turn of the century, the decline in fertility was already under way in the urban areas of European Russia.[94]

Who, then, looked after the baby of a female factory operative? If the father was around, then the parents might work different shifts, exchanging the baby at the factory gates. Perhaps they would pay a landlady, or a neighbour, or a peasant girl too young to find paid employment, in which case the mother would have two 'babies' to care for when she returned from work. In her study of working-class life in Moscow in the mid 1920s, E.O. Kabo gives examples of women still working in their fifties who, because of their families' poverty, had had to begin earning when very young, often starting as a children's nanny until able to get a job in a factory, usually around 14. One woman had entered paid employment as a nanny at the age of seven, returning to her family at 15 to help run the home for six months, and then striking out for the city at the age of 16. She was attracted by the examples of other peasant girls who had migrated for work. She found a place in a factory bottling scent. Married at 17, she had a child a year for the next seven years. With such a large young family, she had to remain at home; but she longed for the day she could return to the factory.[95]

More urban women, however, worked outside factories than inside, and their situation was even more precarious. Pokrovskaia described the conditions of a young dressmaker in St. Petersburg at the turn of the century, who had recently completed her apprenticeship and found a position in a shop, for which she was paid ten

91. Lapitskaia, *Byt rabochikh Trekhgornoi manufactury*, p. 51.
92. Bervi-Flerovsky, *Izbrannye ekonomicheskie proizvedeniia*, vol. 1, pp. 515–25.
93. M.N. Lyadov, 'Koe-chto o zhenshchine rabotnitse', *Literatura Moskovskogo Rabochego Soiuza* (Moscow, 1930), p. 168.
94. Rashin, *Naselenie Rossii*, pp. 167–8.
95. E.O. Kabo, *Ocherki rabochego byta* (Moscow, 1928), vol. 1, p. 95.

roubles a month, with food (on average such workers got two meals a day), for a working day which stretched from 9 a.m. until 10 p.m., stopping only to eat. Such wages were barely enough for subsistence. Pokrovskaia also described an attempt by another dressmaker to make her own way. The woman decided that to attract customers she would need superior accommodation, and rented a room at 18 roubles a month, but her small savings were spent before she built up a clientele. She then moved to a hostel for young women run by a philanthropic society, and rented a bed at three roubles a month. She was allowed to use her sewing machine in the hostel, to enable her to pay for her keep. In order to make the 20 roubles a month which she needed, she frequently put in a twelve-hour day. As for all dressmakers, the work was not constant, so that she had to earn enough in the high season to tide her over during slow periods, such as holidays, which could mean no orders from mid December to mid January, and the summer, when dressmakers could be without work for up to two months. Still Pokrovskaia claimed that independent dressmakers were better off than those who worked in a shop: average monthly wages for the former were 15 roubles, 22 kopecks, and for the latter 12 roubles, 60 kopecks. Pokrovskaia budgeted for the independent dressmaker, calculating that she would earn at most between 200 and 250 roubles in the year, of which 108 would be spent on food, which with the three roubles a month for rent at the hostel left very little for everything else. Any major expense would be at the cost of her health, since she would have to cut down on an already basic diet. Seamstresses, who made underwear and finished off garments (for example, by sewing on buttons), had similar conditions to dressmakers, though wages could fall as low as six roubles a month.[96]

Still the biggest urban employer of women was domestic service. Indeed, unless a peasant woman had an introduction to a factory through her family, then she was most likely to find her first job in the city as a servant. According to Rose Glickman, contemporary observers saw domestic service as a form of 'white slavery', the least desirable and most degrading of all women's work. The irony is that these same observers depended on such servants to allow them to perform their professional and/or philanthropic work.[97] There was a variety of work in service, with floor washers on the lowest

96. M.I. Pokrovskaia, 'Peterburgskaia rabotnitsa', *Mir bozhii* (1900), vol. 12, pp. 32–7.
97. Rose Glickman, *Russian Factory Women: Workplace and Society, 1880–1914* (Berkeley, Calif., 1984), p. 60.

rung of the hierarchy. In the late 1880s, servants were often seasonal workers (in St. Petersburg, up to 70 per cent), who went to
a hiring market in groups, yet who were generally employed on
an individual basis. Once they found a job, they had to surrender
their passport, without which they could not legally move, to their
employer.[98]

In 1897, there were 1,621,755 female and 1,586,450 male servants in Russia. Most of the women entered service at the age of 20.
As supply outstripped demand, wages were low, and conditions
harsh. Even married women were forbidden to have a male guest,
while single women were effectively denied the chance to marry.
Having studied the lot of the domestic servant in the early twentieth
century, L.N. Lenskaia revealed her findings in a lecture addressed
to women who would themselves have been reliant on domestic
servants: long hours and low pay in a context of relative, and sometimes considerable, luxury, and sexual vulnerability, not only to the
men of the house, but to the shop assistants and janitors with whom
they came into contact. Lenskaia provided an example of a domestic
servant, Dunia, who had a good employer. She rose at 6 a.m., cleaned
and set the fires, cleaned the floors and dusted the furniture, orna-
ments and pictures of seven rooms; served meals for seven in the
family and cleared up afterwards, cleaned their shoes, ironed their
clothes and prepared their beds. She also answered the door to
callers. Dunia could not go to bed until her employers had, which
was often not until 2 a.m. She did not have a room of her own;
instead her bed was in the hall, behind a wardrobe. She had no set
meal times. Her remuneration amounted to 30 kopecks a day, or
ten roubles a month. However low that might appear, she was lucky;
at the turn of the century, a servant could be found who was willing
to accept as little as half Dunia's earnings. Indeed, in a famine year
(as in 1901–2), the wages a servant could command plummeted to
three roubles a month.[99]

Dunia's employers were reckoned to be 'good'. Yet they still had
the power to dismiss her at will. Moreover, they might renege, whatever they promised to pay her, or give her the money irregularly.
If the mistress took in lodgers, then the maid would be expected
to clean for them in addition to her employers. Lenskaia claimed
that if a servant worked for a 'bad' employer, she could easily slip

98. A.A. Bakhtiarov, *Briukho Peterburga. Ocherki stolichnoi zhizni* (St. Petersburg,
1887), p. 149.
99. L. Lenskaia, 'O Prisluge', *Doklad chitannyi vo vtorom zhenskom klube v Moskve v
fev. goda* (Moscow, 1908), p. 13.

into prostitution. Why? Lenskaia pointed out that many servants sent money back to their families in the village, which left them with precious little. In addition, they worked such long hours that they had little time for leisure, even if they could afford any. How tempting to be wined and dined by a man, in exchange for her sexual favours. In a study of illegitimacy in pre-revolutionary Russia, David Ransel described the position of a domestic servant in the late nineteenth century:

> With few qualifications and no legal protection, the female domestic often lived and worked in a kind of personal bondage. With a good employer, she may have had a more desirable situation than the factory worker, one that shielded her against the shock of urban life. But frequently her position was far from secure and subject to great abuse.[100]

Again, Lenskaia provides case studies of domestic servants who entered prostitution, including Stepanova, a 14-year-old from a village in Novgorod province. On arriving in the city, she had been taken on as a nanny, and changed jobs several times. A janitor in one of her places of employment threatened to reveal that her passport was not up-to-date unless she had sex with him. Having lost her job, Stepanova spent her meagre savings on a corner flat, and then resorted to the streets. After only two days, she was arrested by the police. She had already contracted a venereal disease. She fell foul of the police because she was unregistered. Lenskaia gave a second case study, this time of a registered prostitute, Nadezhda M., who when a servant had been seduced by a shop assistant, and abandoned once she was pregnant. Nadezhda felt that she had little choice but to go on the streets, and she took the 'yellow ticket' as a registered prostitute. Prostitution had been regulated since 1843, though by no means all prostitutes registered.[101] Lenskaia was of the opinion that it was difficult for a prostitute to 'reform', despite any help offered by philanthropists, because prostitution often paid so much better than domestic service.[102]

100. David Ransel, 'Problems in Measuring Illegitimacy in Pre-Revolutionary Russia', *Journal of Social History* (Winter 1982), vol. 16, no. 2, p. 122.

101. See for example Richard Stites, 'Prostitution and Society in Pre-Revolutionary Russia', *Jahrbucher für Geschichte Osteuropas* (1983), vol. xxxi, part 3, pp. 348–64; Laurie Bernstein, 'Yellow Tickets and State-Licensed Brothels: The Tsarist Government and the Regulation of Urban Prostitution', in Susan Gross Solomon and John F. Hutchinson (eds), *Health and Society in Revolutionary Russia* (Bloomington, Ind., 1990), pp. 45–65.

102. Lenskaia, 'O Prisluge', p. 14.

Of course, it also paid better than casual day-labour and some trades, especially seasonal ones such as dressmaking, seamstressing, millinery and shoemaking. Unless a woman became a brothel keeper, however, it seems that the longer she remained a prostitute, the lower in the hierarchy she slipped, and consequently the lower her earnings. Barbara Engel has revealed that less than a third of the prostitutes in St. Petersburg in the late nineteenth century remained in the trade longer than four years, and moreover, by the age of 30, 80 per cent of registered prostitutes had left the trade for good.[103] Of prostitutes throughout the Russian Empire in 1890, four-fifths were introduced to the trade when they were between 17 and 21 years of age. One study calculated that 72.8 per cent remained in the trade for up to five years; 19.9 per cent up to ten years; 5.2 per cent up to 15 years; 1.6 per cent up to 20 years; 0.4 per cent up to 25 years; and only 0.1 per cent for over 25 years.[104]

A quarter of a century earlier, Kuznetsov had identified four types of prostitutes: there were the 'public women', who worked in brothels; registered streetwalkers; those women who plied their trade on trains; and the unregistered. Within the last category, there were the cheapest prostitutes mentioned by Stites, and also a few upper-class women who might sell their bodies in order to buy something extra for themselves. However, contemporary observers were convinced that once their rich lovers tired of them, such 'camellias' would become common prostitutes.[105] There was considerable disagreement over what drew women into prostitution, with some claiming that they entered the trade willingly, and others insisting that they were driven into it either by force of circumstances, or because they fell into the snares of pimps who met them when they came to the city alone. Yet it was not necessarily a full-time occupation. Prostitution might be combined with another job: Oliunina reported that in the early twentieth century female tailors who were employed in workshops also worked as prostitutes to augment their pay.[106] According to Richard Stites, while a female domestic servant might be paid as little as five roubles a month, the cheapest prostitute could earn 40; a few could even bring in as much as 500 roubles

103. Barbara Alpern Engel, 'St. Petersburg Prostitutes in the Late Nineteenth Century: A Personal and Social Profile', *The Russian Review* (1989), vol. 48, pp. 21–44: 43.
104. A. Dubrovsky, *Prostitutsiia v Rossiiskoi Imperii* (St. Petersburg, 1890), p. xxx.
105. See M. Kuznetsov, *Prostitutsiia i sifilis v Rossii* (St. Petersburg, 1871).
106. Oliunina, *Portnovskii promysel v Moskve*, p. 267.

a month.[107] In the late nineteenth century, prostitutes working in the upper-class areas of St. Petersburg might themselves come from that social milieu. While these women were known as 'ladies' or mistresses of wealthy men, the lower-class prostitute with many more customers was referred to as a 'woman of ill repute'.[108]

In turn, of course, prostitution provided upper-class women with an urgent cause, calling for philanthropic measures both to 'save' the prostitute and to campaign against registration and legalisation.[109] While working towards these long-term goals, they successfully lobbied to raise by two years the minimum age at which a prostitute could register with the police, which until 1895 had been 16. Stites shows that from 1900 these upper-class saviours, working through the Russian Society for the Protection of Women, campaigned to raise the legal age for brothel women from 18 to 21, which was achieved in 1909.[110] One result was to push young prostitutes (some only 9 years old) on to the streets, or into unlicensed brothels. In addition, prostitution was so prevalent by the early twentieth century that the impact of Magdalene shelters was extremely limited. Indeed, war in 1914, with the vast numbers of refugees, including homeless and abandoned children, rendered them almost totally ineffective.

Yet to a woman without skills or contacts in the factory, what were the alternatives to domestic service and prostitution? There was waitressing, which like domestic service entailed very long hours for low pay, and was even more open to the sexual advances of customers. There was also casual employment as day-labourers, but again that was very insecure and poorly paid. Women could be hawkers, selling for example fruit, herring and pies, as well as socks, pens and pencils and balloons. Pokrovskaia pointed out in 1903 that street hawkers were not always successful in selling all their wares on the same day, which meant that they had to store what was left in their corner flats, where the only space available was under the bed.[111] They provided a vital service to the city's poor, as did those women who ran refreshment stalls in the markets. Not all the hawkers were self-employed. Those peasant women who came into the city to work on allotments between May and August were

107. Stites, 'Prostitution and Society in Pre-Revolutionary Russia', p. 352.
108. I. Eremeev, *Gorod Sankt-Peterburg s tochki zreniia meditsinskoi politsii* (St. Petersburg, 1897), p. 4.
109. Laurie Bernstein, *Sonia's Daughters: Prostitutes and their Regulation in Imperial Russia* (Berkeley, Calif., 1995), especially chs 6, 7 and 8.
110. Stites, 'Prostitution and Society in Pre-Revolutionary Russia', p. 360.
111. Pokrovskaia, *Po podvalam, cherdakam i uglovym kvartiram Peterburga*, p. 24.

sometimes also expected to sell the produce.[112] Often, hawkers were older women unable to find any other work. Given the alternatives, it is not surprising that prostitution was not simply a last resort but a welcome escape to many young women.

In addition, although illegal, a prostitute could evade arrest by registering with the police and so had some protection not afforded women who committed other crimes. Women were regarded as less likely to commit criminal offences other than sexual or domestic, while female crime was commonly associated with the city rather than the village. The city was seen as a corrupting influence, where women were more likely to be single and alone, lacking in male supervision. Yet a study of women murderers aged between 20 and 60 in central Russia at the turn of the century revealed that village as well as urban women would resort to crime in certain circumstances, related either to their family situation or to their poverty. Dr. Tarnovskaia, who made a study of female murderers at the beginning of the twentieth century, found that most killed out of passion, and that their victims were known to them: a husband, a son-in-law, illegitimate children or grandchildren, for example. The motive might be jealousy, revenge, or an 'accumulation of upsets', such as continual violent abuse by a partner. Tarnovskaia was most interested in the murder of husbands. She noted that the majority of the peasant women whom she interviewed had married before they had begun menstruating (the average age for the onset of menstruation was, she calculated, 16 or 17 in the village, 14 in the city). In her view, these women were not sexually mature enough for marriage, and she argued that a simple change in peasant customs, with brides becoming older, would lead to fewer wives poisoning their husbands.[113]

On closer inspection, however, it seems that 'greed' was also a significant motivating passion. Women committed crimes for gain, either to tide them over in an emergency, or as an opportunity to supplement earnings. Thus one woman robbed and murdered a landowner who had sacked her when she was pregnant. The child had died soon after birth, but the landowner would not reinstate her. Her attempt to steal from him may have been an act of desperation or revenge, but she had regularly resorted to petty theft whenever she had been out of work. Three other women killed the wealthy female peasants with whom they lodged, for money and

112. Bakhtiarov, *Briukho Peterburga*, p. 150.
113. P.N. Tarnovskaia, *Zhenshchiny-ubiitsy* (St. Petersburg, 1902).

clothes. Tarnovskaia even recorded cases of women who were hired to murder someone, with payment either in cash or kind. Indeed, one of the most popular of crime stories was *Sanka of the Golden Hand*, published in 1903 by M.D. Kleftorov, whose heroine was, unusually, a professional criminal, based on the life of the bandit Sonia Bliuvshtein.[114] She was eventually imprisoned in the penal colony of Sakhalin Island, her fame attracting such visitors as Anton Chekhov. Indeed, the colony capitalized on her notoriety by selling her photograph as a postcard.

Sanka was exceptional. Much more common was Sonia, the prostitute character of Dostoevsky's novel *Crime and Punishment*. She had worked in a garment shop to contribute to her family's income, had resorted to prostitution on losing her job, and then taken the 'yellow ticket'. To conform to regulations, Sonia had to move out of the home which she was supporting. What happened to the fictional Sonia was seen to reflect reality for many thousands of poor women in the city, and knowledge of their plight played a significant part in raising the social and political consciousness of upper-class women in the late nineteenth century. As we shall see in the next chapter, some concentrated on improving the position of women within the established order, but others, seeing the treatment of and attitudes towards lower-class women as an indictment of that order, sought to destroy it.

114. See Brooks, *When Russia Learned to Read*, p. 203.

CHAPTER THREE

Women and Politics before the First World War

A key moment in her political awakening was when Anna Pavlovna Pribyleva-Korba witnessed a group of prostitutes in St. Petersburg being marched by police to their compulsory medical inspection:

> It was as if I had been struck on the head. I had never heard of anything so dreadful in my life, nor could I have imagined such outrageous treatment of women. It seemed to me that the insult was directed against all women, and me personally – me especially, since I felt the weight of humiliation as I was powerless to stop other women from being degraded.[1]

Anna Pavlovna had just settled in the capital with her new husband, who was a banker. She was so upset by the sight of the prostitutes that her health suffered. Her doctor advised her that her illness was not physical, and suggested that she broaden her outlook and understanding of urban life by improving her education. She studied mathematics at the higher courses for women, which brought her into contact with active revolutionaries. She moved with her husband to Moscow and then, in 1874, to Minsk, where she continued to educate herself through reading, and engaged in charitable work. In 1877, during the Russo-Turkish War, she joined the Red Cross, and when her training was complete, she went as a nurse to the front. That experience, as well as the news of the great trials of revolutionaries (including Sofia Bardina) in Petersburg, convinced her both that her marriage was dead, and that she too should become a full-time revolutionary. Within two years, in 1880, she had joined the People's Will, a terrorist group dedicated to assassinating the tsar and any of his officials in the hope of provoking a peasant revolution. She manufactured and carried explosives, forged passports, researched,

1. *Entsiklopedicheskii slovar' 'Granat'* (Moscow, 1926), vol. 40, p. 369.

translated and wrote articles for the group's newspaper, and ran 'safe houses'. In 1883 she was arrested and sent into exile in Siberia, where she remained until the 1905 revolution.

Anna Pavlovna thus travelled a road which thousands of women from the upper classes and the intelligentsia (Anna Pavlovna's father had been a transport engineer, her mother a homeopath) followed in the late nineteenth century: from dutiful daughter and wife to active revolutionary, via higher education, philanthropy, a job in a caring profession, and limited contact with the mass of people to whom she had nevertheless dedicated herself. She and the more famous Sofia Perovskaia were heroic examples for many others to admire, though most opted for a career of service in the professions rather than revolution. What is interesting about Anna Pavlovna is that it was concern with the plight of women, rather than with the people as a whole, which was her initial starting-point. Yet she would not have seen herself as a feminist. Even those who did accepted that the aim was not self-advancement but social utility.

> The Russian women's movement has one characteristic feature in which it differs from the similar movements elsewhere – it holds to the idea of progress. In other countries, however, women sometimes strive for their own rights alone, for their own well-being, and in their eagerness to secure them they leave themselves open to the manipulations of church and conservatism. Russian women don't separate their cause from the great cause of human progress. No retrogressive element in our society can count on the aid of one woman battling for equality.[2]

From 'small deeds' to revolution: the origins of female involvement in the revolutionary movement

Feminists, like revolutionaries, devoted their work to the service of the people, or rather to the mass of women. The usual feminist tactic was to work within the system, trying to achieve reform by gradual, peaceful and legal means, which inevitably involved compromising with the established order. Until the 1905 revolution, feminists in Russia concentrated on philanthropic and educational

2. Marie Zebrikoff, 'Russia', in Theodore Stanton (ed.), *The Woman Question in Europe* (New York, 1884), p. 422.

activities. Indeed, as political reaction had followed the reforms of the 1860s, upper-class feminists had tried to distinguish themselves from the revolutionaries. Such prominent feminists as Nadezhda V. Stasova (1822–95), Anna P. Filosofova (1837–1912) and Mariia V. Trubnikova (1835–97) looked to the women's movements in the West, and imitated in particular the philanthropic tradition and the methods of petitioning and lobbying those with power and influence. Russian feminists were concerned with women's rights in general, while they were also trying to help particular women, notably from the gentry whose families had been impoverished by the abolition of serfdom in 1861. Hence, while campaigning for the entry of women into higher education and the professions, they ran charities for the education and employment of gentry women, and for the cheap accommodation of single women in towns. Such hostels were seen as offering refuge to potential victims of the moral dangers and temptations which the city, it was believed, held in store for the unprotected female.

However, these upper-class feminists were socially isolated, while their moderation and willingness to trim their goals in order to win official sanction, as well as the often patronising regime of their charitable institutions, gradually alienated them both from the more radical feminists, and from the hapless recipients of their benevolence.[3] There was a similar lack of understanding over the issue of temperance, which became an important feminist campaign by the early twentieth century. Indeed, far from bridging the social gulf between the upper-class philanthropists and working-class women, as the former had hoped, the anti-alcohol movement may have strengthened it. Feminists argued that legal rights for women were essential to underpin the crucial role of the mother in the home in ensuring that her husband was sober, and of the educator in school turning boys away from the traditional notion of associating alcohol with adulthood.[4] Working-class women, however, were not opposed to a man frequenting the tavern, so long as he did not spend all his wages there. Wives and children would take action to prevent such an abdication of responsibility by waiting outside factory gates on payday, and embarrassing the men into handing over the housekeeping money.[5]

3. *Sbornik pamiati Anny Pavlovny Filosofovoy* (Petrograd, 1915), vol. 1, pp. 125–36; E.A. Shtakhenshneider, *Dnevniki i zapiski* (Moscow, 1934), pp. 349–57.
4. See E.A. Chebysheva-Dmitrieva, *Rol' zhenshchin v bor'be s alkogolizmom* (St. Petersburg, 1904).
5. A. Buzinov, *Za nevskoi zastavoi: zapiski rabochego* (Moscow, 1930), p. 26.

This generation of feminists avoided overtly political campaigns, yet still suffered reverses, such as the closing of almost all the higher education institutions by the end of the 1880s. Nevertheless, the feminists were resilient, and continued to raise funds for women's courses, while petitioning the tsar that they be reopened. Indeed, Stasova was active in this cause until her death in 1895. She worked tirelessly to improve female education at many levels, successfully campaigning for the establishment of a boarding-house for female students, technical courses for female and male factory workers, supporting Sunday schools (established to spread literacy among workers who could not attend classes on any other day) and reading rooms to promote literacy in St. Petersburg, and setting up a crèche for women workers there in 1893, which took 15 children daily, ranging from babies to 7-year-olds.[6]

In 1894, Stasova accepted an invitation to join the newly formed Russian Women's Society, attending all the meetings and assisting in drawing up the society's charter before she died the following year. The women who had set up this society had to struggle for a year to obtain official recognition. To achieve it, they had to limit their objectives and spheres of activity. Once legally established, Stasova had been unanimously elected the society's chairwoman. She wrote a letter to the revered writer Leo Tolstoy, asking for his opinion on the matter. His negative reply highlighted the very limited impact that such a society could have within both the existing political system and the patriarchal family:

> I am sorry, Nadezhda Vasilievna, if you will find what I am going to say to you about your society to be unpleasant. I never saw anything useful coming out of a society with a charter, which is why I do not think anything useful will come out of your society. That there still exist many centuries-old prejudices towards women is correct; even more correct is the need to fight them. But I do not think that a society in Petersburg which will set up reading rooms and halls for women could become a means for this struggle. I am not appalled by the fact that a woman gets lower wages than a man: prices are set by the value of labour, and if in service a man is given more than a woman, it is not because women are given too little, but because men are given too much. I am appalled that a woman who bears, feeds and rears young children, is also burdened by kitchen work, toiling over the stove, washing up, cleaning, sewing, wiping tables

6. For the origins of the Sunday-school movement, see R.E. Zelnick, 'The Sunday-school Movement in Russia, 1859–1862', *Journal of Modern History* (June 1965), vol. xxxvii, no. 2, pp. 151–70.

and washing floors and windows. Why is such hard work left exclusively to women? Muzhik [male peasant], factory owner, chinovnik [bureaucrat], and any man at times has nothing to do, yet he could lie and smoke, leaving it to women – and they submit – often pregnant, sick, with children, toiling over the stove, or doing the terrible work of washing and caring for a sick child through the night. And all this because of some superstitous belief that it is women's work. It is an awful evil, and because of it wretched women [suffer] untreatable illnesses, premature old age and death; the stupefaction of both themselves and their children. This we have to fight with words, actions and example.[7]

Stasova never replied. She died three weeks later. The society was officially opened a month after her death.

In a sense, within an autocratic system there was basic equality between women and men in that neither had the right of representation, let alone civil rights. Despite their contacts with the Western female suffrage movements, the Russian feminists expressed little interest in the question of political rights for women. Yet not only was their success dependent upon and vulnerable to the whim of the tsar, it was unclear whether the feminist argument, for example, in support of the entry of women into higher education, had been accepted, or whether the regime simply needed a fresh and inexpensive supply of professional labour (especially in teaching and medicine) by the end of the century. By the early twentieth century, moderate feminism, under the leadership now of Anna N. Shabanova (1843–1932) and working through the Mutual Philanthropic Society (established in 1895, and at first under Filosofova's direction), began to approach the issue of suffrage, setting up an electoral department within the society in 1905.[8] Both the conservative Mutual Philanthropic Society and the more overtly political feminists were willing to collaborate with liberal and even left-wing men, notably in 1905.[9] The emphasis was still on service to the people, and the method involved co-operation between women and men against a reactionary state.

Barbara Engel's 1983 study of the female intelligentsia in the late nineteenth century, *Mothers and Daughters*, asked if there were seeds of conflict between women's desire for self-realisation and

7. V. Stasov, *Nadezhda Vasilievna Stasova: vospominaniia i ocherki* (St. Petersburg, 1899), pp. 443–4.

8. Richard Stites, *The Women's Liberation Movement in Russia: Feminism, Nihilism, and Bolshevism, 1860–1930* (Princeton, 1978; 2nd edn 1991), pp. 193–8.

9. See Linda Edmondson, *Feminism in Russia 1900–1917* (London, 1984), pp. 15–28.

the goal of service to the people. The Russians themselves would not have recognised such a conflict, given the absence of an individualistic ethic in the Western sense. Indeed, in the Russian context, a sense of self seems to have developed precisely from working for the community. In 1884 Marie Zebrikoff asserted that 'Russian women who have risen to the consciousness of their right to knowledge and independence consider these blessings as means with which to improve the condition of their native land'.[10] Public service was seen as a step towards independence for the individual woman. In any case, given the role of the state, a woman pursuing a career was most likely to work in the public sector.

However, those who entered the professions, particularly of teaching and medicine, found themselves continually under suspicion of harbouring radical political views. More acceptable to the authorities were those women who devoted themselves to charitable work, though any philanthropic organisation needed official permission, and had to convince state bureaucrats that its activities were apolitical. Hence the philanthropists concerned themselves with orphaned children and fallen women, the poor and the homeless, health and welfare, education and training. However, Bernice Madison has shown that charity could not cope with the scale of poverty in tsarist Russia, as reflected in the persistence of widespread begging and vagrancy.[11] Nor indeed were the services of professional women sufficient to meet the demands of the people. Hemmed in by the weight of officialdom and swamped by the needs of the people, it is perhaps not surprising that so many women followed Vera Figner in abandoning the 'small deeds' of individual service for revolutionary activity.

Barbara Engel believes that there was in these women an absolutism and an intensity of dedication lacking (at least in degree) in most of their male radical contemporaries, but that the result was a sexual division of labour within the revolutionary movement, even though the women enjoyed equal status with the men. It was a division of labour which, Engel claims, left an enduring mark on the quality of female radicalism in Russia. The women were selfless heroines devoted to serving a cause which was led by men. While the women acted alongside men, it was the latter who assumed intellectual leadership.[12] Such altruism and devotion to the general

10. Stanton, *The Woman Question in Europe*, p. 423.
11. Bernice Madison, 'The Organisation of Welfare Services', in Cyril E. Black (ed.), *The Transformation of Russian Society* (Cambridge, Mass., 1967), pp. 515–40.
12. Barbara Engel, *Mothers and Daughters: Women of the Intelligentsia in Nineteenth-Century Russia* (Cambridge, 1983), pp. 5, 173, 183.

good was precisely what was expected of and by women in Russia. Implicit in the judgement that, while women were important in organising and participating in acts of terrorism, they nevertheless failed to take on, or abdicated, intellectual leadership, is an assumed hierarchy within the revolutionary movement which acknowledged theorizing as superior to practical deeds. Yet this was not always the case. Indeed, nineteenth-century Russian intellectuals wanted to impress by the deed and not the word. Writing in the middle of the century, the socialist exile from Russia, Alexander Herzen, had pointed to the intelligentsia's propensity to introspection and apparent impotence to act. In his view, the intelligentsia remained 'eternal spectators, miserable members of a jury whose verdict is never accepted, experts whose testimony no one wants'.[13]

Memoirs and biographies of late nineteenth-century female revolutionaries reveal that they felt such a sense of urgency and such depth of commitment to changing society that they were unwilling to remain onlookers. Perhaps the best-known is Vera Figner. An avid reader and bright, diligent student, she decided to become a doctor, travelling with her new husband to Zurich University in 1870. There she met other radical women who formed a women's study circle (known as the Fritschi) to help them develop confidence in debate without the dominating presence of men. The Fritschi wanted to study and discuss free from male competition and authority.[14] Figner recorded her own development away from study in the 'ivory tower' of university and theoretical debate with her peers, to a medical career in the service of a minority of the people, and then full-time revolutionary terrorism. She returned to Moscow under the influence of revolutionary ideas in 1875, was divorced, qualified as a feldsher, and wrote a programme for the populist (agrarian socialist) movement. She worked as a feldsher in the province of Samara, having to move frequently because of police harassment. Increasingly she felt that her activities as feldsher and propagandist were just a drop in a vast ocean of oppression. She wanted to do more, to act in a way which would have a much greater impact than such 'small deeds'. Hence she persuaded her comrades to allow her to participate in the terrorist campaign. She did not completely give up writing and debating, but she was above all involved in the military wing of the populist movement.

13. A. Herzen, *From the Other Shore* (London, 1956), pp. 76, 87.
14. Vera Figner, *Zapechatlennyi trud* (Moscow, 1964), vol. 1, pp. 116–20; B.S. Itenberg, *Dvizhenie revoliutsionnogo narodnichestva* (Moscow, 1965), pp. 142–4; Amy Knight, 'The Fritsche: A Study of Female Radicals in the Russian Populist Movement', *Canadian Slavic Studies* (Spring 1975), vol. 9, no. 1, pp. 1–18.

In 1873, Vera Figner was betrayed to the police. After being arrested, she spent 20 months in solitary confinement, and after her trial another 13 years in which she was not only kept apart from other prisoners but forbidden to write. She spent another seven years in prison, was released into internal exile in 1904, and because of poor health was allowed to go abroad in 1906, returning to Russia only in 1915. Figner's absence from the intellectual debates and leadership, then, was not simply from choice, not just a case of self-effacement. Deep feelings of frustration at how little she could achieve had led her to terrorist activity; prison had silenced her; exile had isolated her. Ironically, Vera then earned a living from her writing, and she returned to a life of service to some of the people, devoting herself to helping the peasants of her native province and victims of the civil war which followed the Bolshevik revolution.[15]

Figner had been prompted by the question posed in Nikolai Chernyshevsky's novel *What is to be done?*, published when he was in prison for his revolutionary ideals in 1863. The 'going to the people' movement of the early 1870s, in which thousands of young upper-class women and men had gone to the villages to live and work with the peasants, had failed, largely due to peasant suspicion of outsiders and police repression, with the peasants occasionally informing on the radical intelligentsia.Vera Figner wrote that the latter next tried to reach the peasants indirectly through the factory workers, whom they saw as the key to spreading revolutionary ideas among the peasantry. Despite the efforts of intellectuals such as herself and Perovskaia to bridge the social and cultural gap between themselves and the peasants, the latter persisted in regarding the intelligentsia as outsiders. Morever, there was the tsarist secret police to contend with, so that the combination of peasant resistance with government repression meant the work of the intelligentsia in the villages and factories was crushed by 1875. Figner argued that work among the people, both rural and urban, had come to no avail because of the lack of political freedom; and therefore she had arrived at terrorism because 'the people were crushed by poverty, abased by the constant demands made upon them, and did not have the strength themselves to employ such means'.[16] Of the

15. *Entsiklopedicheskii slovar' 'Granat'*, vol. 40, pp. 458–78.
16. Vera Figner, *Memoirs of a Revolutionist* (New York, 1927), pp. 13, 44–5; for the quotation, p. 62. See also V.Ya. Bogucharsky, *Iz istorii politicheskoi bor'by v 70s i 80s gg. XIX veka* (Moscow, 1912), pp. 49–123 for a discussion of terrorism, and pp. 124–41 for this early political activity among workers. For the activities in the 1870s of five female revolutionaries, see B.A. Engel and C.N. Rosenthal (eds), *Five Sisters: Women Against the Tsar* (London, 1975).

generation of female revolutionaries of the 1870s and early 1880s, perhaps Sofia Perovskaia expressed most clearly their feeling of impotence in the face of peasant passivity: 'I want to wake them up from their half-dead sleep, but I haven't the knowledge. I haven't the means.'[17] Unwilling to devote precious time to debating and theorizing, such women struck at the heart of the tsarist system by murdering its representatives.

Yet it is perhaps not the terrorist women who abdicated intellectual leadership, so much as the contemporary perception of their role. They were seen, by liberals as well as radicals, as saints and martyrs for a good cause, particularly if they were either executed, like Perovskaia, or imprisoned for long periods of time, like Vera Figner and Mariia Spiridonova. Some published and gave public lectures abroad, such as Ekaterina Breshko-Breshkovskaia, but it was their practical example which made the strongest impression. Indeed, it was the attempted assassination of the Governor-General of Petersburg in 1878 by Vera Zasulich which became both the model and the catalyst for revolutionary terrorism. Zasulich herself quickly abandoned terrorism for Marxism. A critic of the Bolsheviks, she died soon after they came to power.[18]

Both the 'going to the people' movement of the early 1870s and the terrorism at the end of that decade failed to rouse the peasants. The economic changes of the 1880s, but especially the 1890s, were paralleled by a growing interest among radical intellectuals in the writings of Karl Marx. Marxists tended to view the peasants as backward and superstitious, prone to undisciplined violence, and with aspirations which were fundamentally incompatible with the emerging industrial system. Marxists also identified the traditional patriarchal family, and the subordinate position of women, as a brake on the development of revolutionary consciousness, particularly with the increasing absorption of women into the labour force by the end of the century. In the 1890s, the international socialist movement, based in the Second International, took up the struggle for sexual equality. Many politically conscious workers and intellectuals in Russia, however, dismissed the issue as either secondary or unimportant, and condemned feminism as divisive.

Until the revolution of 1905, the Russian feminist movement focused on the campaign for the entry of women into higher education. Given the high rate of female illiteracy, that demand

17. Quoted in Margaret Maxwell, *Narodniki Women: Russian Women Who Sacrificed Themselves for the Dream of Freedom* (New York, 1990), p. 63.
18. See Jay Bergman, *Vera Zasulich: A Biography* (Stanford, Calif., 1983).

seemed irrelevant to the mass of urban and rural women. Although many socialist women benefited from openings in higher education, they nevertheless refuted the feminist belief that a struggle for women's rights transcended class, and generally accepted the ideological demand that the woman question be subordinated to the class struggle. Socialists, therefore, campaigned for reforms favourable to women as workers and mothers, and tried to make them aware of their social duties in order to break out of the confines of what the revolutionaries saw as the selfish, introverted familial viewpoint so divisive for working-class solidarity. Thus a radical skilled male metal worker claimed that workers were exploited as a class, irrespective of their individual humanity. He recognised, however, that the gulf between the minority of politically conscious workers and the rest was huge, and that the difficult task of arousing the latter included the awakening of women workers to an understanding of their class position: male and female workers must fight together for their common cause, especially in view of the severe repression of workers' unrest.[19]

Women workers were seen as the most backward of their class, and yet they were not unwaveringly passive. They were drawn, and sometimes coerced, into strike action, especially in the larger factories.[20] Occasionally, women took action for themselves, and by themselves, as in the strike wave of the mid 1890s when female workers, notably in textile and tobacco factories, engaged in sporadic and often violent actions. However, given their preoccupation with family interests, as well as their own low level of education, women workers were often reluctant to support strikes, and were used by employers to defeat male worker militancy. Their general political backwardness was seen as a drag on the development of the labour movement. There was an assumption that the conservatism of wives, and their suspicions of the godless intelligentsia, sapped their husbands' opposition to authority. Indeed, Sofia Bardina, who had been carrying out propaganda among factory workers in the mid 1870s, had been betrayed to the police by a woman who believed that her man had been unduly influenced by the female intellectual.[21]

19. Buzinov, *Za nevskoi zastavoi*, pp. 101–3. See also *Literatura Moskovskogo rabochego soiuza* (Moscow, 1930), p. 68; V.G. Gerasimov, *Zhizn' russkogo rabochego: vospominaniia, 1852–1892* (Moscow, 1959), p. 42.

20. M.N. Lyadov, 'Koe-chto o zhenshchine rabotnitse', in *Literatura Moskovskogo rabochego soiuza*, p. 170.

21. S.I. Mitskevich, *Na zare rabochego dvizheniia v Moskve* (Moscow, 1932), p. 111. See also J. Prelooker (Priluker), *Heroes and Heroines of Russia* (London, 1908), ch. xii.

Vera Karelina, a textile worker who participated in the study circles of the early 1890s, understood the position of wives of politically advanced workers; she herself had married one in 1890, and become a mother the following year. In her view, the still illiterate wife was very afraid of both the new skills and knowledge which her man possessed and which might make him dissatisfied with his conditions of work and the object of the attention of the secret police. Nor did she understand why the man no longer spent his time in the tavern, yet did not stay at home; while she was suspicious and resentful of the time he spent reading and discussing with literate, often young and single, women workers.[22] One solution would have been to educate the wives, but the husbands were now preoccupied with their involvement in the labour movement.

Yet the experience of the 1870s had not been completely disheartening. A few women workers at least evinced some interest in the intellectuals' propaganda, and showed a deep desire to learn, as well as a potential for organisation. The radical intellectuals saw their relationship with the masses as that of both teacher and pupil. The early social democrats stressed the need to prepare the workers to lead their own revolutionary movement by raising their intellectual and moral level. A few women intellectuals were involved, such as Ekaterina Koval'skaia, who had been an active revolutionary for almost a decade before she helped establish the South-Russian Workers' Union (based in Kiev) in 1880.[23] Another such female revolutionary was Genrietta Dobruskina, who joined the People's Will in 1882, and its successor, the Socialist Revolutionary party (SRs), at the beginning of the twentieth century. She concentrated her propaganda efforts on urban workers, rather than peasants, and spent a decade trying to draw female workers into the movement.[24]

In this process, in which the intelligentsia performed technical and advisory functions, workers' circles played a vital role. The Brusnev circles of 1890–92, in St. Petersburg and then Moscow, exemplified these tactics. The initiator, Mikhail Ivanovich Brusnev, was a student at the technological institute in St. Petersburg. As early as the winter of 1890, women workers were joining what had hitherto been exclusively male circles, and from 1891 there was a

22. Vera Karelina, 'Vospominaniia: na zare rabochego dvizheniia v S-Peterburge', *Krasnaia letopis'* (1922), no. 4, pp. 12–21.

23. See her memoir, E. Koval'skaia, *Iuzhno-russkii rabochii soiuz, 1880–1881* (Moscow, 1926); see also *Five Sisters*, pp. 206–34.

24. *Deiateli revoliutsionnogo dvizheniia v Rossii: Bio-bibliograficheskii slovar'* (Moscow, 1929), vol. 3, pp. 1196–9.

network of specifically women's circles designed for mainly textile workers. These Brusnev circles attempted to overcome the divisive hierarchies of mental and manual, skilled and unskilled, male and female, and stressed that the workers themselves should take the initiative. The intelligentsia would begin the process by organising study circles of workers, who would then increasingly assume organisational responsibilities themselves.[25]

It had proved extremely difficult to organise in the textile industry, which was backward in terms of its technology and the low cultural level of its workers. Nevertheless, it was a very important industry in Russia, particularly in the Moscow region. By the turn of the century, men were in a minority among textile workers. While some among the small numbers of skilled men tried to educate themselves, generally the unskilled men spent their spare time drinking vodka.[26] Yet it was women who formed the majority of the unskilled textile workforce, and they were seen by the revolutionaries as even harder to reach than their male counterparts, with a tendency to accept and submit to authority.[27] Hence efforts were made in the circles of the early 1890s to overcome the gulf between male and female workers. The propagandists recognised that women were even more harshly exploited by the employers than male workers.

The Brusnev group included such female worker-activists as Vera Karelina, Anna Gavrilova, Anna Boldyreva, Fenia Novinskaia and Natalia Grigor'eva. In addition, Natalia Grigor'eva was a female representative from the women workers' circles on the central workers' circle. The women were helped by the male workers in the Brusnev organisation to set up circles such as that aimed mainly at female weavers which Karelina established with the aid of the skilled male worker, Gavrilov, in the winter of 1890–91. The Karelina circle, in which female students as well as male intellectuals carried out propaganda work, may have included as many as 20 women. Through its members, the Brusnev group was able to make contact with a number of factories employing large numbers of women. Vera Karelina has described the lives of some of those women who were touched by the propaganda and entered the study circles:

25. S. Tsederbaum, *Zhenshchina v russkom revoliutsionnom dvizhenii 1870–1905* (Leningrad, 1927), pp. 154–60; V.I. Nevsky, *Ocherki po istorii rossiiskoi kommunisticheskoi partii* (Leningrad, 1925), vol. 1, pp. 276–8; R.A. Kazakevich, *Sotsial-demokraticheskie organizatsii Peterburga kontsa 80kh-nachala 90kh godov* (Leningrad, 1960), pp. 144–8.
26. Mitskevich, *Na zare rabochego dvizheniia v Moskve*, pp. 75–7.
27. Kazakevich, *Sotsial-demokraticheskie organizatsii Peterburga*, p. 148.

On the Vyborg side we lived in a genuine commune. Four young girls lived there: myself, Natasha Aleksandrova (a seamstress), Varya Nikolaeva (a housemaid) and Aleksandrova's sister who worked at the dye works. A number of wives of the workers at Rasteryaevsky foundry also lived there . . . We lived as a commune: money was paid into a common fund, we shared a common table, laundry and library. Everyone did the housework and there were never any quarrels or arguments.

Young women in general played a large role in the organisation. We were young, healthy and lively, and we attracted young male workers. Our meetings took on a social character. With many young girls, love matches occurred.[28]

These worker activists, female as well as male, held that their interests were basically the same, and that unity between the sexes was essential.[29] The women workers in the Brusnev organisation experienced little hostility from the men. Rose Glickman argues that they were perhaps 'too exhilarated by acceptance into a milieu that uplifted them' to provide a more realistic assessment. In her view, the high regard for women in the circle movement was not sustained.[30] Certainly, the highly skilled, well-read male workers of the Brusnev circles were a far cry from the vast majority of the Russian working class. Many of the male workers, skilled as well as unskilled, were sceptical about the idea of women participating in the revolutionary movement. Moreover, the initial contact with workers was often made by the radical male intelligentsia in the taverns, which were male havens. The fact that revolutionary men sought contact with workers in taverns was not simply because they saw men as more receptive than women to their propaganda. In an absolutist state, there were few public places other than the tavern which would not automatically draw the attention of the secret police. However, the need for relative security reinforced the image of women as politically unreachable. With male workers lacking confidence and trust in women, it was only slowly that respect for women workers developed.[31]

The circles were quickly crushed by the authorities. Certainly too, study circles could reach only a minority who were then, by virtue of their self-development, often cut off from the majority of their uneducated co-workers. Yet the attention paid to women

28. Karelina, 'Vospominaniia', p. 12.

29. *Literatura Moskovskogo rabochego soiuza*, p. 68.

30. R.L. Glickman, *Russian Factory Women: Workplace and Society, 1880–1914* (London, 1984), p. 179.

31. Kazakevich, *Sotsial-demokraticheskie organizatsii Peterburga*, pp. 44, 147.

workers by the Brusnev group did not end with the arrests of the summer of 1892. It had set an example in a region which was dominated by the textile industry. By this time, the social democratic movement had recognised the need to reach much larger numbers of workers, and to organise around their immediate economic demands. Thus the Moscow Workers' Union of 1893–95 published a series of popular agitational leaflets aimed at the mass of factory workers, including Lyadov's pamphlet on working women. He recognised that there were grievances and needs specific to women, and the union accepted that women already constituted the majority of the labour force in many mills. Nevertheless, Lyadov argued that the basic interests of the women were no different from those of the men, so that they must 'grasp each other by the hand' and present a united front in the struggle for the liberation of both sexes from capitalist oppression.[32]

The necessity of including women in their agitational efforts was underlined for the Union members by the behaviour of the female textile workers at Tsindel's cotton mill in 1894, when many of them had to be forcibly restrained from strikebreaking: the male workers locked the women in the factory's living quarters. The women's conservatism was partly caused by profound suspicion of the radical intelligentsia. For example, the wife of the skilled worker Konstantinov, was resolutely, indeed vociferously, opposed to his participation in the labour movement.[33] Among both radical intelligentsia and skilled workers there was a certain condescending frustration with these confounded babas [old biddies] who were delaying the urgent organisation of the working class. However, given the importance of female labour, especially in the textile industry, the 'woman question' had to be addressed. Hence the Moscow union, like the Brusnev group before it, supported, financially and otherwise, a number of women in their efforts to set up women's circles.[34]

The hostility of women workers to the trade-union activities of male workers led the Moscow female social democrats in 1894 to the decision to try to reach women workers by infiltrating the Sunday schools and evening classes as teachers, from where they tried to organise women's circles. Since women propagandists were generally students, teaching in Sunday schools was a common method of making contact with factory workers. At the same time, the agitators continued to address those male workers whom the

32. Lyadov, 'Koe-chto o zhenshchine rabotnitse', pp. 163–70; Mitskevich, *Na zare rabochego dvizheniia v Moskve*, pp. 79–85.
33. Ibid., p. 111.   34. Ibid., p. 85.

propaganda was reaching on the woman question in general, and specifically on the need to involve working women in their struggle.[35]

Through a contact with the head of a Moscow Sunday school, the upper-class student Muralova got a teaching job.[36] From the town of Taganrog, where she had been involved in a circle consisting mainly of intelligentsia, Muralova had gone to Moscow in 1893 knowing that a workers' organisation existed there, and influenced by a rumour that the city's workers were on the brink of a mass rising. Her aim was to teach and carry out propaganda work among the industrial workers. At her first lecture, Muralova met Pelageia Vinokurova and A.I. Smirnova, who invited her to join a circle of female students. There she began by studying Kautsky, and the first volume of Marx's *Capital*. When Vinokurova was sure of Muralova's theoretical education, she introduced Muralova to practical work, and to male revolutionaries who were all engaged in printing leaflets and distributing illegal literature to the workers. One of them, N.I. Perekrestov, who apparently enjoyed great popularity with Moscow workers, acquainted Muralova with some women who were employed in a local tobacco factory. These women were almost totally illiterate. In addition, at her first Sunday school class, she met three young illiterate factory girls whom she found alert and able, and eager to learn. Muralova worked regularly with them, teaching them to read and write, and gradually introducing them to political pamphlets. Within three months, she had a circle of seven women workers, two of whom were beginning to carry out their own propaganda activities among other female workers in their factories. Of course, the attendance of women workers at Sunday school indicated some level of, or desire for, cultural, if not political, awareness.

What did Muralova teach? She was intent on exposing the inequities of the capitalist system by making the women workers aware of their particularly onerous conditions of labour and pitifully low wages. She pointed out that they worked long hours, often as many as 16 a day, in conditions which debased their human dignity. She focused specifically on the fact that, in order to get employment at a factory in the first place, young women were often expected to please the foreman sexually, and that he would take advantage of them for a long time, publicly humiliating them, and perhaps sacking them if they resisted his demands.

35. Ibid., pp. 79–85.
36. The following discussion is based on S.N. Muralova, 'Iz proshlogo', ibid., pp. 153–5.

However, given the numbers and the low cultural base, Muralova's work was of a necessarily long-term perspective, a process of enlightenment. The conscious male workers who were organising the unskilled men were convinced that the women were not yet fit enough to become full union members because of the depth of their ignorance and general lack of preparation. Thus work among the women was generally carried out separately. In addition, the Moscow Workers' Union was smashed by early 1896. Still, in the strike wave of that year, many women were involved and they were as harshly treated as the men, for the cossacks did not discriminate in their charges on strikers and demonstrators, so that even pregnant women were their victims.[37] Indeed, textile workers were much more militant in the mid 1890s than the more skilled and better organised metal workers. This presented revolutionaries with a dilemma, since they saw the skilled workers as their natural recruiting ground, yet it was those workers generally considered more backward who were most likely to protest. The usual explanation is couched in gender terms: the often illiterate female workers were prone to act irrationally and spontaneously; they were both submissive and easily aroused, perhaps by some minor action which made their position suddenly seem no longer bearable. They were volatile, but lacked leadership, direction and staying power.

In his study of the 1905 revolution in St. Petersburg, Gerald Suhr has criticised such explanations as simplistic. He points out that not all women workers were militant in the 1890s. In addition, while female tobacco workers went on strike and demonstrated, it was never on the scale of the textile workers. Suhr sees a possible explanation in the fact that those who took the initiative, often the spinning assistants, lacked authority among the textile workers.[38] Indeed, the way the industry was organised, in huge mills, overseen by foremen who were often non-Russian-speaking foreigners, with a work process which depended on masses of unskilled and at most semi-skilled labourers isolated from each other by an extreme division of labour, served to prevent any sense of solidarity from being developed. Badly paid and dominated by the mill's machinery, textile workers had no real opportunity for a sense of community, let alone an organisation, to grow.

The tiny majority of politically conscious women such as Karelina, Gavrilova and Boldyreva continued throughout the 1890s and into the twentieth century to organise female workers, but their efforts

37. Karelina, 'Vospominaniia', p. 20.
38. G. Suhr, *1905 in St. Petersburg: Labour, Society, and Revolution* (Stanford, Calif., 1989), pp. 68–70.

were constantly thwarted by the secret police. When the Brusnev group was smashed in 1893, Karelina was arrested and imprisoned in solitary confinement for six months. On her release, she had to remain in exile under police supervision.[39] Yet still she organised, and participated in strikes in 1897, and notably in the 1905 revolution. Such heroic efforts, however, had only fleeting success, as Karelitsa continually had to move, whether under arrest or avoiding it. Given the conditions in which the few women such as Karelina practised their revolutionary vocation, it is not surprising that the organisation of women workers was not sustained, and leadership not developed.

Yet a minority at least of female workers had shown an interest in trade unions. Between 1896 and 1902 unskilled and semi-skilled women workers, notably in the tobacco and confectionery industries, were drawn into the organisations set up by Sergei Zubatov, the head of the Moscow secret police, as part of an experimental strategy of government involvement in industrial relations. Although the numbers who joined were very small, the meetings which were organised reached thousands of Moscow workers. While the experiment was stopped by the authorities as soon as the rank and file had shown signs of taking over the movement, it had provided valuable organisational and educational experience for workers who had not previously been reached by the social democratic movement.

Certainly, there had been attempts by a minority of skilled male workers and radical intelligentsia in the previous decade to develop textile workers' political consciousness and organisational experience. Yet not only did such efforts have a very limited impact and prove short-lived, but in the context of political repression, the labour movement in Russia had to be organised around individual factories, effectively cutting workers in different industries off from each other. Victoria Bonnell's study of the labour movement in Petersburg and Moscow before the First World War reveals the importance of the short-lived government-sponsored Zubatov experiment, which might be seen as a precursor to the Assembly of Russian Factory and Mill Workers set up in St. Petersburg in 1904. In the latter, women comprised as many as 1,000 out of its 9,000 membership in the revolutionary year of 1905.[40] However, during

39. Karelina, 'Vospominaniia', pp. 19–20.
40. For Zubatov, see Victoria E. Bonnell, *Roots of Rebellion: Workers' Politics and Organizations in St. Petersburg and Moscow, 1900–1914* (Berkeley, Calif., 1983), pp. 80–6. For the Assembly of Russian Factory and Mill Workers see P.F. Kudelli (ed.), *Rabotnitsa v 1905g. v S-Peterburge: Sbornik statei i vospominanii* (Leningrad, 1926), pp. 14–26.

the revolution, skilled male workers often set up trade unions with the objective of protecting their craft from dilution of skills, including the entry of female labour.

In addition, Zubatov had adopted a dual strategy: besides his unions, there were police informers. Often these were revolutionaries who were 'turned' by Zubatov's methods, which were more psychological than physical. One female informer was Zinaida Zuchenko, who, even when unmasked, declared that she acted from conviction. Another was E.N. Shornikova, who was partly responsible for the arrest of the social democratic faction in the second duma. Once Shornikova had performed her service to the state, she was left unprotected, despite having been exposed as a police agent. Eventually, after much red tape and concern that she might compromise the authorities, she was recompensed and left Russia. As an informer, Shornikova had been seen by the authorities as insignificant, whereas one of the most outstanding of tsarist secret police agents was another woman, Anna Egorovna Serebriakova. She informed on the revolutionary movement from the 1880s to the 1905 revolution. As a student, she had entered revolutionary politics in the 1870s, but the arrest of her husband and herself, leading to him breaking under the pressure, left her as the breadwinner. She agreed in the early 1880s to become an agent of the secret police in order to stop their harassment of her husband. Zubatov, on becoming head of the Moscow secret police in 1896, recognised the value of her work, and she became indispensable to his repression of the revolutionary movement, not only during the strike wave of the mid 1890s, but into the twentieth century, ceasing only at the end of 1905, 'retiring for the sake of her children (or so she claimed)'.[41]

Taking militant action, then, was for most women workers effectively the only way of articulating their grievances. The women lacked opportunities to develop skills, organisation and leaders. Their protests, however, revealed that women workers could not be simply relied upon by employers to submit passively. However, when the period of industrial prosperity came to an end in 1898, and unemployment grew, the strike movement weakened. Given tsarist success in the 1890s in destroying the nascent workers' organisations, along with any links between the radical intelligentsia and the working class, more and more stress was placed by revolutionaries

41. Frederick S. Zuckerman, *The Tsarist Secret Police in Russian Society, 1880–1917* (Basingstoke, 1996), pp. 55–7 for Serebriakova, p. 42 for Zuchenko, pp. 52–4 for Shornikova.

on the need to establish an organisation capable of operating within such an oppressive system, and less on preparing workers to lead themselves.

The success of the secret police was one reason for the gulf between workers and radical intellectuals remaining wide, since it often meant that the latter found it impossible to make contact with, let alone have any impact on, the former. Thus in Odessa in April 1903, male social democrats had refused to carry out work in the commercial docks for fear of arrests. A woman member, however, had been distributing leaflets among the dockers and volunteered to do organisational work among them. The men worried that her appearance did not lend itself to conspiratorial work, since Liia had

> a short, fragile, almost childlike build, with a freckled, typically Jewish face, and sleek bright red hair. All this made her easy to spot in a crowd, and to remember. We were mostly concerned by her unhealthy shyness.

At first her male comrades turned her down, but as no male volunteers stepped forward she was, reluctantly, given the assignment. Within a few weeks, she had organised a meeting of around 40 dockers, which invited the social democratic organiser in Odessa to speak to them. He recorded his astonishment at the way in which the dockers treated Liia:

> I watched them secretly. I expected to see carnivorous, dirty looks directed at Liia, the kind of looks men use to meet and see off babas. There were no such looks here. The dockers looked at Liia as an elder brother looks at his favourite sister.

Having quickly formed three circles she was soon in need of help from her comrades. The decision was made to send in another woman, since the men did not have a good track record in the docks. There were only two other female social democrats in Odessa at that time: Ania, who already worked among artisans, and Marusia, who had recently joined the party. Physically quite different from Liia, but still as striking ('tall, slender, strong, and unusually beautiful'), Marusia joined Liia in the dock strikes in 1903. Both women were arrested, imprisoned and exiled. Their story was related partly to show the difficulties and dangers of clandestine organisation. The male comrade who recorded their revolutionary activities pointed out that such women were largely unknown, because for conspiratorial reasons their own names were not used. His account also revealed the particular position of female radicals, a minority within their political parties, not always taken seriously either by their male comrades or by the workers whom they tried to propagandise. Working among male workers, moreover, made them an obvious target for police repression.[42] Both women were clearly committed revolutionaries, and were active again during the 1905 revolution. Yet, however dedicated, their contacts with workers proved short-lived.

Besides the obstacles to working-class activity generally, very few female workers had been reached by the women's circles. Moreover, there was increasing controversy over the way in which women workers should be organised, while the wider woman question was seen as a long-term concern, to be resolved only when the urgent and elementary task of organising revolution was achieved. Attention was still paid to the woman worker, though it was minimal. In a pamphlet published in 1901, the social democrat Nadezhda Krupskaia pointed out that female peasants and industrial workers shouldered a double burden, as women and as workers. Thus social democracy had to recognise the specific grievances of women workers, and demand protective legislation for them as part of its minimum programme. For Krupskaia, however, the sexual inequality and oppression of women should not set them apart from male workers. Rather, she maintained, women must join with their male comrades in the general struggle against capitalism, for only a socialist society could resolve the woman question.[43]

Women and the 1905 revolution

Not everyone was prepared to wait, and while the efforts of revolutionary intellectuals were now focused on theoretical debates and building an organisation, events of 1904–5 revealed that some at least continued to work with and educate women workers. Once again, Vera Karelina played a crucial role in drawing women into political activity. Both she and her husband, Aleksei Karelin, a lithographer who had also been active in the Brusnev movement, dedicated themselves to working with those whom the intelligentsia in the social democratic movement considered virtually unreachable: the unskilled workers. They retained the Brusnev emphasis on the workers taking the initiative, rather than simply waiting on the

42. Sushkin, *Bezvestnye: zhenskie siluety revoliutsionnogo podpol'ia kanuna 1905g.* (Moscow, 1930), pp. 5–29.
43. N.K. Krupskaia, *Zhenshchina-rabotnitsa* (Geneva, 1901).

intelligentsia to organise them. Both were prepared to co-operate with the priest, Father Gapon, whom many suspected was a secret police agent, in his Assembly of Russian Factory and Mill Workers. Both Vera and Aleksei were seen by the workers as people of unquestioned integrity, devoted to their cause.[44]

At the same time, Vera Karelina was realistic about the uphill struggle which she faced. She wrote that the mass of male workers felt that social (that is, public) activity was not a woman's affair; that her sphere for action was the machine in the factory and the stove at home; and that her task was to bring up the children. Yet in 1905, female workers insisted that they too were human beings, and not inferior to male workers. They pointed out that they suffered a double oppression, exploited as workers and as women in countless ways, but above all both economically and sexually. Moreover, they realised that the male workers did not understand or appreciate their specific needs. Karelina observed that the male comrades tended to dismiss women's demands as relating to the home and not the factory. Indeed, she claimed that even in industries exclusively staffed by women, they were treated as if they did not count as workers.[45] She persisted in trying to raise the political consciousness of women workers, and encourage their active participation in the struggle for a better life for all workers. Father Gapon supported her efforts to organise women within his assembly, despite his apparent acceptance of peasant notions concerning women's inferiority. Gapon was convinced of the need to draw women into the assembly, believing, as the social democrats did, that the women's lack of education, their 'illiterate nature', distracted their husbands from politics. Yet still Gapon believed that 'more use will come of the women's meetings than of the men's'.[46] By the beginning of 1905, Karelina had involved almost 1,000 women on a regular basis.[47]

As in the early 1890s, Karelina's aims were the enlightenment of women workers, and the wives of workers. She hoped to develop their understanding by beginning with a focus on their specific situation and showing them how it fitted into the wider social, economic and political position. Ultimately, she wanted to involve

44. See Walter Sablinsky, *The Road to Bloody Sunday* (Princeton, 1976), p. 99; Suhr, *1905 in St. Petersburg*, p. 117.
45. Karelina, 'Vospominaniia', p. 19; P.F. Kudelli, *Rabotnitsa v 1905g.*, pp. 9–11, 14.
46. A.E. Karelin, '9 Ianvaria i Gapon; Vospominaniia', *Krasnaia letopis'* (1922), vol. 1, pp. 107, 114.
47. Kudelli, *Rabotnitsa v 1905g.*, pp. 14–26.

them in the labour movement, which would be strengthened by unity between the sexes.[48] However, the women workers in her study circle refused to allow male workers to attend their meetings, fearing that the men would judge them wanting.[49] Karelina observed that women workers often wanted to say something, to contribute to a meeting, but were afraid of the possibility of ridicule. Hence they sat in frustrated silence, hearts 'enflamed'.[50] Karelina, herself a worker and mother, was responsive to the gender aspects of the oppression of women workers, and acutely aware of the men's lack of consciousness of and sympathy with such issues. Nevertheless, she saw the way forward as convincing women and men that they had to join in a common struggle.

Karelina has been described by Gerald Suhr as 'a very remarkable person in her own right'.[51] Yet she was not the only social democratic woman trying to organise female workers in 1905. There were a few women's circles based at particular factories in which women predominated in the workforce.[52] Nor were they restricted to the capital: there was a special women's section, aimed at developing the political consciousness of female workers, in the Bolshevik party in the textile centre of Ivanovo-Voznesensk in 1904–5.[53] Moreover, Karelina's comrade from the Brusnev days, Anna Boldyreva, was one of only seven social democratic women elected to the Petersburg soviet of workers' deputies in October 1905. She was joined by Ermolina from a spinning factory, Barkova from a tobacco factory, Bagrova from the shop assistants' union, Razuvaeva, from a printing works, Zvonariova from the railway workers, and Karelina herself, though she soon became ill and had to retire from politics. The most active in the soviet were Boldyreva, Barkova and Bagrova, all whom were Bolsheviks and who served on the soviet's executive committee.[54] The soviet, however, was short-lived, as tsarism was able to reassert itself within a month. In November, there were arrests of deputies, including Boldyreva. In December, workers, women as well as men, were on the barricades again. Despite the participation

48. Ibid., p. 26. See also Sablinsky, *The Road to Bloody Sunday*, pp. 76–139, and Suhr, *1905 in St. Petersburg*, pp. 118–25.

49. Kudelli, *Rabotnitsa v 1905g.*, pp. 24–5. See Glickman, *Russian Factory Women*, pp. 184–6.

50. Kudelli, *Rabotnitsa v 1905g.*, p. 15.

51. Suhr, *1905 in St. Petersburg*, pp. 118–25.

52. Kudelli, *Rabotnitsa v 1905g.*, p. 9.

53. S.N. Serditova, *Bol'sheviki v bor'be za zhenskie proletarskie massy 1903g.-fevral' 1917g.* (Moscow, 1959), pp. 43–51.

54. Kudelli, *Rabotnitsa v 1905g.*, p. 11.

of a number of women workers in the revolution, however, they had made up only about 1 per cent of the soviet's membership. This was true even of the textile centre of Ivanovo-Voznesensk.[55] In 1905, of the 26 factories (19 of which were textile mills), 17 failed to elect a single female deputy to the soviet. The remaining nine elected a tiny minority of women, though one cotton mill (Kashintsev) returned a majority of female deputies, electing seven women and only one man. Of these seven female deputies, only two were affiliated to a political organisation (the Russian Social Democratic Labour Party, RSDLP). Nevertheless, one of the city's leading social democrats in 1905 was a woman, Olga Afanas'evna Varentsova. She had been active for over a decade, having organised the first Marxist circle there in 1892, the workers' union in 1895, and in 1901–2 she had initiated a southern workers' union, serving as its executive secretary. Another prominent female Bolshevik active in Ivanovo-Voznesensk in 1905 was the textile worker Matrena Ivanovna Golubeva, who was a deputy and speaker at the soviet, and kept weapons as well as illegal literature in her flat.

The textile worker Elena Avtonomovna Razorenova was also elected to the soviet in Ivanovo-Voznesensk. From a peasant background, she had worked in a factory in the city since she was 14 years old. By the time of the 1905 revolution, she was a working mother of two children. As a result of her political activities, she was sacked. To escape further repression, she moved to Baku and found work in a fish-processing factory. Another politically active female textile worker, Anna Ivanovna Smelova-Perlovich, also came from a poor peasant background, and had worked in an Ivanovo-Voznesensk textile factory since 1895. She had been a participant in workers' meetings and in strikes, and had become a member of the RSDLP before the revolution. Like Golubeva, she kept illegal literature and weapons in her flat. She managed to continue her political activities into the next year, when her flat was used as an organising centre for the metal workers' trade union. Often such women worked in partnership with their husbands. Thus Dar'ia Ivanovna Sergiecheva-Chernikova and her husband kept a clandestine printing press in their flat, producing leaflets for the RSDLP. She too was dismissed from her job as a result of her revolutionary work in 1905; she was also beaten by cossacks, and suffered frequent arrests.

55. See V.A. Balukov *et al.* (eds), *Pervyi Sovet Rabochikh Deputatov Ivanovo-Voznesenska, mai-iiul', 1905g.*, 2nd edn (Yaroslavl', 1971) for the following discussion.

Also active in the textile workers' strike in Ivanovo-Voznesensk was Kanareika, the party name for the social democrat Razumova. Her background of family poverty and her employment history was typical of many village women who moved to the cities. Born in the village of Nekrasova in Kostroma province in 1882, her widowed mother had worked in the textile industry of Ivanovo-Voznesensk, but did not earn enough to feed her family. Razumova had worked as a nanny from the age of 11 until she was 15, when she had followed her mother into the textile industry of Ivanovo-Voznesensk. In the city, Razumova gradually acquired literacy skills. At first, this had increased her religious feelings, and she had contemplated entering a convent. However, two years before the revolution, she had come under the influence of a politically conscious young male worker, who introduced her to a social-democratic group. As a result of studying revolutionary literature, including fiction, she drastically revised her views. In 1905, she was a key organiser of the strike of textile workers in Ivanovo-Voznesensk, and was elected to the soviet. The police became increasingly interested in her activities, which like these other women included transporting weapons as well as distributing illegal literature. Razumova went underground to evade police harassment. She did not stop such revolutionary activities, however, while she continued to support herself by working in a textile factory in another town. By 1907, she was back in Ivanovo-Voznesensk, trying to organise a strike which failed. Although arrested, she was soon released. She persisted in her political work, keeping a 'safe house' used by the local Bolsheviks in her mother's old flat until 1908, and distributing thousands of leaflets. Although she remained one jump ahead of the police, Razumova was repeatedly sacked by her employers, who considered her a dangerous influence on the factory floor.[56]

Besides such revolutionary activities, women workers had tried to contribute to the Shidlovsky commission. It had been set up by the tsar in an attempt to deflect the workers from revolution, by offering the prospect of improvements in their situation. Women workers (excluding domestic servants) could vote, but only men were allowed to be representatives, and when as a protest one woman was elected, Shidlovsky refused to recognise her. Women workers insisted that this was unjust, particularly since they predominated in many factories, notably textiles and spinning. They complained that they were treated in a particularly degrading way, and that their pay was much less then that of male workers:

56. *Kommunistka* (1920), no. 5, p. 28.

When the announcement about setting up your commission was made, our hearts filled with hope: at last the time has come, we thought, when Petersburg women workers will be able to speak loudly to the whole of Russia on behalf of all our sister-workers about the oppression, the offences and the insults, which no man can understand. And when at last we had elected a woman-deputy we were told that only a man may become a deputy. We hope that this decision is not final.[57]

A strike of seamstresses in Samara in May 1905 had called for the representation of women workers on the Shidlovsky commission, and textile workers presented specifically women's demands to the commission, but the crushing of the December uprising made it irrelevant.[58] Yet women workers had shown that they were capable of more than sporadic action. Vera Karelina recorded strikes by women workers in 1905 in a variety of industries, including tobacco and thread factories, and a bindery.[59] One example of an industry which employed women and men and whose workforce demanded equal pay for women in 1905 was tailoring. Throughout Russia in 1897, 326,470 people were employed in dressmaking, of whom about a fifth (69,000) were women. In Moscow, by 1902, as much as 17 per cent of paid employment was in tailoring, with women making up 52 per cent (12,200) of the labour force.[60] On the whole, Moscow workshop owners preferred to employ women and children to men.

Until the revolution, the nature of the industry, with workers scattered in numerous small workshops, had prevented them from taking any concerted action to improve their situation. Until the spring of 1904, there had been no strikes in the industry. However, the revolution radicalised the tailors, women as well as men, and by November 1905 their demands included: the eight-hour working day, a ban on overtime, wage increases, equal pay for women, no child labour (indeed, no employment of anyone under 16 years of age), the substitution of technical education for the apprenticeship system, and the abolition of work from home. The tailors' union was legally registered in August 1906 and of the 3,415 members, 400 were women. After registration, a series of strikes organised by the union had, by May 1907, achieved a decrease in working hours

57. Kudelli, *Rabotnitsa v 1905g.*, p. 10.
58. Kollontai, 'Avtobiograficheskii ocherk', *Proletarskaia Revoliutsiia*, 1921, no. 3, pp. 271–2.
59. Kudelli, *Rabotnitsa v 1905g.*, pp. 64, 67.
60. E.A. Oliunina, *Portnovskii promysel v Moskve i v derevniakh Moskovskoi i Riazanskoi gubernii* (Moscow, 1914), p. 166. Extracts from Oliunina's work are included in Victoria E. Bonnell (ed.), *The Russian Worker: Life and Labour under the Tsarist Regime* (Berkeley, Calif., 1983), ch. 5.

and increase in pay, though not equal pay for women. However, that month the government banned the union.[61]

In the eyes of revolutionaries, the conditions of life and work in the tailoring trade were poor and their barely subsistence pay explained the women's lack of political awareness. It also accounted for the absence of solidarity between women and men, since the former were used by employers to displace the latter wherever possible. Yet a significant minority of female tailors at least had been radicalised by the revolution. In many ways their situation reflected the impact of a modernising economy on what had been a village craft. As we have seen, ready-made clothes based on foreign designs had hurt the peasant woman's craft of making traditional dresses. By the early twentieth century, the extreme division of labour characteristic of large factories had further diluted the skills in the tailoring trade, and allowed for the increased hiring of women on low wages. In 1902, there were 6,550 individual tailors, of whom 5,469 were women.[62] Among dressmakers in workshops catering for individual or private orders, there was narrow specialisation, with some just making sleeves, for example. Some workshops hired women with sewing machines, and women to iron the finished clothes. Another way of cutting costs had been the widespread use of apprentice labour.

Women were employed on very short-term contracts, sometimes by the day, sometimes the month. Any days off work would be deducted from the monthly wage. The woman with children was more likely than a man to miss work. One male textile worker calculated that in the fifteen years of his marriage, there had been nine baptisms and six funerals, and that his wife had been the one to take time off work to deal with all of them (and the births of course; she had had a pregnancy almost every eighteen months). He gave an average of three to four days a month in unpaid leave caused by childbirth, the care of sick children, and the burial of the majority, which seriously affected his wife's earnings.[63]

If she worked in the tailoring trade, those wages would have been low and seasonal. When not at work, female tailors often had to supplement their earnings by 'moonlighting' – taking in sewing at home. In large workshops women were paid 55 per cent of men's wages, in smaller ones, 85 per cent. However, in the latter, the wages were generally lower than in the former. In high season,

61. Oliunina, *Portnovskii promysel v Moskve*, pp. 289–302.   62. Ibid., p. 48.
63. M. Davidovich, *Peterburgskii tekstil'nyi rabochii* (Moscow, 1919), p. 25.

overtime was unavoidable; indeed, given the ups and downs of the trade, it was essential. It was also badly paid, with women getting between a third and a half of the male rate. Low and slack seasons forced many into prostitution. Indeed, some female tailors were very open about their prostitution, referring to their encounters with men as adventures, rather than as simply the last resort of a desperate woman. In the workshop, women, and especially young female apprentices who had no bargaining power, were vulnerable to sexual harassment by the owners and their sons.[64]

Not only were wages low, but, before the revolution, payment was often in kind, which might include board and lodging. One effect of the tailors' action during 1905 and 1906 was to accelerate the move from wages in kind to money; and yet by the eve of the First World War, as many as 27 per cent of men and 18 per cent of women in small workshops in Moscow still had much of their payment in kind, usually in the form of board and lodgings.[65] Where wages were in cash, women would spend more, as a proportion of their pay, on accommodation than men, as we saw in the previous chapter. What other factors affected wages? Expertise and dexterity were two factors, so that young girls (and especially apprentices) and older women earned less than those in the age group 20 to 35. A literate woman would earn more than an illiterate.

All these factors have been used to explain the lack of political consciousness among female workers in late nineteenth- and early twentieth-century Russia: low levels of literacy, de-skilling through the introduction of extreme division of tasks, subsistence pay-rates, long hours at work, family responsibilities, competition with men for jobs, sexual harassment at work and seasonal prostitution. Yet the demands of the tailors' union in 1905 and 1906, notably for equal pay, an end to the use of apprenticeship to undercut wages, a set working day, and no compulsory overtime showed that the organised workers, who included a sizeable minority of women, could articulate their grievances and were prepared to fight for improvements. Of course the first two demands may be seen as an attempt by men to stop the practice of replacing them with women and youths. By the same token, it was a recognition that women were co-workers whose unequal pay kept down wage rates across the board. In an economy in which a man did not earn enough on his own to support a family, the demand for equal pay for women was a recognition of the crucial nature of the female contribution,

---

64. Oliunina, *Portnovskii promysel v Moskve*, p. 267.   65. Ibid., p. 198.

whether from wives or daughters but especially the former, to the household economy.

Indeed, despite the suppression of the union in 1907, there were continual efforts to involve women in any attempt at trade-union organisation. The second union of tailors in Moscow, which was active between 1908 and 1911, attracted 700 members, of whom 89 were women. In November 1912, a third union registered in Moscow: of the 1,648 members, 150 were women, and of the 97 apprentices who joined, 34 were girls.[66] Economic recovery around 1909 encouraged tailors to organise to improve their situation. In the autumn of 1913, and notably in October, there was a significant increase in labour protests by tailors, and women accounted for 44 per cent of the strikers. On the eve of the First World War, there was a special 'women's commission' set up by active tailors with the specific task of raising the level of female tailors' political awareness, and so attract them into the trade union.[67] Employers responded by separating male and female tailors, with women increasingly specialising in ladies' clothes, and men more likely to be hired as pressers and machine operators.

Nor was it only in industries which employed large numbers of both men and women that female workers took action in 1905. Indeed, Kollontai claimed that in 1905 there was 'no corner in which, in one way or another, the voice of a woman speaking about herself and demanding new rights was not heard'.[68] Though their efforts proved short-lived, working women, including domestic servants, organised themselves during the revolution. Indeed, some women who did not take action themselves had expressed their support for the strikers by cooking and taking the food to them.[69] Despite all the handicaps and obstacles in their way, women had organised, struck, demonstrated and made their own demands, including equal pay. Nor did the reassertion of tsarist power stop efforts to protect themselves. In 1906, laundresses in St. Petersburg tried to set up a trade union, and made the following appeal:

> Comrade laundresses, all men and women are uniting in the trade-union movement to defend their interests. The conditions of our work are very harsh. We toil between 15 and 18 hours a day in damp, cold, and very hot conditions, and in the process lose our health prematurely. Our masters oppress and exploit us. We have endured enough. It is time for us to unite and join the struggle. That is why

66. Ibid., p. 309.   67. Ibid., p. 317.
68. A.M. Kollontai, *Sotsial'nye osnovy zhenskogo voprosa* (St Petersburg, 1909), p. 21.
69. S. Lapitskaia, *Byt rabochikh Trekhgornoi manufactury* (Moscow, 1935), p. 96.

we, the undersigned, call on all our fellow workers to form a union of laundresses in order to strengthen our efforts in the fight for higher wages, a reduction in the working day, improvements in food and accommodation, and for respectful treatment.[70]

In the revolutionary year of 1917, the laundresses would establish a union and strike for the redress of these grievances. Given the scattered nature of the industry, and the variety of establishments, ranging in size of workforce from only a few laundresses to as many as 80, that was no easy task. Even more difficult to penetrate was domestic service, given its concentration in private homes. Yet 5,000 servants went on strike in Moscow in November 1905, the first meeting of a union of female and male servants took place in the city that month, and within a week it had a membership of 300. After the revolution was suppressed, membership dropped to a tenth of that, yet by March 1906 it had grown again to 200. In keeping with the wages of its members, the fee was low (two per cent of earnings). The union sought to recruit house-servants especially, and tried to help unemployed servants financially, by setting up a bureau to register them and help find them places, charging prospective employers a rouble for their recommendation. The servants' union also set up literacy classes, meeting twice a week after 8 p.m. During the revolution, the union had complained that servants had not been included in the Shidlovsky commission franchise. Two years later, the union addressed the second duma:

> We demand that the State Duma pass a special law, for the protection of house-servants; and in the first place we ask that the following demands be met: limit the working day to between nine and ten hours; set up an institute of women inspectors and extend the remit of the factory inspectorate to house-servants; open free agencies [to place servants] paid for by the city; establish state insurance in case of unemployment or illness; establish procedures for examining standards of living accommodation with trade-union representatives; secure equal rights for women; give women ten weeks' maternity leave (four weeks before and six after birth); and provide each servant with a work book recording wages, conditions, and reasons for leaving a job.[71]

Such unions were set up in other towns and cities. Ekaterinoslav in southern Russia had a special section for servants who worked in restaurants, hotels and taverns. In response to such agitation,

70. *Zhenskii Kalendar'* (St. Petersburg, 1906), pp. 391–2.
71. L.N. Lenskaia, 'O Prisluge', *Doklad chitannyi vo vtorom zhenskom klube v Moskve v fev. 1908 goda* (Moscow, 1908), p. 20.

the St. Petersburg duma even discussed the possibility of banning female labour in eating and drinking places, though the case was based more on moral than economic reasons. Such a ban would have resulted in 1,500 unemployed women.[72] However, political repression after 1907 led to the closure of all servants' unions.

Some female intelligentsia, members of the Bolshevik, Menshevik and SR parties, played important roles in 1905. The latter continued with terrorist activities, usually in retaliation against brutal attacks on peaceful crowds. The social democrats, both Menshevik and Bolshevik, attempted to organise urban workers. Female revolutionaries generally acted as couriers, printed and distributed leaflets which they only occasionally wrote, and kept 'safe' houses – all under constant police surveillance. These were dangerous activities. Three female students, Bloch, Masharina and Fridenson, were all arrested in January 1905, having been caught carrying leaflets.[73] Indeed, female radicals were treated with equal brutality by the counter-revolutionaries. Moreover, the nature of some of the attacks on these women seemed to be spurred on by rage that females were taking such a public stance.[74]

What of the feminists in 1905? The *Women's Calendar* for 1906 records that women in the professions were involved in political meetings, drawing up and signing resolutions, and participating in strikes, though there was by no means unanimity.[75] Linda Edmondson suggests that the example of Vera Karelina's work for Gapon's Assembly may have provided feminists for the first time with a model of a mass organisation of women.[76] At the same time, it seems that it was only when the feminist movement appeared to be gaining some support among the female workers that the social democrats turned their attention to the task of drawing women into the labour movement.[77] In general, however, Bolsheviks distrusted separate organisations for women, preferring that women participate with men in strike committees and soviets, as in Kostromo where female textile workers were elected to both.[78]

72. Ibid., p. 21.

73. V. Nevskii, 'Ianvarskie dni v Peterburge v 1905 godu', *Krasnaia letopis'* (1922), no. 1, pp. 71–2. For the SRs. see Maxwell, *Narodniki Women*, pp. 179–80.

74. See Stites, *The Women's Liberation Movement in Russia*, pp. 270–5.

75. For a dispute among women pharmacists over support for a strike see Mary Schaeffer Conroy, *In Health and in Sickness: Pharmacy, Pharmacists, and the Pharmaceutical Industry in Late Imperial, Early Soviet Russia* (Boulder, Colo., 1994), pp. 129–30.

76. Linda Edmondson (ed.), *Women and Society in Russia and the Soviet Union* (Cambridge, 1992), p. 82.

77. Kollontai, *Sotsial'nye osnovy zhenskogo voprosa*, pp. 102–6.

78. Serditova, *Bol'sheviki v bor'be za zhenskie proletarskie massy*, pp. 43–51.

Certainly, the revolution revitalised the feminist movement by opening up questions of constitutional change, not least, of course, the vote. By then, liberals in the Union of Liberation had been turning to the feminists for support, and liberal women set up the Union for Women's Equality in 1905, in the wake of the massacre of Father Gapon's supporters in January.[79] The union attracted very few factory and peasant women, while some social-democratic and SR women sought to radicalise the union from within.[80] The union's platform included a call for protective legislation and compulsory insurance for wage-earning women, and equal rights for peasant women in any land reform. Although it was open to both sexes, and sought links with the constitutional movement as a whole, the Union for Women's Equality failed to win the wholehearted support of male liberals. The feminists claimed that those men who argued for women's rights did so from principle, whereas those who argued against did so either from prejudice (politics would corrupt women, harm the family, and lower the birth rate) or expedience (the time was not ripe for female suffrage, the cultural level of the mass of women was too low, female suffrage would alienate potential conservative supporters of constitutional reform).[81] Yet feminists were themselves divided on suffrage. Some were prepared to petition for the right to vote in local elections only; some to accept suffrage based on property-owning and taxation.[82]

In terms of political tactics, the union of women focused on the zemstvo, hoping to influence progressive members. The socialist supporters of the union complained about the neglect of agitational work among the masses of women. Generally, however, the union recruited above all from the intelligentsia, and despite seeking some reforms in the conditions of lower-class women, the union's main interests lay in gains for the educated, in terms of higher education and equal rights to posts in the civil service and the professions. In 1905 and 1906, the union campaigned vigorously through lobbying, holding public meetings, distributing pamphlets, and gathering petitions. Yet though a few made efforts to reach remote districts with their petitions, the Union of Women failed to win mass female support. Indeed, peasant women were more interested in land rights than women's rights.

79. See N. Mirovich, *Iz istorii zhenskogo dvizheniia v Rossii* (Moscow, 1908), pp. 1–4; Stites, *The Women's Liberation Movement in Russia*, pp. 198–208.

80. Mirovich, *Iz istorii zhenskogo dvizheniia*, pp. 6–10.

81. Ibid., pp. 4–16, 22–4; M.I. Pokrovskaia, *Zashchitniki i protivniki ravnopraviia zhenshchin v pervoi gosudarstvennoi dume* (St. Petersburg, 1907), p. 34.

82. Mirovich, *Iz istorii zhenskogo dvizheniia*, pp. 12–13.

The stereotype of the Russian female peasant is of a woman so downtrodden that she would fight any attempt to change her position for the better, and the assumption has been that she either remained passive during the 1904–5 upheaval, or tried to restrain her man from action. Maureen Perry, however, has drawn a different picture in her study of the peasant movement in this period. During the revolution, peasant women generally shared the attitudes of their men; indeed, frequently the women spurred on any men who were slow to take action with taunts and reproaches. Whereas the prominence of women in any rural disturbances reflected their traditional role as the shock troops of the food riot, female field hands took an active, and occasionally leading, part in the strike movement. Indeed, while it was generally the younger generation of the peasantry who participated in the 1905 revolution, Perry quotes from a report from Tambov, which noted that support for the movement came from 'the old women in particular, who had experienced the oppression of serfdom'.[83]

Of course, these examples do not suggest that women participated in the peasant movement on an equal basis with men in 1905. The All-Russian Peasant Union which organised much of the action and articulated peasant grievances certainly had national concerns, including interests in civil rights and demands for the reform of local government. However, whether directed by the union or the communal assembly, the peasant movement in 1905 was shaped above all by the male peasantry. When it came to the land held by a peasant household, the women did not see their interests as different from the men: both thought in terms of the family. In addition, female peasants also had grievances against the local government, including the irregular payment of allowances to the wives of soldiers who had been sent into the war against Japan in 1904, the conflict which had precipitated the revolution in the cities. The fact that urban feminists concentrated on lobbying zemstvo officials, whom the peasants considered treated them in a disrespectful and often coarse manner, could not win village women to the feminist cause.

Of the feminist organisations, the more conservative Mutual Philanthropic Society ignored the peasant, stood aloof from the political groups, and continued instead to lobby the authorities, without success, except perhaps in marginalising itself within the

83. Maureen Perry, 'The Russian Peasant Movement of 1905–1907: Its Social Composition and Revolutionary Significance', *Past and Present* (Nov. 1972), no. 57, pp. 123–55: 144–6.

wider feminist and general reform movements. Mariia Pokrovskaia, the feminist physician, founded the Women's Progressive party in 1905, which was more liberal than the society but, unlike the union, was not open to men. However, the party was troubled by dissension within its ranks from the beginning, over whether it should focus exclusively on women's issues or adopt a broader political platform, as was favoured by Pokrovskaia.[84] Its activities over the next year had a very much lower profile than those of the union. Indeed, despite Pokrovskaia's obvious sympathy with working-class women, as reflected in her writings, her party seemed to stand aloof from the lower classes, whom Pokrovskaia tended to portray simply as the victims of the men of their class.[85] The success of the feminist movement, which eschewed violence and pursued legal means, depended on the fate of the duma, the institution set up by the tsar in response to the 1905 revolution. The prospects were unfavourable. The union feminists continued their tactics of lobbying and petitioning. They remained committed to moderate reforms, and resisted any recourse to militant action. As the duma moved to the right after 1907, and the tsar restricted the franchise to favour forces which supported the established order, the feminists found their room to manœuvre very limited. Indeed, some peasant women believed that the political changes which had been gained as a result of 1905 worked to their disadvantage, in the context of a period of political reaction. Peasant women argued that the total lack of political rights had at least enforced a form of equality between women and men, which was lost in the reform which granted limited, male suffrage:

> There was a time when, although our men might beat us now and then, we nevertheless decided our affairs together. Now they tell us: 'You are not fit company for us. We shall go to the state duma and take part in the government – perhaps not directly, but we shall elect members. If the law had made you equal with us, then we would have asked your opinion.' . . . This law is wrong; it leads to discord between men and women, and even enmity. . . . [Before] we lived in misery together, but when it was changed so that we all have to live according to the law, we women find we are not needed. . . . The men do not understand our women's needs. We are able to discuss things no worse than the men. We have a common interest in all our affairs, so that the women should take part in deciding them.[86]

84. Edmondson, *Feminism in Russia 1900–1917*, p. 53.
85. Kollontai, *Sotsial'nye osnovy zhenskogo voprosa*, pp. 328–37.
86. Vera Bilshai, *Reshenie zhenskogo voprosa v SSSR* (Moscow, 1956), p. 65.

From revolution to world war

Linda Edmondson argues that the Union of Equal Rights influenced such open letters from peasant women, asking for land and the vote.[87] However, all their petitions and letters achieved nothing as the tsar proceeded to dismiss, emasculate and ignore the duma, while the feminist movement itself fragmented in the wake of the 1905 revolution. A women's congress, for which official permission was obtained in 1908, was seen as a means of uniting and reviving the movement.[88] The congress was to be as broadly based as possible, and would include men. Upper-class women dominated in an attendance of over 1,000, whereas peasant women were absent, and the working class a tiny minority. The programme provided for discussion on the activity of women in various fields: philanthropy, the economic situation of women, the political and civil aspects of women's situation, both in Russia and abroad, female education, and questions of ethics in the family and in society in general.[89]

Police intervention prevented any serious criticism of existing conditions. Nevertheless, there was debate and disagreement, for example on the tactics of the movement and on the question of marriage.[90] The relationship between the feminist movement and political parties also aroused controversy. For example, some feminists called for the employment of female factory inspectors to inspect women workers, but others saw the underlying argument as less altruistic, simply the opening up of another professional opportunity for women from the intelligentsia.[91] In addition, the working-class delegates, led by the social democrat Alexandra Kollontai, as well as the more conservative feminists, objected to the contention that women constituted an oppressed class and must, therefore, fight for their own liberation, apart from men.[92] In Kollontai's view, the feminists were supporters of capitalism who saw the woman question as one of rights and justice within the existing system, whereas the working-class woman experienced it as a question of

87. Edmondson, *Feminism in Russia*, p. 71.

88. See Linda Edmondson, 'Russian Feminists and the First All-Russian Congress of Women', *Russian History* (1976), vol. 3, no. 2, pp. 123–49.

89. *Trudy pervogo vserossiiskogo s'ezda pri Russkom zhenskom obshchestve v Sankt-Peterburge 10–16 dekabria, 1908* (St. Petersburg, 1909), pp. x–xvi; N.V. Orlova, *O zhenskom dvizhenii v Rossii* (St. Petersburg, 1911), pp. 4–5.

90. *Trudy 1908*, pp. 367–8, 348.   91. Ibid., pp. 730–40.

92. Ibid., p. 786; A.A. Kalmanovich, *Zhenskoe dvizhenie i otnoshenie partii k nemu* (St. Petersburg, 1911), p. 15.

'a morsel of bread'.[93] Nevertheless, the working-class women won support at the 1908 congress on the issues of female and child labour in the factories.[94]

What of the relationship between socialists and feminists after the 1905 revolution? The 1908 congress highlighted what women held in common by virtue of their sex, but it also underlined fundamental social and economic divisions among women, which had political implications. The feminists criticised what they saw as the limited, opportunistic or even merely lip-service support of the socialists for women's rights. The socialists in turn criticised the upper-class nature of the feminist movement generally, a judgement which seemed borne out by the ban on the participation of workers' groups by the organisers of a later congress on women's education at the end of 1912 (although some workers still took part.)[95]

The polemics between the liberal feminists and socialists continued after the 1908 congress, partly through Kollontai's book, *The Social Foundations of the Woman Question* (1909). As at the congress, she argued in this book for the interrelationship between economic change and changes in the situation of women. In her view, co-operating with upper-class women in a united feminist movement was a dangerous diversion from the struggle against the common enemy of both female and male workers: capitalism. She insisted that women workers had to fight together with male workers within the organisations of their class for the liberation not just of individual women but of all humankind from the yoke of capitalist wage slavery. Yet she accepted, as Vera Karelina had done before her, that special efforts were needed to organise women workers.[96]

The feminist movement was divided and demoralised by the political reaction which set in from around 1907. Kollontai nevertheless worried about the impression it might make on women workers because some had attended feminist meetings and agitators from the equal rights union had received invitations to speak at their factories.[97] She sought to counteract feminist influence by addressing numerous public meetings, trying to organise a bureau for women workers, and encouraging socialist clubs for working women. She insisted that feminist demands for equal rights between

93. *Trudy 1908*, p. 792.
94. Ibid., pp. 791–2; Kalmanovich, *Zhenskoe dvizhenie*, p. 15.
95. Ibid., p. 11; Serditova, *Bol'sheviki v bor'be za zhenskie proletarskie massy*, pp. 79–80.
96. Kollontai, *Sotsial'nye osnovy zhenskogo voprosa*, p. 4.
97. A.M. Kollontai, 'Avtobiograficheskii ocherk', *Proletarskaia revoliutsiia* (1921), no. 3, pp. 261–302: 268–70.

the sexes could not cover the differences between women of different, indeed opposing, classes. She claimed that working-class women disappointed the feminists by proving to be more interested in demands for a minimum wage, a standard working day, and a day off work, than in women's rights.[98]

Yet in contrast to Karelina's experience, Kollontai had little support from within the social-democratic movement for her efforts to combat feminist inroads into the working class. Kollontai claimed that her comrades even accused her of feminism because she organised women separately, in their own clubs, which she had done since 1907, and because of her determination to participate in the 1908 feminist congress. Whereas they saw this as a distraction from the class struggle, Kollontai hoped that the congress would help educate the textile workers who attended. Ironically, she in turn criticised Menshevik women for co-operating with the feminists.[99]

According to Kollontai, her plans were only reluctantly sanctioned by the Petersburg committee of Social Democrats. She saw their ambivalence reflected in the thwarting of one of her attempts to organise a meeting of women workers. Despite the promise of the committee to provide a venue, when Kollontai and several women workers arrived, they found a sign on the door which read: 'The meeting for women only has been cancelled; tomorrow there will be a meeting for men only.'[100] Yet the Bolsheviks had supported, albeit reluctantly, the organisation of women's groups within the social-democratic movement. Kollontai's negative experience when trying to implement that decision was indicative of the tension between the strategy of class solidarity, and the tactics of raising female political consciousness around women's issues. One woman worker who attended the socialist Sunday schools and women's clubs of 1907, and later became a member of the Bolshevik party, described the raising of her consciousness. Through the radical intelligentsia, she learned the names of revolutionary women such as Sofia Perovskaia and Vera Figner. She read in secret (because the government had deemed it subversive) N.G. Chernyshevsky's novel of 1863, *What is to be done?*. That novel's main character, Vera Pavlovna, came to see that economic independence was essential for a woman to enjoy sexual equality. Self-confident and socially conscious, Vera Pavlovna represented all the characteristics of the 'new woman' to which this female Bolshevik aspired. Later in the underground, she turned to Marx, Engels and Lenin:

98. Kollontai, *Sotsial'nye osnovy zhenskogo voprosa*, pp. 102–6.
99. Kollontai, 'Avtobiograficheskii ocherk', pp. 276–8.   100. Ibid., p. 272.

We understood that the enslavement of women occurred together with the establishment of private ownership of the means of production and the beginning of the exploitation of man by man, and that real equality and real freedom for women would only be found in socialism where there would be no exploitation. Therefore, the most reliable path to the liberation of women was the path of political struggle against capitalism in the ranks of the proletariat.[101]

An article published in 1913 in a newspaper aimed at metal workers, who regarded themselves as the élite of their class, revealed fear of, as well as condescension towards, women workers:

At the new Aivaz factory, women have begun to do metal work. This has produced a stunning impression on worker circles. Slight irony has gradually passed into fright: the grey metal workers have begun to curse the babas [old crones] who 'get in' everywhere and take work away from the men. To the conscious [male] worker has occurred the unhappy possibility of the lowering of the already too low rates [of pay], with the procession of the new 'barbarians' to the vices. The imagination has sketched the unlimited prospects of an expansion of female labour. The factory has already begun to seem alien, like an odious 'women's city'. . . .

Only a short time ago, a woman came to the factory, at first to do clean-up work; then as a machine-operator. In the clean-up work, she replaced the unskilled [male] worker, performing purely male worker functions for lower pay. She went to the machine tools when a type of simplified machine tool became widespread in the factories, the work on which required no professional training. Initially, the unskilled [male] worker had been placed at these machine tools. They, too, were replaced by women, again offering labour at a lower wage than men. . . .

But capital always calls new strata of workers to the factory because it is advantageous to it. The same was observed at factories when the unskilled [male] worker ousted the trained [male] worker from almost all positions. The arrival of women at the vices was consequently inevitable. [If] not today, then tomorrow; [if] not in 1913, then in 1914. Machine tools are modernised, the division of labour proceeds all the more deeply and broadly; work is increasingly simplified; and consequently with every passing day capitalism's appetite grows for cheap, untrained labour, among whom are women. Female metal workers, therefore, are the inevitable result of all technological development, of the entire capitalist system.[102]

Yet women in 1905 had shown that they were prepared to strike and demonstrate, while their increasing numbers in the workforce,

101. A. Artiukhina *et al.*, *Zhenshchiny v revoliutsii* (Moscow, 1959), p. 21.
102. A. Zorin [Aleksei Gastev], *Metallist'* (Dec. 1913), no. 13 (37), pp. 2–3.

and particularly in factories which the social democrats saw as their main recruiting ground, forced the revolutionaries to pay more attention to drawing women into the labour movement. Indeed, this interest in working women pre-dated the war, coinciding with the upsurge in strikes from 1912, in which women workers, too, were involved. Thus on the eve of the First World War, both the Bolsheviks and Mensheviks devoted new journals, the former *Rabotnitsa (The Woman Worker)*, the latter *Golos Rabotnitsy (Voice of the Woman Worker)*, to the task of organising women workers.[103] The Menshevik journal was published only twice, and until 1917 little more attention was paid to work with women.[104]

The Bolshevik journal, however, survived for seven issues in 1914, appearing between February and June, and was then suppressed when war was declared. Editorial work was conducted in St. Petersburg by Anna Ul'ianova (Elizarova), in Cracow by Nadezhda Krupskaia and Lilina Zinovieva, and in Paris by Lyudmila Stal' and Inessa Armand. According to Krupskaia, the main instigator in setting up *Rabotnitsa* was Armand.[105] While Lenin was in favour of the initiative, the same could not be said of the majority of the Bolsheviks. Armand appealed to them and to the male working class in general not to forget that they shared the same cause with working women. Indeed, failure to include the female proletariat in their struggle constituted an immense obstacle which could only harm the movement. Armand exhorted male workers to encourage and help the women in their attempts to organise themselves.[106]

The editorial of the first issue of *Rabotnitsa* declared that it was clear to politically aware women that the interests of the working class and of the bourgeoisie were diametrically opposed, and that women's place in society was determined by class divisions rather than sexual differences. Thus as far as the proletariat was concerned, the woman question centred on the problem of how to involve female workers, whom the journal described as the 'backward masses', in their class organisations. The urgent task was to make the women comrades in the common struggle as quickly as possible. Solidarity between working men and women, their common cause, and the common path to these goals: such in the view of *Rabotnitsa* was the resolution of the 'woman question' for the working class.[107]

103. Artiukhina, *Zhenshchiny v revoliutsii*, p. 21.

104. Robert McKean, *St. Petersburg Between the Revolutions: Workers and Revolutionaries June 1907–February 1917* (New Haven and London, 1990), p. 120.

105. N.K. Krupskaia, *Pamiati Inessy Armand* (Moscow, 1920); see the introduction.

106. A.F. Bessanova (ed.), 'K istorii izdaniia zhurnala *Rabotnitsa*', *Istoricheskii arkhiv* (July–Aug. 1955), no. 4, p. 31.

107. Ibid., pp. 37–9, for the quotation and following discussion.

In 1914, *Rabotnitsa* aimed to raise the social and political awareness of women workers. The journal pointed to women's double burden, being responsible for the housework as well as having a job outside the home. Indeed, instead of widening her horizons, this double burden ensured that the woman worker's world remained relatively closed, still centred on the family which perpetuated peasant attitudes towards women. Married women, and women with children, simply had no time outside work, and were preoccupied with domestic worries, which in turn prevented them from participating in class actions for fear of the dire consequences which might befall their families. *Rabotnitsa* acknowledged and set out to overcome the restraining influence such women were perceived to have on the labour movement. Thus, women workers were seen, by political parties as well as by politically conscious male workers, to act as a drag on the revolution which, *Rabotnitsa* explained, the women in turn saw as a male indulgence at the expense of their families. The women were convinced that they at least knew where their responsibilities lay, and would continually remind the men of theirs. *Rabotnitsa*, however, was determined to open the women's eyes; at the same time, the journal recognised that this task also involved a change in male attitudes to women.

To achieve this goal, the journal tried to relate contemporary events, both in Russia and elsewhere, to the position of women workers, in order that the latter might be able to relate their personal and familial position to the wider political and economic context. It described in a variety of ways, including contributions from women workers in the form of articles, letters and poems, the conditions of life and work under which the female labour force struggled to support their families as well as themselves. *Rabotnitsa* propagated the theory of class struggle, claiming that the interests of the women workers could lie only with their class. It reasoned that instead of an autonomous organisation for women, female workers must support and be brought into the struggle of male workers against their common oppressor, capitalism. The outbreak of war in the summer of 1914, however, put an end to Bolshevik efforts to organise women workers through *Rabotnitsa*, until after the February revolution in 1917.

PART TWO

From World War to the New Society, 1914–1930

CHAPTER FOUR

From World War to Revolution

In 1920, the Bolshevik Konkordia Samoilova recorded the development of political awareness among working-class and peasant women
since the 1905 revolution:

> If prior to 1905 Russian women workers had participated only in
> economic strikes, if in 1904 during the Japanese War, female workers
> and peasants had protested against their husbands' conscription only
> by means of 'isolated rioting' which was quickly and forcibly put
> down, then on the other hand action by Petersburg women workers
> on International [Women's] Day in 1917 led to the February revolu-
> tion because the ground for it had been prepared by all the eco-
> nomic and political conditions of the development of Russia and by
> the last Russo-German war.
>
> That destructive and bloody war built up in the workers a revolu-
> tionary hatred of the Tsar's government, the landowners and capital-
> ists. That fratricidal, predatory war opened the eyes of the old tsarist
> army which used to be a blind weapon in the hands of the ruling
> classes, forcing the soldiers to join the rebelling working class. At
> last, the very war which took women away from housework and put
> them, instead of their husbands, into the factories to earn a living –
> this war undoubtedly gave a start to the political development of
> women workers, 'it cooked them in the factory pot' and compelled
> them to participate more actively in the common struggle of the
> working class for its liberation.[1]

Alfred Meyer has shown that the First World War affected
Russian women in many different ways, according to class, status
and geographical location.[2] In terms of work, many peasant and

1. Konkordia Samoilova, *Rabotnitsa v rossiisskoi revoliutsii* (Moscow, 1920), pp. 4–5.
2. Alfred G. Meyer, 'The Impact of World War I on Russian Women's Lives', in
Barbara Evans Clements, Barbara Alpern Engel, Christine D. Worobec (eds), *Russia's
Women: Accommodation, Resistance, Transformation* (Berkeley, Calif., 1991), pp. 208–24.

working-class women became the main breadwinners, often by replacing male workers, because of the military conscription of their
men; while educated women had more opportunities for employment in white-collar posts and in the professions, and even more
scope in philanthropy. Only upper-class, educated women seemed
to view the war as potentially beneficial for women, providing them
with opportunities to prove both their patriotism and their talents.

Women, work and the First World War

Linda Edmondson has argued that the feminist use of women's
contribution to the war effort as propaganda for the granting of
equal rights once the emergency was over was not simply opportun-
ism, but rather a demand that society recognise how crucial women
were in the defence of their country.[3] They used both philanthropy
and paid employment to prove themselves as citizens, and the length
that the war dragged on, and the increasing numbers of men who
were conscripted, provided the feminists, and indeed women in general, with a wide variety of vital work. War opened up more and
new professional jobs to women. Women who did not need to work
for wages volunteered to serve as nurses at the front, out of patriotism as well as a sense of adventure. Mary Britnieva, for example,
who came from a very privileged background, joined the Red Cross
to serve as a nurse in the war, and married the chief doctor.[4] Others
threw their energy into vital charitable work, providing relief for refugees, including thousands of abandoned children. Women trained
as drivers for the military; female technical students received government recognition as engineers, to relieve shortages of personnel in
transport and essential utilities. Given the terrible defeats and massive
loss of life in 1914 and 1915, any sense of excitement may well have
been quickly lost, but memoirs of such women show their determination to play their part in their country's struggle.[5]

Other women, many from the peasantry, joined the army, often
initially disguised as men. There was no planned involvement of
women in the military in Russia, though as many as 5,000 fought.
Since the late nineteenth century, Russian women had been involved
in violence against the state, through terrorism, while peasant women
had taken part in rural unrest, and lower-class women generally were

3. Linda Edmondson, *Feminism in Russia 1900–1917* (London, 1984), p. 163.
4. Mary Britnieva, *One Woman's Story* (London, 1934).
5. See ibid. For other examples, see Meyer, 'The Impact of World War I', p. 209.

the major protagonists in bread and conscription riots. It was perhaps the scale of female involvement at the front, and the fact that it included aristocratic as well as peasant women, which differentiated the war experience. It also brought out differences between women, as many more women lost than retained their initial patriotic enthusiasm for the war. There was, in addition, a huge social and cultural gulf between the upper-class women and the lower-class men they nursed to return to the front.

In discussing the military contribution of women to the war effort, historians usually focus on the person of Maria Bochkareva, a peasant woman. Of the declaration of war in August 1914, she wrote:

> There was something sublime about the nation's response. Old men, who had fought in the Crimean war [and they would indeed have been old], in the Turkish campaign of 1877–78, and the Russo-Japanese war, declared that they never saw such exaltation of spirit. It was a glorious, inspiring, unforgettable moment in one's life. My soul was deeply stirred, and I had a dim realisation of a new world coming to life, a purer, a happier and a holier world. . . . 'Go to war to help save the country!' a voice within me called. . . . My heart yearned to be there in the seething cauldron of war, to be baptised in its fire and scorched in its lava.[6]

Perhaps because of her military opposition to the Bolshevik seizure of power, Bochkareva became the most famous of the female combatants. On trying to join the army in November 1914, she was told that no women were allowed, but the commander advised her to send a telegram to the tsar, seeking his permission for her enlistment, which he granted. Before the war, Bochkareva had cut her hair and donned men's clothes in order to escape an abusive husband, but she did not disguise her sex when she became a soldier. In her study of women and the military, Julie Wheelwright claims that in assuming the male role Bochkareva was attempting to shed a feminine identity which she had experienced as a form of enslavement, after a brutal father and two abusive husbands.[7] Yet even in combat, women were expected to fulfil their traditional role of self-sacrifice, rather than the more masculine role of fighting hero. In her memoirs, Bochkareva claimed that she was often called on to give medical attention to women in the villages wherever she was

---

6. *Yashka: My Life as Peasant, Exile and Soldier*, by Maria Bochkareva, Commander of the Russian Women's Battalion of Death, as set down by Isaac Don Levine (London, 1919), pp. 64–5.

7. Julie Wheelwright, *Amazons and Military Maids: Women Who Dressed as Men in Pursuit of Life, Liberty and Happiness* (London, 1990), p. 30.

stationed.[8] Still, Bochkareva fought alongside the men, was wounded
four times, and was decorated for her bravery with all four of the
prestigious Georgii crosses.[9] Indeed, it seems that Bochkareva specialised in rescuing wounded soldiers from under enemy fire.[10]

While many women combatants did not disguise their sex, they
sought to suppress their sexuality in an effort to be taken seriously
by the men, to ensure that they would indeed serve as soldiers and
not be relegated to domestic service, and to obviate any suspicions
that they might be prostitutes. This is reflected in an incident related
by Marina Yurlova, who fought with the cossacks. She had been
taken on as an orderly for an afternoon by an officer who expected
her to clean up his filthy quarters. When he entered his room:

> He seemed a little nervous, I thought. He walked to and fro, picking
> up papers and putting them down. He lit a cigarette, and crushed it
> before he had taken two puffs. At last he came over to me, where
> I stood waiting to be dismissed.
> 'You are a good girl, making my room so clean for me. Are you
> always a good girl, heh?'
> He looked at me so oddly that I began to blush, and hated myself
> for blushing. I did not want to be thought a girl – I was a soldier. But
> something had to be said, so:
> 'I – I think so, your nobleness,' I stammered at last.
> 'You think? You don't know a thing like that?'
> . . . As a little saliva crept out of the corner of his lips, I grew fright-
> ened. But I dared not move.
> He pinched my ear, and put one hand round my shoulders; he
> unbuttoned my jacket with the other hand and his fingers crept
> inside, stroking me gently. And then – I suppose because I was shak-
> ing all over – he muttered:
> 'What is the matter, child?'
> I was so terrified that I said the first thing that came into my mind.
> 'I want that herring, your nobleness.'
> At that he started, like a man shaken out of a trance, laughed wear-
> ily, and pushed me away.

She was given the herring, and dismissed.[11] For Marina the safe
quarters away from the front and the plump herring revealed the gap
between the officers and the ordinary soldiers. Yet that experience

    8. Bochkareva, *Yashka*, p. 116.
    9. See I. Rozenthal, 'Smertnitsy na fronte', *Argumenty i Fakty* (1994), no. 31.
    10. Anne Eliot Griesse and Richard Stites, 'Russia: Revolution and War', ch. 3 in
Nancy Loring Goldman (ed.), *Female Soldiers – Combatants or Noncombatants? Historical
and Contemporary Perspectives* (Westport, Conn., 1982), p. 64.
    11. Marina Yurlova, *Cossack Girl* (London, 1934), pp. 126–7.

also made her painfully aware of her sexual vulnerability. Being so few among so many men convinced women such as Yurlova and Bochkareva that they had to remain chaste, while both memoirs show how difficult it was to be accepted by the men. Indeed, perhaps because she was so young, fighting with the cossacks when she was just 15 years old, Yurlova found that older male comrades would assume the role of her protector and mentor. She might even have been her company's mascot. Certainly, neither she nor the other female soldiers sought to promote sexual equality. None saw themselves as pioneering women, or role models for their own sex, though some feminists lauded them.[12] Indeed, none sought out other female comrades. Having joined for a variety of personal reasons, they each remained the exception in their particular unit.

Women who fought at the front came mainly from the upper classes, such as Yurlova, and the peasantry, like Bochkareva, and they did not mix. Moreover, they were a tiny minority of Russian women, whose main contribution to the war effort was to serve on the home front. In doing so, feminists hoped that such a national emergency would dissolve the differences between women.[13] They won the support of some prominent radical women, including Vera Figner, Breshko-Breshkovskaia, and Kuskova. However, Meyer's study of women's journals published between 1914 and 1917 reveals the opposite: feminists certainly hoped to gain legal, civil and employment rights as a result of women's contribution to the war effort, yet generally upper-class and educated women were remarkably unaffected by the privations which beset the home front. Moreover, these women were not slow to criticise both female servants for their lack of domestic skills, and factory women whenever they sought to organise in their interests.[14] However much they sympathised with the plight of women workers, feminists nevertheless saw strikes and demonstrations as undermining the war effort.

As we saw in the previous chapter, after the revolution of 1905, peasant women in Russia had been drawn into the industrial labour force in increasing numbers. Indeed, the revolution had heightened the trend for employers to displace male workers wherever possible, particularly in the cotton-weaving industry.[15] For the most

---

12. See Richard Stites, *The Women's Liberation Movement in Russia: Feminism, Nihilism, and Bolshevism, 1860–1930* (Princeton, 1978; 2nd edn 1991), pp. 298–9.

13. A. Bogdanov, *Voina i zhenshchina* (Petrograd, 1914), pp. 31–2.

14. Meyer, 'The Impact of World War I', p. 223.

15. A. Riazanova, *Zhenskii trud* (Moscow, 1923), p. 34; A.G. Rashin, *Formirovanie rabochego klassa v Rossii: istoriko-ekonomicheskie ocherki* (Moscow, 1958), pp. 235–6.

part, women workers remained unskilled, and showed little interest in trade unions – not surprisingly, perhaps, given that male workers sought trade-union protection from the bosses' growing preference for female labour. The First World War quickened this process of female replacing male workers, though the initial impact was to increase unemployment among women workers in both town and countryside, especially those who worked in luxury trades and crafts, and generally among those in both blue-collar and white-collar jobs unrelated to the needs of a wartime economy. With millions of men conscripted, their wives were in a desperate situation, given the very low level of assistance to soldiers' families. Hence increasing numbers of women sought jobs in war-related industries, where employers welcomed them as cheap labour.

The proportion of women in the industrial workforce as a whole soared in Russia from 26.6 per cent in 1914 to 43.4 per cent in 1917; the numbers of factory women rose from 732,000 in 1914 to over a million in 1917.[16] During the war, the increase in the employment of female and child labour was especially marked in those areas where large factories predominated. Thus in the Moscow industrial region, the percentage of women workers rose from 39.4 in 1914 to 48.7 in 1917; in the cotton industry from 49.5 in 1914 to 60.6 in 1917; and in the metal industry from 7.4 in 1914 to 18.6 in 1917. The percentage of women employed in the Petersburg district (renamed Petrograd during the war) was similar: it rose from 25.3 in 1913 to 33.3 in 1917. Before the war, men had constituted three-quarters of the Petrograd labour force. Towards the end of 1917, less than half the total number of workers employed in Petrograd were men. Even in the male-dominated industries such as the metal and chemical industries, the numbers of women and children employed towards the end of 1916 amounted to at least a third.[17] At the same time, however, while women made up 37.5 per cent of the unskilled metal workers in the Moscow province in 1918, they constituted less than 1 per cent of the skilled toolworkers.[18] Besides the factories, of course, there were thousands of women employed in sweatshops and as domestic servants, for whom demand remained high: by January 1917, around 130,000 women worked in Petrograd factories, while there were approximately 80,000 employed as domestic servants, 50,000 as office workers,

16. Ibid., p. 43.
17. S.O. Zagorsky, *State Control of Industry in Russia during the War* (New Haven, 1929), pp. 54–5.
18. Rashin, *Formirovanie rabochego klassa v Rossii*, p. 541.

and another 50,000 as shop workers. Women replaced male care-takers and gatekeepers. In addition, women took over jobs (both white- and blue-collar) in other sectors which had previously been considered the monopoly of men, such as transport, including the railways and the postal service, while more professional posts were also open to women, for example in secondary teaching and accountancy.[19]

The demand for labour for the war industries was so intense that, in the absence of enough men, women and youths were drawn even into areas previously monopolised by skilled male workers. Some girls and women simply moved out of domestic service, un-skilled and seasonal work, and trades which had been hit by the war, to take on factory jobs; some female peasants who worked in rural manufacturing moved to the cities for higher wages. In terms of geographical mobility, the war did not simply push peasant women and youths to the cities. There were mass movements of refugees, of troops between fronts, and, especially in 1917, of deserting soldiers and revolutionary agitators. Hence the context of this tremendous growth in female labour was great demographic instability, the dis-integration of the economy, and the collapse of the transport system. Rural craft industries were cut off from urban markets, peasant out-workers from urban employers, towns from rural supplies. While industry looked increasingly to female labour, agriculture became dependent on it.

Nowhere did women earn as much as men. The skilled male workers, however, feared that the flood of women into their work-places would lead to dilution of skills, as had already happened with the spread of 'scientific management' practices in the early twen-tieth century, and the weakening of their trade-union organisation, which employers had been attempting since the 1905 revolution. Indeed, the number of women who joined trade unions remained relatively insignificant, while only a minority of those women who took action to protect their conditions were attached to any par-ticular political group. More immediately, however, any men who protested were liable to be sent to the front as punishment, and as an example to others. Nevertheless, Kondratev's memoirs of the Bolshevik party's activities with the Petrograd working class record

19. I. Gordienko, *Iz boevogo proshlogo, 1914–1918gg.* (Moscow, 1957), p. 34; Z.V. Stepanov, *Rabochie Petrograda v period podgotovki i provedeniia oktiabr'skogo vooruzhennogo vosstaniia* (Moscow, 1956), pp. 33–6; N.D. Karpetskaia, *Rabotnitsy i Velikii Oktiabr'* (Leningrad, 1974), p. 19; S.A. Smith, *Red Petrograd: Revolution in the Factories 1917–1918* (Cambridge, 1983), p. 23.

that a number of women had approached party organisers for help in developing their education and organisation, and that at the end of 1914 a small group of female workers had been formed, meeting sometimes at a party member's flat and sometimes in a tearoom. It was not an exclusively female circle, however; indeed, its leadership was male.[20]

The Bolshevik position had been clearly explained by Nadezhda Krupskaia, who held that male and female workers had to collaborate in order to solve the woman question, which she believed had a quite different meaning for the working class than it did for the bourgeoisie. Feminists, in her eyes, fought for women's rights against the opposition of their men. For feminists the woman question was narrowed to the issue of equal rights within an exploitative society. Politically conscious workers, however, saw class as the basis of that unjust society, and recognised that each class had its own interests which clashed with those of the others. Krupskaia pointed to the harsh lives led by women workers and by their children. She declared that workers had only each other to rely upon, so that while female workers should indeed fight for their specific interests, they should do so within the common struggle of their class: one for all and all for one.[21]

For the Bolsheviks, the First World War exposed the underlying divergence of interests between working-class women and female professionals, between feminist and socialist women. While the feminists continued to see patriotism as a way to achieve their political demands, the latter would come to condemn the war as an imperialist struggle, as a slaughterhouse for the masses who had no stake in it. The Bolsheviks believed that feminist support for the war effort would serve to alienate increasing numbers of peasant and working-class women who bore the brunt of the war effort on the home front.[22] There had been elections for worker representatives to sit on the War Industries Committee which had been set up by the government in 1915 in an attempt to run the war more efficiently. Not one woman had been elected out of the total of 198 representatives. The Bolsheviks accepted this 'sad fact' as evidence of the strength of all the old prejudices concerning women among the majority of the male labour force, and their refusal to allow women to develop and cast off their age-old subservience.[23]

20. K. Kondratev, 'Vospominaniia', *Krasnaia letopis'* (1922), no. 5, p. 234.
21. A.F. Bessanova (ed.), 'K istorii izdaniia zhurnala *Rabotnitsa*', *Istoricheskii arkhiv* (July–Aug. 1955), no. 4, pp. 31–8.
22. V. Bilshai, *Reshenie zhenskogo voprosa v SSSR* (Moscow, 1956), pp. 83–7.
23. E. Bochkareva, S. Liubimova, *Svetlyi put'* (Moscow, 1967), pp. 49–50.

Yet it was not only workers who persisted in this traditional view of the essentially domestic nature of women's work. In response to serious food shortages in 1915, one agitational leaflet had stressed that it was precisely their domestic role which made women particularly well equipped to deal with such a problem as the food supply. The leaflet also asserted that besides this specifically domestic campaign, there were wider issues which should engage them: 'the struggle to raise pay and shorten the working day is possible only with the most active participation of women workers'.[24] In a sense, then, while the Bolsheviks recognised that women bore a double burden, they also accorded women, but not men, a dual role in the labour movement, expecting them both to take on work which reflected their experience in organising the household and to join their men as equal partners in the general struggles of their class. The idea of relying on women's expertise in domestic areas of work, rather than challenging men to equip themselves with such skills, was reiterated after the Bolsheviks took power by the leading female Bolshevik, Alexandra Kollontai. She argued, during the civil war, that women who knew how to bring order out of chaos in their households would also be capable of doing so on the larger social scale; and moreover, working-class and peasant women would be able to do so more effectively than upper-class women ever could.[25]

With war in 1914, conditions of life and work began to deteriorate owing to the worsening problems of transport and distribution, the rationing and the ever-lengthening queues.[26] The severe wartime privations made the lives of working women particularly difficult, leading to a further deterioration in their general situation of long hours, low wages and crude treatment from male supervisors. With the mobilisation of millions of men, the war had forced many women to become effectively the sole provider for the household. Revolutionaries had to come to terms with the fact that any strikes or demonstrations could only be carried out if women were involved. In practice, women were not passive in the face of worsening conditions. Indeed, the mass poisoning of women workers at a Petersburg rubber factory on the eve of the war, in March 1914, had provoked strike action with the women protesting against the management's cost-cutting.[27]

24. S.N. Serditova, *Bol'sheviki v bor'be za zhenskie proletarskie massy, 1903g.–fevral' 1917g.* (Moscow, 1959), pp. 118–19.

25. See A.M. Kollontai, *Rabotnitsa za god revoliutsii* (Moscow, 1918), and *Bud' stoikim bortsom!* (Moscow, 1919).

26. A. Artiukhina *et al.*, *Zhenshchiny v revoliutsii* (Moscow, 1959), p. 153.

27. *Vsegda s vami: sbornik posviashchennyi 50-letiiu zhurnala 'Rabotnitsa'* (Moscow, 1964), pp. 206–11.

As the military conflict dragged on, feminists remained loyal to the war effort; indeed, the longer it lasted, the more chance women had to prove themselves worthy of equal rights. Women workers, however, became increasingly concerned with the acute shortages of bread and fuel, and the high death rate among Russian soldiers.[28] Yet still the Bolshevik party worried about the potential dangers of feminism and separatism for the unity of the working class. The specific exploitation which women faced simply because of their sex was recognised, but the party tended to stress what united rather than what divided the working class. Hence it dwelt on issues which affected the physical and material well-being of all workers, including the petty and arbitrary nature of management, and the lack of dignity with which it treated workers.

In his study of Petrograd factory workers in 1917, David Mandel insisted that it was not sex but the level of skill and the social characteristics associated with it in Russia which were the primary determinants of political culture, and that in the Russian labour movement the term 'conscious worker' embraced an entire code of conduct which included relations with women.[29] Yet skill continued to be seen as a masculine characteristic. Few women workers rose above the level of the semi-skilled, and indeed few jobs which women did were recognised as skilled. Moreover, a general complaint found in the journal *Rabotnitsa* and in the memoirs of skilled male workers such as Kanatchikov was that women workers were too narrowly focused on the problems of everyday life, concerns for which limited their interests and served to inhibit their men from fighting for an ideal. Yet Mandel's point might be more telling if applied to the worker's place in the hierarchy, rather than skill. For example, in June 1917, female workers at the Treugol'nik rubber factory in Moscow forced management to dismiss more than twenty forewomen who had been promoted during the war, and whom the workers claimed had used their new position of authority to act with excessive zeal and to treat them with contempt and arrogance, much like male supervisors. The latter went on strike in support of their female colleagues, and in defence of the established pecking order.[30] The women workers resisted all efforts to allow the forewomen to return to the shop-floor, even if demoted.

28. A.M. Kollontai, 'Avtobiograficheskii ocherk', *Proletarskaia revoliutsiia* (1921), no. 3, pp. 261–302: 296; Samoilova, *Rabotnitsa v rossiiskoi revoliutsii*, pp. 3–12.

29. David Mandel, *The Petrograd Workers and the Fall of the Old Regime* (London, 1983), pp. 16–27.

30. Diane P. Koenker, William G. Rosenberg, *Strikes and Revolution in Russia, 1917* (Princeton, 1989), pp. 140, 224.

Mandel has further conjectured that the inertia of the unskilled workers, their low level of participation in the labour movement in general, had parallels in the peasants' fatalism and passivity.[31] Yet he also acknowledges that this passivity did not preclude periodic outbursts of extremely militant collective action. Shliapnikov, the Bolshevik leader in Petrograd during the February revolution of 1917, argued that the privations of the war served to politicise women workers and soldiers' wives. He pointed out that the burden of the food crisis struck above all at working-class women, who were forced, with very limited resources and time (given the long hours they spent at work), to find ways and means of rooting out hoarded products. These women became the first to struggle against those who speculated and profited from the war.[32] Previously, revolutionaries had concentrated their efforts on drawing male workers into trade unions, and trying to turn strikes over everyday issues into political acts against the state. Bread riots had been categorised as isolated, apolitical and predominantly female disturbances. However, in the conditions of the First World War, the bread riot was as significant an expression of collective suffering and communal demands as the strike, reflected in the direct, spontaneous action taken by female textile workers in February 1917 which proved to be the starting-point of the revolution.

Indeed, a study of the relationship between bread and revolution in February 1917 reveals that only a year or so after the war had begun, Petrograd and cities in the north were already experiencing serious food shortages. By the end of 1916, the woman worker was spending on average 40 hours a week simply queuing for food, the quality as well as the quantity of which continuously deteriorated.[33] Although wages rose during the war, they never kept pace with inflation, which hit the lowest paid and the unskilled, the majority of whom were women, and those low-prestige white-collar and professional workers on fixed salaries, again including many women. This brought additional heavy burdens to women workers, especially if they headed families. After a ten-hour shift in their factories, they formed long queues outside bakeries and other food shops. As the transport and distribution systems collapsed, many shops were forced to close, so that women often had to travel considerable distances from their place of work and from their home to find an outlet. As the shortages grew and the queues lengthened, the women had no option but to camp outside bakeries, unable to

31. Mandel, *The Petrograd Workers*, pp. 27–31.
32. A. Shliapnikov, *On the Eve of 1917* (London, 1982), p. 118.
33. I.P. Leiberov, S.D. Rudachenko, *Revoliutsiia i khleb* (Moscow, 1990), pp. 17–20.

make the long journey home before trudging back to work after hours spent queuing. On their stools and makeshift beds, spending so much time together, these lines of women developed into discussion groups, as they grappled with the causes of their privations, and their fears for the men at the front.

Another Bolshevik, Samoilova, who was involved with organising women workers in 1917, agreed with Shliapnikov that the First World War was an important catalyst for the development of the female proletariat, in terms of both numbers and consciousness.[34] In her view, the war wrested many more women from the household and threw them into the cauldron of factory life, in place of their husbands, fathers and brothers, not just to earn their own daily bread but to support their families: in effect to assume the traditionally male role. Factory work helped mould these women, pressing them into active participation in the general class struggle. Samoilova pointed out that the life of these women was especially hard and brutal, with long hours of heavy toil for low and unequal pay; with base and degrading treatment from male employers and foremen. These women workers were veritable 'slaves of capital who sold not only their strength, but also often their own bodies for a piece of needed bread'. Their sufferings intensified with the shortages caused by the war and in the context of the general absence of political rights. Samoilova believed that through the experience of industrial work, the greatly expanded labour force came to place their own miserable situation in the wider context not only of the horrifying war, but also of the class struggle.[35]

Certainly, by the beginning of 1917, women workers' patience was exhausted: 'rising before dawn, we ran to the shop for bread, and then, downtrodden and drained from standing in the queue, we went to work. Cursing god, the tsar, and our wretched life, we slumped down at the machines.'[36] Yet no one, except perhaps the secret police who were aware of the level of unrest, expected a revolution, least of all one begun by women workers. In his memoirs of 1917, the Menshevik Nikolai Sukhanov, who was working in Petrograd for the tsarist government, recorded his thoughts and feelings on the eve of the revolution:

> Tuesday, February 21st. I was sitting in my office in the Turkestan section. Behind a partition two typists were gossiping about food difficulties, rows in the shopping queues, unrest among the women, an attempt to smash into some warehouse.

---

34. Samoilova, *Rabotnitsa v rossisskoi revoliutsii*, pp. 3–12.   35. Ibid.
36. Artiukhina, *Zhenshchiny v revoliutsii*, p. 153.

'D'you know,' suddenly declared one of these young ladies, 'if you ask me, it's the beginning of the revolution!'

These girls didn't understand what a revolution was. Nor did I believe them for a second. . . .

Not one party was preparing for the great upheaval. Everyone was dreaming, ruminating, full of foreboding, feeling his way . . .

These philistine girls whose tongues and typewriters were rattling away behind the partition didn't know what a revolution was. I believed neither them, nor the inflexible facts, nor my own judgement. Revolution – highly improbable! Revolution! – everyone knew this was only a dream – a dream of generations and of long laborious decades. Without believing the girls, I repeated after them mechanically: 'Yes, the beginning of the revolution.'[37]

International Women's Day and the collapse of tsarism

On the morning of 23 February [1917], I could hear women's voices in the lane which the windows of our section overlooked: 'Down with the war! Down with high prices! Down with hunger! Bread for the workers!' In a flash, I and several comrades went to the windows. . . . Masses of women workers filled the lane, and their mood was militant. Those who caught sight of us began to wave their arms, shouting: 'Come out! Down tools!' Snowballs flew through the window. We decided to join their demonstration.[38]

When it was decided to mark International Women's Day with a demonstration against the war, the Bolsheviks, aware that the mood of the workers was very tense, nevertheless resolved to preserve their energies for May Day, and determined to maintain control. They sought to prevent isolated outbreaks of action which might detract from the orderly direction which they hoped to impose on a demonstration to which they had been reluctant to agree in the first place. As far as the Bolsheviks were concerned, the task was to lead and discipline the female workers, who were renowned for their militant spontaneity. The Bolsheviks sought to limit International Women's Day to a rational protest against the war. In fact, none of the socialist parties put much effort into organising for women's day, failing to appreciate the urgent desire for action felt by the female workers and mothers. According to Shliapnikov,

37. N.N. Sukhanov, *The Russian Revolution 1917: A Personal Record,* edited, abridged and translated by Joel Carmichael (Princeton, 1984), pp. 3, 5.
38. I. Gordienko, *Iz boevogo proshlogo, 1914–18gg.* (Moscow, 1957), pp. 56–7.

the leading Bolshevik in Petrograd in February, the party had been unable to produce a leaflet for the day because their press had broken down. He recorded that, nevertheless, some Bolshevik women tried to persuade the reluctant local party committee in Vyborg (a working-class district in Petrograd) to hold a meeting on 23 February, on the theme of war, inflation and the situation of working women.[39] The party had set up a Petrograd women's circle, charged with carrying out propaganda and organisational work among female factory workers. It was this circle which decided that International Women's Day should be commemorated with an anti-war demonstration. A brief appeal was issued:

> Dear women comrades, are we going to put up with this in silence much longer, now and then venting our smouldering rage on small shop owners? After all, they're not to blame for the people's suffering, they are being ruined themselves. The government is to blame! It started the war and cannot end it. The government is ruining the country and causing us to go hungry. The capitalists are to blame! The war brings them profits. It's high time to cry out to them: 'Enough! Down with the criminal government and its whole gang of robbers and murderers! Long live peace!'[40]

In the militant Vyborg district, women from several textile mills went on strike and moved from factory to factory. As was later reported, threadworkers at the Neva Mills heard a commotion in the streets, and when they looked out found other textile workers imploring and demanding that they leave their machines and join them:

> 'Into the streets! Stop! We've had it!' And the entire first floor of the thread mill opened its windows in a flash, or rather they were knocked out with sticks, stones and pieces of wood. The women threadspinners surged noisily into the passageway.... All the doors were thrown open. And crowds of thread-makers pushed out into freedom.[41]

The women went *en masse* to the nearby metal works where they called on the men to join them in their demands for bread and an end to the war. Some, notably in metalworking plants, struck and went home, but many more went into the streets, demanding bread. This was not simply a bread riot, however, for it began in the factories, and was then joined by the women from the queues for bread

39. A.G. Shliapnikov, *Semnadtsatyi god* (Moscow, 1923), pp. 60–1.
40. E. Burdzhalov, *Russia's Second Revolution: The February 1917 Uprising in Petrograd*, translated by Donald J. Ralegh (1967; Bloomington, Ind., 1987), p. 105.
41. Ibid., p. 107.

and kerosene. The metal worker and Bolshevik, Kaiurov, had earlier addressed a women workers' meeting, urging them to follow the directives of the party committee. He recorded later that, on hearing of the strike by female textile workers, he had been extremely indignant at their blatant disregard of the call for self-control and discipline.

> Taking into account the rising temperature of the masses, the district committee resolved to discontinue its agitation for immediate strike action, etc., and to concentrate instead on maintaining discipline and conserving energy for future action.
>
> On the eve of Women's Day, the night of 23 February, I was sent to the Lesnoy district to address a women's meeting. I first spoke on the significance of Women's Day and on the women's movement in general, and then went on to discuss the current situation, stressing the need to refrain from isolated outbursts and to act solely on the directions of the Party Committee.
>
> I was sure that we were strong enough to enforce our decisions in the district.
>
> Imagine my astonishment and indignation when, on the following day, 23 February, at a contingency meeting in the corridor of the [Erikson] factory, comrade Nikifor Il'in informed us that several textile factories had gone on strike and that women delegates had come to demand the support of the metal workers.
>
> I felt deeply aggrieved by the behaviour of the strikers. For one thing, they had blatantly disregarded the decision of the district committee of the party, and for another, I had urged restraint and discipline on the women workers just the night before, and suddenly they had gone on strike. It seemed there was no rhyme or reason for it, unless it was the recent increase in the length of the bread queues – which in essence is why the strike began. But what was to be done? We would have to make the best of it. The meeting continued, with the Mensheviks and SRs now present. We decided (albeit reluctantly) to support the women on strike, and my proposal was accepted, that since we had decided to protest it was incumbent upon us to take the lead in the strike and the demonstrations, and direct all workers without exception into the streets. . . .
>
> It was a strange thing, but neither the district committee nor the representatives of the workers on the shop-floor were surprised at this decision. Clearly the idea of going to the streets had long been ripening among the workers, only at that time, no one imagined where it would lead.[42]

42. V. Kaiurov, 'Shest' dnei fevral'skoi revoliutsii', *Proletarskaia revoliutsiia* (1923), no. 1, pp. 157–70: 157–8; translated by James D. White.

The implication in Kaiurov's memoir is that only the skilled male workers could provide political direction and leadership, and that the women acted out of desperation and hunger. It was also a view held by opponents of the revolution:

> The Russian revolution was begun by hungry women and children demanding bread and herrings. They started by wrecking tram cars and looting a few small shops. Only later did they, together with workmen and politicians, become ambitious to wreck that mighty edifice the Russian autocracy.[43]

Again there is the implication that women, like children, would not behave in a political way, that they had to wait for the men to provide that ingredient. In practice, the women's initial economic demands swiftly took on a political meaning in the context of the war. Indeed, the previous month, the tsarist secret police had recognised the revolutionary potential of the working women:

> mothers of families, exhausted from the endless queues at shops, suffering at the sight of their ill and half-starved children are at this moment much closer to revolution than [the Duma liberals]; and they are, of course, more dangerous because they constitute a mass of inflammable material which needs only a spark for it to burst into flames.[44]

The women workers' actions, moreover, had put the Bolsheviks, and indeed all the revolutionary groups, on the spot, especially since the rank and file members of their parties supported the women, as revealed by the Bolshevik Gordienko's memoir. Yet at first not all workers responded. In his study of the February revolution, the soviet historian Burdzhalov recorded that some workers with large families to support were afraid that if they went on strike, they would simply be dismissed. Other men were afraid that the penalty for taking strike action would be conscription and being sent to the front.[45] Hence some male workers adopted the cautious stance usually associated with women. They held back, waiting to see what would come of the women's actions. A female tram conductor described how the revolution spread:

43. P. Sorokin, *Leaves from a Russian Diary* (Boston, Mass., 1950), p. 3.
44. Zoya Igumnova, *Zhenshchiny Moskvy v gody grazhdanskoi voiny* (Moscow, 1958), p. 11.
45. Burdzhalov, *Russia's Second Revolution*, p. 109.

We began to leave the yard to board the municipal trams when suddenly we saw a crowd of workers coming towards us, shouting 'Open the gate to the yard!' There were several hundred people. They stood on the rails and on the stairs of the Garnyi Museum which was opposite the yard. The workers were from a pipe plant, a tannery and a paper factory. They told us that today all the plants in our city were on strike and the trams were not running. The strikers were taking the tram drivers out of the control of the management. From all sides we heard 'Down with the war!', and a woman shouted 'Return our husbands from the front!'[46]

From the beginning, the women workers tried to win over the soldiers, or at least to neutralise them, recognising that these defenders of tsarism were vacillating. Indeed, according to Shliapnikov, from the start of the war in 1914, women workers had been aware of the crucial role of the conscripted soldiers:

> An extremely active part in propaganda was taken by women workers, the weavers and the millgirls: some of the soldiers were from the same villages as the women workers, but for the most part, the young people came together on the basis of 'interests of the heart' and thus kinship relations were established between barracks and factory.[47]

Thus in February 1917, it was women workers who took action, and the men who hesitated. Despite bloodshed and beatings by the cossacks and police, the women refused the military's call to disperse, responding that they were not to be dismissed as babas, for they were sisters and wives of soldiers at the front. The strikers and demonstrators would surround the cossacks and describe their miserable situation to them, exploited for profits while their men were slaughtered. They pointed out that the cossacks had mothers, wives and sisters, as well as children suffering from terrible privation. A Bolshevik female worker, A.I. Kruglova, described one encounter between her factory and soldiers and cossacks:

> A detachment of cossacks bore down on us quickly. But we did not waver; we stood in a solid wall as though turned to stone. An officer of the cossacks yelled: 'Who are you following? You are being led by an old crone!' I said: 'No old crone; but a sister and wife of soldiers at the front.' What happened next was totally unexpected. The soldiers of the Novocherkassk regiment lowered their rifles. . . . Someone at the rear yelled: 'Cossacks, you are our brothers, you can't shoot us . . .' And the cossacks turned their horses around.[48]

---

46. *Vsegda s vami*, pp. 100–1. 47. Shliapnikov, *On the Eve*, p. 7.
48. Burdzhalov, *Russia's Second Revolution*, pp. 114–15.

The result of the women's determined and brave actions was increasing confusion in the ranks, and the refusal of soldiers to fire on the crowds.[49] The revolutionary groups had hesitated, reluctant to condone, let alone support, what they considered to be the women's typically precipitate action. The demonstration by the Petrograd women was indeed spontaneous, in the sense that it had no direct, conscious, formal structure of leadership, or strategy for overthrowing tsarism. Yet it should be remembered that despite the low level of organisation by women, textile workers had been militant since the mid 1890s, while they were to play a significant part in the strike movement after February 1917. Unrest had been growing since 1915, and urban women, notably textile workers, had been involved in numerous strikes across Russia, for example in Ivanovno-Voznesensk and Kostroma.[50] At the beginning of 1917, there had been widespread strikes over wages, conditions and mistreatment by superiors. For example, in January there had been a strike by female textile workers at a large Petrograd mill when the employers had tried to extend the working day by one hour (the women were already working twelve-hour shifts). The women destroyed a list with signatures of those workers who had agreed to the extra hour, and then went on strike. The factory owners reversed their decision, though they tried to victimise and isolate some of the strike leaders by taking them away from the shop-floor, and putting them to work in the factory's food store. The women workers, however, successfully insisted that all the strikers be reinstated.[51] What happened in February, therefore, was also the culmination of long pent-up anger at the privations their families had been suffering and which they were expected to accept with meekness and stoicism as their contribution to the war effort. A woman who was then working on the trams recalled years later her impressions of the February demonstrations:

> The streets were packed with people. The trams had stopped running, cars lay overturned across their tracks. At the time, I didn't know, didn't understand what was happening. I screamed along with the rest, 'Down with the tsar!', yet when I wondered 'how will it be without a tsar?' I felt as if a bottomless pit had opened up in front

49. Gordienko, *Iz boevogo proshlogo*, pp. 56–7; T. Hasegawa, *The February Revolution: Petrograd 1917* (Washington, 1981), pp. 215–24.

50. Serditova, *Bol'sheviki v bor'be za zhenskie proletarskie massy*, p. 105; Bochkareva and Liubimova, *Svetlyi put'*, pp. 47–8.

51. V. Perazich, *Tekstili Leningrada v 1917g.* (Leningrad, 1927), p. 8.

of me, and my heart sank. Yet still I shouted over and over again, 'Down with the tsar!' It felt as if my old life was collapsing, and I rejoiced in its destruction.[52]

Between the two revolutions

Nevertheless, despite the prominent part which they had played in the overthrow of tsarism in February, there were very few women – around ten – in the first Petrograd soviet, while it was mostly men who were elected to the factory committees. Men retained their dominant position, despite the fact that by 1917 women in Russia accounted for around 47 per cent of the total workforce, and were entering sectors of the economy previously dominated by, or even exclusive to, men. With women remaining for the most part unskilled and still forced to spend so much time queuing for food, it is not surprising that skilled male workers continued to dominate all working-class organisations.[53] Sukhanov recorded a conversation he had had not long after the February revolution with a woman to whom he often turned for information on what people in the streets were saying:

'Well, how about the queues? Have they got any smaller? Are they more orderly now or less, without the police?'

'Just the same,' said Anna Mikhailovna; 'the queues – well the queues haven't got smaller in the least; I think they're even bigger. You stand half the day just as before.'

'And what are they saying?'

'What are they saying? They say – liberty-flibberty, it's all the same, there's nothing to be had. They say it's just the same, the rich keep fleecing the poor. The shopkeepers are the only ones making money.'

'Aha!'

People . . . were fond of repeating in 1917 that the women in the queues made the revolution. I wondered what these women wanted to do now. What would it bring forth, this talk – reaction or future Bolshevism? . . .

It seemed that in the new conditions the 'lower depths' were in deadly earnest about the question of prices and the struggle against the high cost of living.[54]

52. *Zhenshchiny goroda Lenina* (Leningrad, 1963), p. 89.
53. Kollontai, 'Avtobiograficheskii ocherk', p. 296; S. Kingsbury, M. Fairchild, *Factory, Family and Women in the Soviet Union* (New York, 1935), pp. 15–16.
54. Sukhanov, *The Russian Revolution*, pp. 182–3.

As in 1905, the women were themselves aware that their political development was as yet only a spark. They acknowledged their need for a comrade who could brave a public meeting, speak on their behalf, explain things to them, and tell them what they should read and what was to be done. The majority of women workers continued to view the trade unions as male bastions. Nevertheless, women workers did not lapse into passivity. Indeed, in the interval between the two revolutions of 1917, one of the most prolonged and bitter disputes involved women: in May, 40,000 laundresses struck for increased pay, for the eight-hour day, and for more machinery to lighten their load. Alexandra Kollontai, who supported the laundry workers, also organised a movement of soldiers' wives.[55]

However, it seems that in the factories, female workers were impeded in their efforts at organisation by men who continued to believe that women were still not capable of organising or leading.[56] Positions of responsibility were monopolised by the minority of politically active, organisationally experienced, skilled male workers. Eva Broido recorded that female metal workers in some factories were simply not accepted by the men, who were in the majority, as suitable to represent them on the factory committee. This was not a view held only by men. Even in plants making sweets, chocolates and biscuits, which employed a majority of women, very few were elected as representatives.[57] At the same time trade unions made some attempts to increase their female membership, such as the special women's commissions set up by the leather workers.[58] On the eve of the Bolshevik seizure of power, one female textile worker acknowledged that the predominantly male factory committee had done a great deal to organise the 'dark masses'; but she also complained that this same male vanguard seemed to want to retain their monopoly of the leadership, dominating in this case a cotton-spinning mill in which women comprised over 90 per cent of the workforce. She accused the male leadership of acting undemocratically, of beginning 'to boss their backward comrades', and of treating the workers with rudeness and arrogance.[59]

That factory worker had her grievance published in the Bolshevik journal *Rabotnitsa*. In March 1917, the Petrograd committee of the party had again recognised the need and potential for systematic work among women. A bureau was set up and publication of

55. Kollontai, *Rabotnitsa za god revoliutsii*, pp. 18–19.
56. *Rabotnitsa* (19 July 1917), no. 7, p. 4.
57. Eva Broido, *Zhenshchina-Rabotnitsa* (Petrograd, 1917), p. 8.
58. *Rabotnitsa* (30 May 1917), no. 4, p. 15.
59. Ibid. (18 Oct. 1917), no. 11, p. 15.

Rabotnitsa was resumed in May. It was, however, emphasised that no independent women's organisation was being formed. According to Nadezhda Karpetskaia, the soviet historian of women in the 1917 revolution, it was Vera Slutskaia who suggested the need for both a centre to organise Bolshevik work among women, and the resumption of *Rabotnitsa*.[60] Yet Slutskaia was cautious to stress the limits of such activities: they would be purely agitational, and, in general, the woman worker would be involved within the political and trade-union organisations of the working class. The women's bureau would be subordinate to the Petrograd party committee. Still, although it was not explicitly stated, Slutskaia implied that the party representatives on the bureau would all be women.

The Bolshevik leadership appeared to be reacting to, rather than initiating, the upsurge in the actions of women workers, while there was some fear that the feminist movement, which had been revitalised by the war, might make inroads into the working class. In Kollontai's opinion, a special Bolshevik party apparatus devoted to work among women was essential precisely to counteract what she believed to be the influence feminists were winning among the workers.[61] However, she and Slutskaia failed to convince many of their comrades, who effectively sabotaged the proposed centre. Another female Bolshevik, Liudmilla Stal', noted that, following the February revolution:

> attempts were made to begin organisational work among the female proletariat, following the example of German social democracy. But these efforts were undermined by resistance from our party workers. In their view, conducting special work among women reeked too strongly of feminism, and they would on no account split party work among the proletariat along sex lines. The attempts of the Petersburg committee to organise a city-wide centre for work among proletarian women was, therefore, a failure. The only organisational centre for such work was the journal of the central committee, *Rabotnitsa*.[62]

Karpetskaia's work, published in the Soviet Union in 1974, not surprisingly stresses the role of Bolshevik women in organising female workers in 1917, and neglects the activities of other revolutionary groups as well as the feminists. The latter were conspicuous by their absence from the February revolution, but soon declared their support for the war efforts of the provisional government which

60. N.D. Karpetskaia, 'Vovlechenie trudiashchikhsia zhenshchin Petrograda v revoliutsionnoe dvizhenie, mart–iiul' 1917g', in *Vestnik Leningradskogo Universiteta* (1966), no. 8, p. 46. See also her *Rabotnitsy i Velikii Oktiabr'* (Leningrad, 1974).
61. Kollontai, 'Avtobiograficheskii ocherk', p. 197.
62. L. Stal', 'Rabotnitsa v Oktiabre', *Proletarskaia revoliutsiia* (1922), no. 10, p. 297.

replaced the tsar. Indeed, the feminist movement revived its campaign for female suffrage, lobbying liberal and left-wing politicians
and activists, and staging mass demonstrations. Universal suffrage,
with equal rights for women, was proclaimed by the government in
July. By then, women had finally been granted the right to serve on
juries and entry into the law profession on equal terms with men.
In August, further reforms gave women in the civil service equal
rights, including equal pay.[63] By August, however, lower-class women
in the cities had become even more radicalised, partly by the still
deteriorating economic situation, partly by the threat to the revolution which had been posed by the attempted military coup in August,
headed by General Kornilov. It had provoked a tremendous response
from the workers, with women as well as men prepared to defend
Petrograd against the general. Although he had been defeated,
there was widespread fear of future counter-revolutionary actions,
and popular suspicion that the leader of the provisional government, Kerensky, had conspired with the general. Hence the feminists had little hope of winning the support of working-class women
for the government and the war it persisted in pursuing, particularly as Kornilov had been appointed commander-in-chief of the
armed forces by Kerensky himself.

Certainly, Karpetskaia acknowledges the influence of female
activists who were not Bolshevik, but she insists that they made
headway only with the more backward elements among women
workers. It seems that women workers were unwilling to commit
themselves to a particular political group, though they might accept
an individual activist's help in organising their protests.[64] Yet both
the Mensheviks and the Socialist Revolutionaries (SRs) essentially
agreed with the Bolsheviks on the dangers of separatism, and the
need to organise women alongside men. Thus it is hard to distinguish between the Bolshevik line and the position of the Menshevik
Eva Broido. She wrote in 1917 that women workers should join men
in trade unions to fight for improved conditions; that the task of
involving women necessitated a change in men's attitudes, so that
they would look on women as comrades and not competitors; and
that special attention to women workers would help convince both
the women themselves and male workers that women were capable
of organisation, that their backwardness was not 'natural', but rather
a result of their position in society.[65] Certainly, Bolshevik women

63. Stites, *The Women's Liberation Movement*, p. 295.
64. Perazich, *Tekstili Leningrada*, p. 5.
65. Broido, *Zhenshchina-Rabotnitsa*, pp. 13–14.

emerge from Karpetskaia's history of women in the 1917 revolution much more positively than their male comrades. Moreover, despite the imbalance in Karpetskaia's treatment of the subject of women workers and their organisation in 1917 and bearing in mind, of course, that it is a history written by the victors, ultimately it was the efforts of Bolshevik women which seem to have been the most successful.

Moreover, Diane Koenker and William Rosenberg have shown that, whatever the supportive, organisational and leadership roles of the various socialist groups, strikes by women workers, and not only factory but service workers, were more widely reported in Bolshevik newspapers (and not only in *Rabotnitsa*) than in any others. Koenker and Rosenberg argue that what distinguished the Bolshevik reports was 'the apparent recognition that activist behaviour by generally dormant workers like salesclerks and laundresses was itself a matter of real political import, reflecting class struggle in stark form, and worthy of extensive reporting in part as an example to others'. Hence, the strike by laundresses in Petrograd in May 1917 received much more attention in the Bolshevik party newspaper *Pravda* than any other paper.[66] Perhaps, too, the reports of female workers' strikes were to demonstrate to men that women had the capacity for sustained organisation.

While many Bolsheviks, female as well as male, continued to resist the notion of special work among women, there are competing claims for who first championed the establishment of a Bolshevik women's centre. Carole Eubanks Hayden records that Alexandra Kollontai proposed the creation of a women's department to a meeting of women delegates at the Seventh All-Russian Conference of the Bolsheviks in April 1917, but received little if any support.[67] Certainly, Kollontai's memoirs give the impression that she was the often isolated instigator and driving force behind the Bolshevik party's efforts to organise women workers, a view which has been reinforced by her Western admirers.[68] Yet, as Karpetskaia has shown, there were a number of female Bolsheviks who recognised the need for special work among women, including Slutskaia, who had made the suggestion for a bureau in March, and Samoilova, who put her

66. Koenker, Rosenberg, *Strikes and Revolution in Russia*, pp. 228–9.

67. Carole Eubanks Hayden, 'The *Zhenotdel* and the Bolshevik Party', *Russian History* (1976), vol. 3, no. 2, pp. 150–73: 152.

68. See for example Moira Donald, '"What did *you* do in the Revolution, Mother?" Image, Myth and Prejudice in Western Writing on the Russian Revolution', *Gender and History* (Apr. 1995), vol. 7, no. 1, pp. 85–99.

efforts into making *Rabotnitsa* the organisational centre for such activities.[69]

The journal not only published articles by and about women workers, but convened local and factory meetings to address issues which were of general interest to workers. Such issues covered improved pay and conditions, the eight-hour day and child labour. Issues of specific interest to women included workplace crèches, protective legislation for women, and equal civil and political rights. *Rabotnitsa* publicised women workers' strikes, while Bolshevik women tried to organise not only workers but soldiers' wives and domestic servants, and to mobilise them on issues which were not simply confined to the workplace, including protests against war profiteering, food shortages and inflation.[70] Public meetings were important for those workers who did not have factory committees, but who were scattered between workplaces, such as laundresses and waitresses.

The women who edited and wrote for *Rabotnitsa* (including Krupskaia, Stal' and Slutskaia) did not remain in the journal's offices, but agitated and organised women workers and soldiers' wives throughout the city. Karpetskaia records that a school was established to prepare women as agitators and organisers in their own places of work.[71] Of course, the stress remained on the unity of the working class, and there were constant warnings about the divisive nature of feminism, but in practice these women would be concentrating their efforts on their sisters. Rose Glickman wrote that women workers had shown even in 1914 that they did not need *Rabotnitsa* to explain their problems. In the tumultuous months of 1917, however, *Rabotnitsa* played a crucial role, according to Richard Stites. He contends that Bolshevik newspapers, journals and pamphlets 'reduced the complexities to everyday categories that any proletarian housewife could understand' and that they reached thousands of women.[72] In addition, the party helped pressure male workers into recognising women as comrades in their struggle. In a Petrograd textile factory in March, male apprentices shouted down two women who tried to address a meeting. Both these workers were Bolsheviks, but the opposition seemed related more to their gender and to the fact that one of them appeared Jewish. Another woman was

69. For Samoilova, see L. Katasheva, *Natasha: A Bolshevik Woman Organiser* (London, 1934), pp. 41–5.

70. See for example Artiukhina, *Zhenshchiny v revoliutsii*; Hayden, 'The *Zhenotdel* and the Bolshevik Party', pp. 152–3.

71. Karpetskaia, *Rabotnitsy*, pp. 44–51.

72. Glickman, *Russian Factory Women*, p. 280; Stites, *The Women's Liberation Movement*, pp. 303–4.

rejected as a representative because she worked at the factory shop, rather than at the machines. A strong Bolshevik campaign strengthened the position of all three women on the factory committee.[73]

Kollontai observed that as the economic situation worsened, notably from June, with spiralling inflation, falling real wages, and increasing unemployment, it was women workers who suffered most.[74] Indeed, some factory committees, notably munitions and metal works, attempted to combat the latter by forcing women workers whose husbands, brothers or fathers worked in the same factory to leave their jobs.[75] *Rabotnitsa* protested that women's labour should be defended and not opposed by male workers, pointing out that dismissing women could not solve the immense problems caused by the war which was destroying Russian industry and distorting the economy.[76] The Menshevik Eva Broido similarly insisted men had to overcome their prejudices, accept women as equals and welcome them into the workplace.[77] The metal workers' union, that bastion of skilled men, also condemned attempts of factory committees to make women workers bear the brunt of redundancies. The Bolsheviks and the metal workers' union, in which the former had considerable influence, argued not in terms of women's rights, but of class solidarity, wanting the factory committees to treat women as equal members of the working class.[78] Yet this call for equal rights for women from a predominantly male union may in fact have been an attempt to push women out of the metal industry, once they were no longer seen as cheap labour by the employers. Ironically, the committees were thinking in terms of narrow family interests (continuing to see the man as the main breadwinner, whose job was therefore more important to save than a woman's), which was more usually the criticism made by activists of women workers.

Thus the experience of working with female workers and soldiers' wives in 1917 had convinced a number of prominent Bolshevik women, who had previously dismissed special efforts to organise women as separatist and who still resisted the notion of a special women's department, of the necessity for conferences of working women to raise the general level of female consciousness. In

73. Perazich, *Tekstili Leningrada*, p. 28.

74. Kollontai, *Rabotnitsa za god revoliutsii*, p. 4.

75. Bochkareva, Liubimova, *Svetlyi put'*, pp. 59–69.

76. *Rabotnitsa* (1 Sept. 1917), no. 9, p. 9.

77. Broido, *Zhenshchina-rabotnitsa*, p. 14.

78. Stepanov, *Rabochie Petrograda v period podgotovki i provedeniia velikogo oktiabr'skogo voorozhennogo vosstaniia*, p. 146.

particular, the editors of *Rabotnitsa* had found through practical activity and contact with women workers that it was vitally necessary to overcome their profound cultural backwardness and centuries of silence. Samoilova explained why they had changed their minds:

> though the February revolution provoked the rise of revolutionary fervour among a great number of women workers, it had not yet forged a lasting class-consciousness. That's why many of these women workers sometimes became despondent on their thorny revolutionary path and wavered, especially under pressure from Black Hundred [extreme right-wing, anti-Semitic] agitation which was carried on among the working class by all their enemies. This wavering in the mood of women workers became especially apparent during the July Days, when the counter-revolutionary scum started its dirty persecution of the party of the working class, spreading the most absurd rumours and slanders about the Bolsheviks, calling them 'German spies' and so on. . . . The most backward and irresponsible women workers, who easily believed the various rumours spread among them in the queues and wherever else it was possible, fell for the bait of the enemies of their class. They would come to the party organisation and throw away their membership cards, asking to be struck off the Bolshevik party membership list.
>
> This expression of the political instability of women workers, of their inadequate class consciousness, prompted the Bolshevik party of the working class to pay attention to work among the female proletariat.[79]

Thus the Bolshevik party was forced to conduct more intensive propaganda among women workers, through special sections attached to party organs. Krupskaia recorded that from the start of *Rabotnitsa*, she and Inessa Armand had addressed female workers not only through this specialist journal, but also in pamphlets and meetings dedicated to women's issues, and in the pages of the party's newspapers, urging women to become involved in the struggle against counter-revolution, and in the Bolshevik party. They believed that systematic work among women by female delegates from the party was vital if peasant and working-class women were to be absorbed into active participation in building a new society.[80] However, in his biography of Armand, R.C. Elwood has shown that in 1917 *Rabotnitsa* was very much a Petrograd initiative. In Moscow, Armand, Varvara Iakovleva and then Sofia Smidovich tried to conduct work among factory women first through their new journal, *Zhizn' rabotnitsy (The*

79. Samoilova, *Rabotnitsy v rossisskoi revoliutsii*, p. 7.
80. Krupskaia, *Pamiati Inessy Armand*, pp. 24–6, 31.

Woman Worker's Life), and then through the Moscow region's 'Commissions for Agitation and Propaganda among Working Women'. Thus while, in Elwood's view, the Moscow journal was a pale imitation of *Rabotnitsa*, the commissions resembled those sections which Kollontai had unsuccessfully proposed in Petrograd in May. Armand, however, soon retired to her family estate to care for her 13-year-old son, who was ill.[81]

Whether in Moscow or Petrograd, these leading Bolshevik women criticised the persistent opposition within the party to special work among women as short-sighted dogmatism. Indeed, Samoilova claimed that the time devoted to women workers produced clear results, reflected in a growth of their political awareness, and in their active participation in the class struggle.[82] This was seen in women workers' response to the attempted military coup in August by the Chief of Staff, General Kornilov. In defence of the revolution, women worked with men to repel the general's forces, building barricades and organising medical aid, in the form of Red Sisters.[83] However, Stal' was less sanguine about progress, seeing the slow growth of the Bolshevik organisation among women as not simply the result of such hidebound theory, but because *Rabotnitsa* itself was run too intellectually to have any real impact on the majority of women workers.[84]

Certainly, it was women from the intelligentsia who dominated *Rabotnitsa*, since they had by far the widest experience of organisation, and were more articulate than women workers. Still, the reporting of strikes and demonstrations by the latter in Bolshevik newspapers was generally detailed in terms of the participants' organisation, demands, and the obstacles which they encountered. Koenker and Rosenberg provide two case studies of how such actions were reported, in both of which women constituted a significant proportion of the participants. The first, in May, was a prolonged strike of 350 workers, mostly women, in dye and dry cleaning works, along with around another 150 sales people from affiliated shops in Petrograd. The second, in June, was of the capital's teashop and restaurant workers. Both were reported in the liberal and non-Bolshevik socialist press, but it was the Bolshevik papers which seemed most clearly to grasp the significance of the actions, and of

81. R.C. Elwood, *Inessa Armand: Revolutionary and Feminist* (Cambridge, 1992), pp. 211–13.

82. Samoilova, *Rabotnitsy v rossiisskoi revoliutsii*, pp. 7–8.

83. Artiukhina, *Zhenshchiny v revoliutsii*, p. 59.

84. Stal', 'Rabotnitsa v Oktiabre', p. 297; Artiukhina, *Zhenshchina v revoliutsii*, p. 108.

the issues raised by these service workers.[85] Nor were the issues limited to material demands. The waitresses and waiters demanded respect as human beings, including an end to tipping, which they felt was degrading. In common with all workers in the service sector, including domestic servants, they wanted to be addressed with the formal 'you' instead of the usual practice of the familiar 'you' which they associated with serfdom. Equal pay was not a universal demand in 1917; indeed women workers seemed more concerned with immediate improvements of their appalling situation, maternity benefits, the abolition of child labour, and an end to demeaning practices, such as body searches.[86]

Most historical accounts of working-class unrest in 1917 tend to generalise, and to focus mainly on factory workers, without reference to gender. Yet one of the most bitter struggles which radicalised women workers in Petrograd was the strike in May of between five and eight thousand laundresses. Female worker Bolsheviks were prominent in the laundry workers' trade union. In addition, Alexandra Kollontai certainly encouraged the laundresses at mass meetings, and publicised their demands (including an eight-hour day, minimum wage, improved work and sanitary conditions, paid annual and sick leave, respectful treatment). Moira Donald claims that the Bolsheviks had not automatically supported the laundresses' strike, but had had to be prodded into action by Kollontai.[87] Yet, from the frequent reports in the party press, it also seems that the Bolshevik leadership saw the strike as an example to other workers.[88] Certainly, the laundresses' dispute was also reported in the Menshevik and Socialist Revolutionary papers; but it was the emphasis in the Bolshevik press on the bitterness of the strike, the sometimes violent retaliatory action taken by employers and scab labour (including attacks with hot irons and boiling water), and the militance of the women which may have better represented the deteriorating state of labour relations generally by the summer of 1917.

Still, the Bolsheviks looked on these women first and foremost in terms of their class, and used their actions to support the Bolshevik view that the separate organisation of women was unnecessary. In contrast, Richard Stites argues that the Mensheviks put little effort

85. Koenker, Rosenberg, *Strikes and Revolution in Russia, 1917*, pp. 229–32.

86. Orlando Figes, *A People's Tragedy: The Russian Revolution 1891–1924* (London, 1996), p. 368.

87. Moira Donald, 'Bolshevik Activity amongst the Working Women of Petrograd in 1917', *International Review of Social History* (1982), vol. xxvii, pp. 129–60: 144.

88. Koenker, Rosenberg, *Strikes and Revolution in Russia, 1917*, pp. 3–4.

into winning the support of Petrograd women workers. Reports of female actions, such as strikes, demonstrations and food and fuel riots, dwelt on the particular material grievances, and avoided wider issues of politics and organisation.[89] In addition, Mensheviks and Socialist Revolutionaries (now members of a coalition government with liberals) sought collaboration between workers and employers. The Mensheviks were seen as conciliators who sought moderate reform. Thus Eva Broido in 1917 was arguing in favour of female factory inspectors who should be responsible for investigating the conditions of all women workers and of their families.[90] Indeed, a study of textile workers in 1917 which was published on the tenth anniversary of the revolution insisted that it was because of the initial high representation of Mensheviks and SRs on the soviet that workers' economic demands were toned down, and moreover that strikers were asked to return to work. On one occasion, female textile workers were so infuriated that they denounced a male Menshevik deputy in no uncertain terms: 'Traitor! . . . Who sent you to the soviet, workers or masters?'[91] As for the SRs, they were still orientated towards the peasantry and, however sympathetic to the plight of the urban women workers, did not consider their specific needs when constructing their political platform.

In addition, the Bolshevik anti-war propaganda gradually won popular support. They were, however, opposed by the female soldier Bochkareva, who sided with the provisional government because of its pledge to continue the war until victory was won. Indeed, she had supported the February revolution largely because she suspected that the royal court and the tsar's ministers responsible for the war effort were in fact traitors, in league with the enemy. After the February revolution, however, the rate of desertion among front-line troops soared, and, as war weariness deepened, female soldiers were to serve as models of military heroism to their male comrades. Bochkareva's response was to secure government approval for the establishment in May, under her command, of a battalion of women soldiers which would shame the men into remaining at their posts. She pleaded with a patriotic audience in May:

> Men and women citizens! . . . Our mother is perishing. Our mother is Russia. I want to help save her. I want women whose tears are pure crystal, whose souls are pure, whose impulses are lofty. With such women setting an example of self-sacrifice, you men will realise your duty in this grave hour.[92]

89. Stites, *The Women's Liberation Movement*, p. 394.
90. Eva Broido, *Zhenskaia inspektsiia truda* (Petrograd, 1917).
91. Perazich, *Tekstili Leningrada*, p. 32.   92. Bochkareva, *Yashka*, p. 162.

Of the 2,000 women who volunteered, Bochkareva initially selected 500, and ultimately around 300 stayed the course. Bochkareva's requirements were strict: irreproachable honesty and a serious attitude towards the cause; cheerfulness, politeness, kindness, affability, cleanliness and tidiness; respect for other people's views, complete trust in one another; and noble aspirations. Many of the rejections were on the grounds of lax behaviour.[93] Richard Abraham has identified a feminist aspect to the women's battalion, and certainly feminists at home and abroad applauded Bochkareva's battalion.[94] In Russia, however, there was often ridicule if not outright hostility. When the women's battalion marched through Petrograd, rude and suggestive remarks were made, and extra watchmen had to be assigned to the women's barracks. Still, the initiative was not restricted to the capital: other women's battalions were formed in Moscow, Saratov, Mariupol', Baku, Ekaterinburg, Kiev, Tashkent, Ekaterinodar, Odessa and Minsk. Only the Petrograd battalion, however, left a lasting impression.[95] Bochkareva was not fighting for women's rights, but to defend the February revolution and continue the war effort. To that end her battalion saw action on the western front in June, in which many died.[96] In addition, it has been claimed that the mass desertion which set in with the rout of the Russian summer offensive by the Germans led to some men assaulting and killing a number of women soldiers.[97]

Women and the October revolution

Better known is the action of Bochkareva's troops in defence of the Winter Palace against the Bolsheviks in October. Around 200 of them were stationed in the Winter Palace, along with two companies of cossacks and some young cadets, making a total of approximately 3,000 defenders of the provisional government. Morale was low, and the cossacks were reluctant to serve with a women's battalion, confirming the impression drawn from Yurlova's memoir of life among the cossacks that female soldiers were acceptable only

93. Rozenthal, 'Smertnitsy na fronte'.

94. R. Abraham, 'Mariia L. Bochkareva and the Russian Amazons of 1917', ch. 6 in Linda Edmondson (ed.), *Women and Society in Russia and the Soviet Union* (Cambridge, 1992), p. 127.

95. See Rozenthal, 'Smertnitsy na fronte'.

96. See for example Louise Bryant, *Six Red Months in Russia* (London, 1918), p. 210.

97. Griesse and Stites, 'Russia: Revolution and War', p. 64.

as unique individuals. Orlando Figes describes as 'hysterical' the reaction of the women's battalion to the blank round fired by the battleship *Aurora*, which signalled the Bolshevik attack on the Palace. Yet it also caused the frightened ministers to collapse on the floor, while the male soldiers and cadets abandoned their posts.[98] The Bolsheviks' opponents insisted that there were mass rapes of the female soldiers, allegations which, it has been claimed, were 'probably unfounded'.[99] The British ambassador in Petrograd, Sir George Buchanan, believed that the women were brutally treated by the Red Guards who had taken them prisoner, and that the women were 'saved from the fate that would inevitably have befallen them had they spent the night in the barracks' only through the intervention of the British General Knox.[100] In fact, three women were raped, and one committed suicide.[101]

What did the Bolsheviks think of these female troops? In the October revolution, Bolshevik women carried arms. Historically, Russian revolutionary women had not shied away from violent actions, reflected both in the prominence of women in the terrorist movement since the 1870s and in the support given to peasant and working-class attacks on persons and property. Bochkareva's actions, however, the Bolsheviks considered perverse, sustaining the state which oppressed her. Soon after the battalion had been formed, Kollontai pointed out in *Rabotnitsa* that most of the women in Bochkareva's 'battalion of death' were not from the working class, and insisted that their level of political consciousness was extremely low. She believed that reasons for joining the army included misguided patriotism, the desire to avenge the death of a husband, father or brother, and even escape from a failed love affair.[102] They may also have shared Yurlova's sense of adventure, or as *Rabotnitsa* less generously expressed it, 'an obscene and sordid thirst for blood'.[103]

Yet larger numbers of women took part in the October revolution, fighting in the Red Guards (among whom they constituted a minority), serving in their medical brigades (where they were in the majority) and maintaining communications between detachments

98. Figes, *A People's Tragedy*, p. 488.

99. Harold Shukman (ed.), *The Blackwell Encyclopedia of the Russian Revolution* (1988), p. 36.

100. Sir George Buchanan, *My Mission to Russia and Other Diplomatic Memories* (London, 1923), vol. 2, p. 208.

101. See Rozenthal, 'Smertnitsy na fronte'.

102. *Rabotnitsa* (25 June 1917), no. 6, pp. 7–8.

103. Karpetskaia, *Rabotnitsy*, p. 90.

of the Guards.[104] Medical personnel who supported either the Mensheviks or the Socialist Revolutionaries refused to support the Bolsheviks in October. According to John Hutchison's work on public health in revolutionary Russia, leadership in the streets of Petrograd in 1917 was provided by a remarkable feldsher-midwife, T.A. Fortunatova, whose organisation of women workers as stretcher-bearers and medics laid the basis for the Proletarian Red Cross. The female physician V.M. Bonch-Bruevich went on to play a major role in the formulation of Bolshevik health policy after the revolution.[105]

Who were these women who supported the Bolsheviks? Mary McAuley has identified two types of Bolshevik women in 1917. On the one hand there was the woman of the intelligentsia, whom she sees personified by Elena Stasova, who came from a wealthy family with a father in the legal profession. Stasova had joined the party in 1898, and so had nearly two decades of political experience behind her by the time of the revolution. On the other hand, McAuley sees the new, young recruits coming from the working class, exemplified by Klavdia Nikolaeva, a bookbinder and party member since 1909.[106] What of the women who joined the party in 1917? Writing in 1929, William Chamberlain relates the story of a woman born into a poor peasant family, in the province of Tver, who received little formal education. She was sent by her father to work in a textile factory, and then married off by him when she was 18 years of age. She went to St. Petersburg with her husband, and both of them found factory jobs. Her husband died at the front in the First World War, and she became radicalised when the commission for the relief of soldiers' wives refused to help her. After the February revolution, she joined the Bolsheviks, and left the factory to work for the party.[107] It seems, then, that since the revolution of 1905 but especially since 1917, increasing numbers of working-class, white-collar and professional women had joined the Bolsheviks. In contrast, the party's base among the female peasantry, which was already tiny, shrank. The social composition of female membership of the Bolsheviks confirmed the urban nature of the party, which was reinforced between the revolutions of 1905 and 1917, as Table 4.1 confirms.

104. *Zhenshchiny goroda Lenina*, pp. 91–2; Bochkareva, Liubimova, *Svetlyi put'*, p. 95.
105. John F. Hutchison, *Politics and Public Health in Revolutionary Russia, 1890–1918* (Baltimore, 1990), pp. 73, 185.
106. M. McAuley, *Bread and Justice: State and Society in Petrograd 1917–1922* (Oxford, 1991), p. 31.
107. William H. Chamberlain, 'Daughters of the Russian Revolution', *The Yale Review* (June 1929), vol. 18, pp. 732–48.

TABLE 4.1   *The social origins of female Bolsheviks*

	Pre-1917 (%)	1917 (%)
Aristocratic	20	12.2
Intelligentsia	16	25.1
White-Collar	4	15.3
Working-Class	43	45.6
Peasant	5	1.8

Source: *Kommunistka*, 1924, no. 4, pp. 8–10.

Women remained in a minority, however, representing about 10 per cent of the Bolshevik party's membership.[108] An analysis of Bolshevik party members in Moscow has shown that the women tended to be older (on average by four years) than the men, and that the women joined the party at a slightly older age (perhaps by two years), though a working-class female was more likely to join at a younger age than a female intellectual.[109] By far the majority of women who joined the Bolsheviks in 1917 were from towns and cities, while there were more from the educated and professional classes than from the working class. It has been suggested that the fact that female Bolsheviks were generally better educated and of a higher social class than their male comrades may be an indication that rebellion was more difficult for women than for men, because the former had to challenge not only the state but the patriarchal family structure and traditional notions of femininity and women's role.[110] It may be, however, that women postponed joining the party because of the difficulties in combining domestic responsibilities with the commitment demanded by membership. Thus P. Sleptsova, whose husband joined the party in 1918, continued to work in a textile factory while rearing her eight children. She showed some interest in politics, becoming in 1920 a women's delegate and a member of the Moscow soviet. Only in 1930, however, did she join the party.[111]

Yet while female membership of the Bolshevik party had increased after the 1905 revolution, and while there were significantly more

108. *Kommunistka* (1924), no. 4, pp. 8–10.
109. W. Chase, J.A. Getty, 'The Moscow Bolshevik Cadres of 1917: A Prosopographical Analysis', *Russian History* (1978), vol. 5, pp. 84–105: 93–4.
110. Barbara Evans Clements, 'Baba and Bolshevik: Russian Women and Revolutionary Change', *Soviet Union/Union Sovietique* (1985), vol. 12, part 2, pp. 161–84: 167.
111. I. Kor (ed.), *Kak my zhili pri tsare i kak zhivem teper'* (Moscow, 1934), pp. 32–3.

women social democrats (Mensheviks as well as Bolsheviks) than
Socialist Revolutionaries, the female proportion of Bolshevik party
membership fell in the context of a massive influx of men in 1917.
Beate Fieseler's study of Russian female social democrats suggests
that they may have embraced the cause more for personal reasons
than for abstract political ones, though it is unlikely that the latter
lay behind the surge in male working-class membership.[112] In addition, the Menshevik Sukhanov would have queried Fieseler's speculation, given that not only was his wife a Bolshevik of long standing,
but that she had hosted the meeting which had decided to go
ahead with the revolution, having ensured that he would be away
that night.[113] There is also the case of Ekaterina D. Kuskova, whose
attraction to Marxism in the 1890s had been based on ideological
conviction, elements of which she retained when she split from the
social democrats at the end of the century. In the 1905 revolution,
Kuskova worked with the liberal Union of Liberation, and in 1917
she supported the provisional government and collaborated with
the feminists.[114] Still, while Fieseler insists that the achievements of
Marxist women in Russia have to be set within the context of a very
limited range of options open to women in such a patriarchal society, her final comment highlights their essentially subordinate and
supportive role: the women were comrades-in-arms but not in
power.[115]

112. Beate Fieseler, 'The Making of Russian Female Social Democrats, 1890–
1917', *International Review of Social History* (1989), vol. xxxiv, pp. 193–226.
    113. Sukhanov, *The Russian Revolution*, p. 556.
    114. Barbara T. Norton, 'The Making of a Female Social Democrat: E.D. Kuskova's
Conversion to Russian Social Democracy', *International Review of Social History* (1989),
vol. xxxiv, pp. 227–47.
    115. Fieseler, 'The Making of Russian Female Social Democrats, 1890–1917', p. 226.

CHAPTER FIVE

Working Women, Civil War and the New Society, 1918–1930

In a 1928 study of working-class life in Moscow the researcher, E.O. Kabo, related the story of a woman worker who had been an active member of the Bolshevik party since 1913. The daughter and then the wife of a worker, she had been brought up in the city. On completing her primary education at the age of 14, she had spent two years learning how to be a dressmaker, and worked at that trade until she was 20, in 1913. At that age, she took a job in a pipe factory, and joined the Bolshevik party. In 1915, she stopped work in order to devote herself to the party on a full-time basis. After the 1917 revolution, she returned to factory work, which she combined with her party activities. During the civil war, she worked with women in the countryside, returning to Moscow in 1920, when she again entered a factory, this time as a white-collar worker. In 1921, however, she ceased both factory and political work because of her poor health. By 1928, she had become a mother, with two children.[1] The consequences of years of poverty, the impact of the deprivations of the First World War followed by civil war, and the demands of motherhood cut short this Bolshevik woman's political career.

Her life, however, had followed a trajectory common to many working-class Bolsheviks, although fewer women than men, in its journey from wage labourer to political activist to party bureaucrat, taking the revolution to the peasants in 1918, and leaving the work bench for the office at the end of the civil war. Another example would be Razumova, a textile worker from Ivanovo-Voznesensk, who had been active in the 1905 revolution and continued her revolutionary activities clandestinely until the 1917 revolution, when she had been quickly elected as a worker's representative, as she had

---

1. E.O. Kabo, *Ocherki rabochego byta* (Moscow, 1928), p. 112.

been in 1905. After the October revolution, Razumova studied in a party school and worked for a time for the party's central committee. She later returned to Ivanovo-Voznesensk where she was active in the party's women's department, the Zhenotdel.[2] Clearly, some women, especially politically aware urban working-class women, benefited from the revolution. Yet Kabo's subject's career was cut short, at the age of 28.

Kabo's research revealed that women's working life began before men's, sometimes from as early as 7 years old. Again this woman seems unusual, having had six years in school. However, her trade was the typically female one of dressmaking, which she abandoned after four years for better-paid factory work. Perhaps because of her schooling and political activity, she postponed motherhood until she was in her twenties; however, she could not escape the ill health which Kabo saw as general among female workers, especially textile workers, by the time they were in their early thirties, ground down by long years of heavy wage labour and housework and too many pregnancies. Indeed, this woman's health might have suffered from the additional burden of political activity in extremely difficult circumstances, not only of civil war, but of peasant hostility to the Bolsheviks, including the distrust felt by peasant women, especially older women, towards urban female Bolsheviks.[3]

Women and the ABC of Communism

The Bolsheviks renamed themselves the Communist party in 1919. Now in government, they needed a new programme. To accompany this, and to help explain in simple terms complex theory to new party recruits, the *ABC of Communism* was published in 1920 promising a new world, including the end of patriarchy.

> We must not forget that 'every cook has to be taught to take her share in governmental administration'. We have learned above all that the really important matter is not the right which is written on paper, but the possibility of realising a right in practice. How can a

2. *Pervyi Sovet Rabochikh Deputatov* (Yaroslavl', 1971); *Kommunistka* (1920), no. 5, p. 28.
3. See for example Barbara Evans Clements, 'The Effects of the Civil War on Women and Family Relations', in Diane P. Koenker, William G. Rosenberg, Ronald G. Suny (eds), *Party, State and Society in the Russian Civil War* (Bloomington, Ind., 1989), pp. 105–22: 108.

working woman effectively realise her rights when she has to devote so much time to housekeeping, must go to the market and wait her turn there, must do the family washing, must look after the children, must bear the burden of all this domestic drudgery?

The aim of the Soviet Republic and of our party must be, to deliver working women from such slavery, to free the working woman from these obsolete and antediluvian conditions. The organisation of house communes (not places in which people will wrangle, but places in which they will live like human beings) with central wash-houses; the organisation of communal kitchens; the organisation of communal nurseries, kindergartens, playgrounds, summer colonies for children, schools with communal dining rooms, etc. – such are the things which will enfranchise woman, and will make it possible for her to interest herself in all those matters which now interest the proletarian man.

In an era of devastation and famine, it is, of course, difficult to do all these things as they ought to be done. Nevertheless, our party must in this manner do its utmost to attract the working woman to play her part in the communal task.[4]

The new Bolshevik regime was committed to sexual equality in general, and to improving women's position in specific ways. Indeed it was only after the October revolution that there were attempts, for the first time initiated and supported by the authorities, to transform the position of women on a massive scale.[5] Hence it appears that the revolution at least brought formal equality between the sexes, enshrined in law and in the declared intention of the state to base that legal status on a firm social, economic, political and cultural foundation. Moreover, this goal of sexual equality was propounded as an essential, integral part of Bolshevik theory and practice. Kollontai encouraged women to participate in defending the revolution and building the new society not simply for the good of the whole, but to strengthen the specific gains which women had made through the revolution.[6]

However, it was impossible to transform the position of women immediately, given the historical context of centuries of subjugation,

4. N. Bukharin, E. Preobrazhensky, *The ABC of Communism* (1920; Harmondsworth, Middlesex, 1969), pp. 227–8.

5. See A.M. Kollontai, *Rabotnitsa za god revoliutsii* (Moscow, 1918), pp. 22–8; A. Artiukhina *et al.*, *Zhenshchina v revoliutsii* (Moscow, 1959), pp. 187–206; E. Bochkareva, S. Liubimova, *Svetlyi put'* (Moscow, 1967), pp. 68–9; V. Bilshai, *Reshenie zhenskogo voprosa v SSSR* (Moscow, 1956), p. 106; R. Schlesinger, *Changing Attitudes in Soviet Russia: The Family in the USSR* (London, 1949), pp. 75–9.

6. A.M. Kollontai, *Rabotnitsy, krest'ianki i krasnyi front* (Moscow, 1920); F. Halle, *Women in Soviet Russia* (London, 1933), pp. 98–103.

as well as the actual situation of socialist revolution led by a small urban party dominated by intellectuals in an overwhelmingly peasant country, now in the throes of civil war, and under siege from the outside world. The divisions and hierarchies in society as a whole were reflected among Bolshevik women: the female intelligentsia and the few politically conscious women workers led the majority, who were not willing followers. Moreover, despite the fact that some women held important posts in party and state organisations, men predominated at all levels. Occasionally, there are glimpses of an ambitious woman. A.F. Ilyin-Zhenevsky was a member of the Petrograd military commissariat in 1918. His memoir of that first year of Communist power is very much a male affair, with little mention of women apart from his wife and the wives of Red Army officers who came to see him about their rations. The exception is Fanny Borisovna Tartakovskaia, also a party member. She was appointed secretary to the board of the commissariat in 1918. Her main job was to take minutes at its meetings. Ilyin-Zhenevsky had previously done the job, but now found that it occupied too much of his time. It was a job he felt could be entrusted to a loyal party woman. He soon found that Tartakovskaia was such 'an enterprising and energetic' woman that

> Mere recording of the minutes did not satisfy her. Soon she was not just writing down the board's decisions, but she was following up their implementation. She also tried to take over some of my functions, but that did not come off. After some slight friction we demarcated our duties and thereafter we worked together very well.

Eventually Tartakovskaia found a broader and more satisfying field of work for herself. She became a member of the board of a political education sub-department which Ilyin-Zhenevsky's commissariat had just established.[7]

There were efforts to involve more women in politics, to prepare them for positions of responsibility; but any success was limited by the resistance of both women and men. As the American observer Jessica Smith wrote, it would take more than one generation to wear away the layers of superstition and fear fostered through the centuries, and persisting in conditions of material insecurity.[8] In any case, the Bolsheviks had more immediate priorities. In addition, there were the circumstances of everyday life which might combine

7. A.F. Ilyin-Zhenevsky, *The Bolsheviks in Power: Reminiscences of the Year 1918*, translated and annotated by Brian Pearce (Leningrad 1929; London, 1984), pp. 40–1.
8. Jessica Smith, *Women in Soviet Russia* (New York, 1926), p. 34.

to force a woman, more so than a man, out of public life before she was 30 years old.

As far back as 1862, a secret proclamation had demanded the abolition of marriage as a 'highly immoral phenomenon, and one incompatible with the full equality of the sexes'. It had been argued that, in order to free women, the care and education of children must become a function of society.[9] That became the Marxist view of women's emancipation, although no blueprint for family legislation after the revolution had been developed.[10] The primary aim was to abolish the traditional patriarchal institution with its conservatism and links to the despotic past. Yet there was no agreement on how this was to be achieved, or even on what should replace it. What was agreed was that the liberation of women would not be complete until they were relieved of the demands of housework and childcare. In practice, rather than change attitudes towards the division of labour in the home, and persuade men to take an equal share of the work with women, the Communist party from 1918 opted for the development of public services, which they reasoned would take the work out of the home. Some even advocated the total destruction of the family, replacing it with the upbringing of children by the collective. Others placed the hopes for the future on the children, who could act as agents of revolution in their own homes once they had been educated away from the conservative influence of the family. Still others had a less antagonistic view of relations between the family and the state, and believed that it was unrealistic, given the material conditions of scarcity and the political insecurity, to dismantle the family. Moreover, it was essential to win the people to the revolution, rather than risk their continuing resistance by setting the generations against each other. Thus it was not enough for the educational institutions of the state to inculcate revolutionary principles and the collective way of life into the children. It was also essential that parents be trained for their role in the new family, and in particular that special courses be provided to help mothers bring up their children.[11]

Whatever the vision of the future relations between the sexes, there was the reality of civil war which absorbed all energies. In the

9. V. Burtsev, *Za sto let* (London, 1897), p. 43.

10. See B.L. Glass, M.K. Stolee, 'Family Law in Soviet Russia, 1917–1945', *Journal of Marriage and the Family* (Nov. 1987), vol. 49, no. 4, pp. 893–902.

11. See for example A.M. Kollontai, *Sem'ia i kommunisticheskoe gosudarstvo* (Moscow, 1918); B. Sokoloff, *Spasite detei! O detiakh Sovetskoi Rossii* (Prague, 1921); L. Trotsky, *Voprosy byta* (Moscow, 1923); N. Krilenko, *Sem'ia i novyi byt* (Moscow, 1926).

struggle for survival, there developed an extremely functional attitude towards sexual relations. Many comrades made a virtue out of necessity, seeing the civil war, and the policy of 'war communism' which developed during it, as a possible short-cut to the new society. What some might see as the disintegration of traditional sexual relations, others saw as a sexual revolution. According to the Soviet scholar A.G. Kharchev, the civil war led to a sharp decline in the standards of sexual behaviour so that, concerning marital and family relations, the new society had to begin from an even lower level than had existed in tsarist Russia.[12] The civil war had a profound impact on society as well as politics. Every aspect of life was subjected to the military analogy, from Trotsky's call for the militarisation of labour to Kollontai's view of the prostitutes as labour deserters.[13] Kollontai in particular was seen as at least a baleful influence on, if not an agent of, the social and sexual chaos. As the Left Communist Victor Serge wrote of Soviet Russia in the early 1920s:

> Doubtless, sexuality, so long repressed, first by revolutionary asceticism and then by poverty and famine, was beginning to recover its drive in a society which had been abruptly cut off from any kind of spiritual nourishment. Promiscuity fed upon the misery of the environment. Books like those by Alexandra Kollontai propagated an oversimplified theory of free love: an infantile variety of materialism reduced 'sexual need' to its strictly animal connotation. The most sophisticated section of youth, the university students, was discussing Enchmen's theory (contested by Bukharin) on the disappearance of morals in the future Communist society.[14]

Yet it was also the case that there was a significant increase in marriage rates, especially in the cities, during the civil war and into the 1920s.[15] Reasons included the reforms brought in by the Communists which simplified, and secularised, the marriage procedure; many marriages had already been postponed because of the First World War; while marriage to a Red Army soldier entitled a woman to rations. It may also have lent an air of stability to an uncertain age. Of course, in such an unstable situation there was also an apparent breakdown in traditional morality, while politically conscious

12. A.G. Kharchev, *Brak i sem'ia v SSSR* (Moscow, 1964), p. 140.
13. A.M. Kollontai, *Prostitutsiia i mery bor'by s ney* (Moscow, 1921), pp. 22–3.
14. Victor Serge, *Memoirs of a Revolutionary* (London, 1963), translated by Peter Sedgwick, p. 205.
15. See Wesley A. Fisher, *The Soviet Marriage Market: Mate Selection in Russia and the USSR* (New York, 1980), pp. 90–1; Koenker, Rosenberg, Suny, *Party, State and Society*, p. 97, table 3.

urban youth were attracted to Alexandra Kollontai's vision of the 'new woman' and her radical theories of the 'new morality and the working class'.[16]

Kollontai argued that the new morality would have no need for regulatory laws since it would be based on consideration of the other person, and no longer on exclusive possession or mere carnal desire.[17] The new morality would ensure that human beings would be able to relate to someone without the need for possession of that person; that they would come to spurn inequality, to recognise reciprocal rights, and to respect the other's independent personality. In her view, it was wrong to postpone addressing such issues. On the contrary, morality was an intrinsic part of the class struggle, and the problems of sexual relations concerned the working class in its daily life. She firmly believed that the ways in which workers structured their personal relations would have a vital influence on the outcome of the revolution.[18]

Kollontai was not advocating 'free love'. She explicitly denied that her ideas propagated any irresponsible or selfish sexual adventurism. 'I would put it the other way: I was always preaching to woman, make yourself free from the enslavement of love to a man.'[19] Sex without love was wrong in Kollontai's opinion because it did not rise above the level of primitive instinct. Such an act was deemed by her to be the 'wingless eros', incapable of absorbing the full force of the human psyche, a one-dimensional attraction, and ultimately boring physical experience which left only a feeling of dissatisfaction and incompletion. However, in the chaotic period of the civil war, perhaps in response to the severe privations, uncertainty and lack of time to concentrate on personal affairs, sexual relationships tended to be encounters based only on the sexual urge. Kollontai recognised that the effort to save the revolution itself demanded all of people's energy and attention. The immediate demands of the civil war effectively precluded meaningful relations between the sexes.

Certainly it is difficult to assess how voluntary or conscious was the new sexual ethos among urban youth in particular. There were attempts to create a new way of living based on 'free love' and the collective. The Communist youth organisation, the komsomol, insisted that it was revolutionary behaviour to go against all the pre-revolutionary moral norms and principles. Hence marriage and the

16. A.M. Kollontai, *Novaia moral' i rabochii klass* (Moscow, 1918) and her *Sem'ia i kommunisticheskoe gosudarstvo*.

17. Kollontai, *Novaia moral'*, pp. 36–7.   18. Ibid., p. 60.

19. I.D. Palencia, *Alexandra Kollontai* (New York, 1947), p. 19.

family were restrictions on freedom, and institutions which incul-
cated a selfish individualism.[20] Without control over reproduction,
however, and without the adequate material base to provide state
services, there could not be genuine equality between women and
men. This continuing dominance of men in sexual relations was
reflected in a song:

> They say that I am a komsomolka
> But I was not a komsomolka.
> I began going out with a boy from the communist league.
> I became a young communist league girl.[21]

Kollontai's 'new woman' was a creature of developed, urban capitalism, and while she saw the peasant woman as a possible agent for
revolution in the countryside, she assumed that industry was Russia's future. Kollontai looked on the past as a burden of subservient
womanhood, and overlooked the vitality of the peasant family. Nor
did she fundamentally challenge the traditional sexual division of
labour, either within the family or within society as a whole. She
recognised that the hierarchical division between skilled and unskilled, male and female not only favoured men at the expense of
women but tended to undermine people's, and especially women's,
control over their everyday lives. Yet whereas Kollontai was fully
aware of women's 'double burden' of housework and childrearing
on top of paid employment outside the home, she seemed to assume
that it would be women who would staff the public institutions
providing childcare and services. Certainly, this was a means of
immediately utilising women and giving them a positive role in
building the new society, as well as recognising that there were
skills in the previously undervalued work of the household. However, it also reinforced the view of certain work as predominantly
'women's work'.

In addition, Kollontai and the Communist party in general saw
motherhood as an innate, natural instinct, almost a sacred duty.
Again, there was a gain for women here, in the recognition of the
dignity and value of motherhood. On the other hand, there was a
suspicion of contraception. Kollontai wrote that in the place of the
slogan of voluntary limitation of the birth rate, the working class
would see only the slogan of greater protection of maternity. She
claimed that in the new society, workers should not hesitate or be

20. V.I. Chekalin, *Liubov' i sem'ia* (Vilnius, 1970), pp. 18–36; P.M. Chirkov, *Reshenie zhenskogo voprosa v SSSR, 1917–1939gg.* (Moscow, 1978), pp. 197–207.
21. Y.M. Sokolov, *Russian Folklore* (1938; Detroit, 1971), p. 641.

afraid to have children, for in doing so they ensured the survival and development of their state. Moreover, the workers' state needed new members, and welcomed the arrival of every new baby born into it.[22] Contraception was an aspect of selfish, capitalist individualism. Thus in Kollontai's view, with the state carrying the burden of childbearing and childrearing, the woman would be able to combine work for the collective with the satisfaction both of personal fulfilment and of playing an honourable and vital social role through giving birth.

There was, therefore, a failure to recognise that the woman's lack of control over her fertility worked against sexual equality. Still, the new Communist regime was the first to legalise abortion. The 1920 measure was seen as one of expediency, necessary in social and medical terms, but a temporary evil. It was assumed that when conditions improved and the cultural level rose, the widespread need for abortion would diminish. That was very much a long-term hope. It was observed that for women workers in the mid 1920s

> the fact of motherhood makes it impossible for most of them to spend as many years in industry as men do. Women's wages consequently average less than those of men, and were only 62 per cent of the latter in March 1926. This shows that motherhood and the care of children are factors which make women's wages less than those of men.[23]

Besides these factors, sexual equality was inhibited by the social instability in the wake of the civil war. As one sympathetic foreign visitor to Russia in 1925 wrote:

> In the early stages of the revolution the most trifling squabbles led to divorce, although this did not lead to moral disintegration. Contrary to the spicy gossip columns of the anti-bolshevik press, promiscuity was rare in the early years of the revolution . . . In fact, people were too absorbed in the new tasks to have much time for what was called 'personal life'. Cold and hunger did not predispose one to it either . . . The men appeared to be the main beneficiaries of the loosened divorce and marriage regulations and they played havoc with their women.[24]

In her study of Russian women in this period, Anne Bobroff contends that although thousands of women workers had participated

22. Kollontai, *Sem'ia i kommunisticheskoe gosudarstvo*, p. 17.
23. S. Chase, R. Dunn, R.G. Tugwell (eds), *Soviet Russia in the First Decade* (London, 1929), p. 221.
24. Rosa Levine-Meyer, *Inside German Communism* (London, 1977), p. 100. See also V. Bystransky, *Kommunizm, brak i sem'ia* (Petrograd, 1921), pp. 64–5.

in the revolutions of 1917, with a few going on to hold positions in the new government, their situation did not improve appreciably over that of tsarist times. She quotes from a woman worker who complained in the 1920s that: 'Our position in many respects remains difficult and unenviable. The kitchen, children, washtubs with laundry, work in the factory – this is our world from which few have leapt to freedom.'[25]

Women and the civil war, 1918–1920

Writing in 1920, the prominent female Communist Konkordia Samoilova acknowledged that, with the exception of the minority of politically aware women workers, most could not understand why there was civil war at all. Indeed, at first they thought that it was the soviets which were waging war, and only gradually did they realise that it had been forced on them by the counter-revolutionaries. Samoilova related how women workers in Petrograd dug trenches around the city, erected defences of wire and bags of sand, maintained communications between local headquarters, and carried arms in the militia, determined to save the city from the advancing counter-revolutionary armies. These women organised to locate and distribute scarce sources of food and fuel, making sure that the cities were fed. Women worked in munitions, and produced uniforms for the Red Army. Women workers also set up groups of Red Army Sisters of Charity to tend to the wounded at the front. Others went to the front not only as nurses but as political commissars who taught basic literacy and disseminated propaganda among the soldiers. Some served as scouts, some as organisers of army supplies.[26]

During the second city conference of women workers in May 1919, Petrograd was attacked by the counter-revolutionary army of General Yudenich. In response all the women delegates at this conference went to the front. When Yudenich attacked again in October, women workers set up their own headquarters in the city to co-ordinate its defence. Each district had its own women's 'fighting cell', numbering between 140 and 300 women. These fighting women worked in all aspects of defence, including handling a variety of weapons such as machine guns and mortars, as well as digging

25. Anne Bobroff, 'Russian Working Women: Sexuality in Bonding Patterns and the Politics of Daily Life', in Ann Snitow, Christine Stansell, Sharon Thompson (eds), *Powers of Desire: The Politics of Sexuality* (New York, 1983), pp. 206–27: 207.
26. K. Samoilova, *Rabotnitsa v rossisskoi revoliutsii* (Moscow, 1920), pp. 10–14.

trenches, serving in communications, and taking care of the dead and wounded. Women raised funds for the war effort, sewed underwear and knitted socks for the Red Army. Women workers would also collect and send gifts to the soldiers at the front, such as tobacco, sweets, penknives and books. They printed party propaganda on cigarette paper so that the soldiers could smoke after reading![27]

Kollontai estimated in October 1920 that around 1,850 female Red Army personnel, from a total of 66,000, had either been killed or taken prisoner.[28] There were many more female front-line fighters in the Red Army than in the First World War, but still the majority of women at the front in the civil war were in support roles, including medical, educational (enlightenment), political and administrative.[29] The non-combatant women tended to be of a higher social status than the soldiers, and to be regarded by the latter as delicate, urban ladies. Their task was essentially to make themselves redundant by teaching male peasant and working-class recruits basic literacy skills and political concepts, with the result that after the civil war the army's political commissariat became male dominated.

Certainly, few women remained in the Red Army once the war was over. However, in whatever capacity women had served at or supported the front they were recognised to have a higher political consciousness than was the norm among women, and were drawn into party work after the war. One example was Pelagheia Kholodova, a factory worker who had participated in strikes before 1917, had been one of the first women to raise the red banner durng the October revolution, and who in the early 1920s became director of a factory employing 3,000 people. Another example was the textile worker Kalyghina, who had been a member of the Bolshevik party since 1915, had been active in both the October revolution and the civil war, and had then become one of the first women to chair a regional soviet.[30]

Few working-class women reached such positions of responsibility in either politics or the economy. Still, the wars since 1914, and particularly the civil war, had shown that women could play vital

27. Ye.D. Emel'ianova, *Revoliutsiia, partiia, zhenshchina* (Smolensk, 1971), pp. 120–2.

28. *Kommunistka* (1920), no. 5, p. 159.

29. See A.R. Bogat, *Rabotnitsa i krest'ianka v Krasnoi Armii* (Moscow, Leningrad, 1928).

30. *Vsegda s vami: sbornik, posviashchennyi 50-letiiu zhurnala 'Rabotnitsa'* (Moscow, 1964), p. 144. Like so many other 'old Bolsheviks', Kalyghina was a victim of Stalin's purges in the 1930s.

military as well as economic roles in the defence of the state. Thus fear of further foreign intervention in 1927, when relations with Britain sharply deteriorated, led to calls on women workers to consider military training, not only as army nurses but as cavalrywomen, riflewomen and machinegunners, and in anti-aircraft defence. The majority of women were still expected to produce supplies for the armed forces and serve as the last line of defence at home, and much stress was placed on women workers raising funds to build aircraft in 1927 (giving the aeroplanes such names as 'the woman worker', 'the woman delegate', 'the housewife'). Nevertheless, there were many articles on military heroines of the civil war. There were also accounts of potential heroines, in the shape of female air pilots and commanders of army and naval units, which were first published in 1926, not only reflecting technological developments since the Communists had come to power, but implying vast improvements in the position of women in terms of education, training and employment opportunities.[31]

Yet another aspect of this development was the militarisation of life in post-revolutionary Russia, reflected in the way in which male Communist party leaders (though not Lenin) dressed, and in the use of military metaphors and images all of which conveyed a relatively straightforward and attainable (at least for younger workers) masculine ideal to complement Kollontai's 'new woman'. In practice, however, the Communist multi-faceted feminine ideal meant a double burden of paid and domestic work in conditions of continuing and severe shortages of goods and services, but with new pressures for active participation in public life.[32] Perhaps it was not so much women's low political consciousness which led them to try to keep the Communist party at arm's length, but rather their exhaustion.

Samoilova's pamphlet of 1920, *Women and the Russian Revolution*, on the part played by women in the revolution and civil war, reflected both the importance the Communists now placed on urban working-class women, and the continuing need to remind women as well as men that they had a further, key role to play in building the new society. Women, particularly factory workers, certainly responded positively, but the majority remained either indifferent or hostile. There was widespread fear that the Communists would

31. Ibid., p. 143.
32. See Eric D. Weitz, 'The Heroic Man and the Ever-Changing Woman: Gender Politics in European Communism, 1917–1950', in Laura L. Frader and Sonya O. Rose (eds), *Gender and Class in Modern Europe* (Ithaca, NY, 1996), ch. 13, p. 351.

nationalise women and abolish the family. Hence the Communist party insisted that the government was pledged to ease the lives of working mothers by providing social services which, rather than destroying, would enhance family life and ensure women equality with their husbands. Indeed, despite her radical theories, Kollontai recognised that, given the circumstances of civil war, it was unclear to women workers and peasants, who were not in the direct line of fire but were suffering severe privations caused by the struggle, just where their interests lay.[33] What Kollontai tried to do, through her agitational pamphlets, was to show women that they had a vested interest in, and a crucial contribution to make to, the victory of the Red Army and survival of the Soviet state. She believed that only through their active participation could women retain the rights so dearly won, and develop them when the situation improved. She attempted to explain, in simple terms, that being equal with men meant that women had to struggle equally with them, as comrades. She returned continually to addressing women in her agitational work, viewing their education and the raising of their consciousness as vital. Hence her pamphlets asserted that women stood to lose most if the Communists were defeated, claiming that it was in capitalism's interests that women remained oppressed by their double burden of wage-earning and domestic labour. She claimed that the capitalists realised that if women turned to the political struggle and took part in public life, capitalism would be deprived of its last stronghold in the working class.[34]

Soviet Russia, according to Kollontai, had at least shaken the basis of the traditional family. The revolution had given women their fundamental right of equality with men. The 'new woman' was being created: an active fighter for the interests of her class. In Kollontai's view, woman was being transformed from a docile creature into a political being.[35] She regretted that the Communist party, distracted by the struggle for survival, had not yet recognised the significance of the 'reserve army' of women for the revolution, and so still did not utilise them systematically in constructing the life of the Soviet state.[36] Nevertheless, the Communist party had called an All-Russian Congress of Women in 1918, to which over a thousand women came as delegates. However low the educational level, the 1918 congress showed that work among women was possible on a large scale. A year later, Zhenotdel, the party's women's

33. Kollontai, *Rabotnitsy, krest'ianki i krasnyi front*, p. 11.   34. Ibid, pp. 16–17.
35. A.M. Kollontai, *Za tri goda* (Moscow, 1920), p. 6.   36. Ibid., pp. 8, 11.

department, had been set up to carry out propaganda and agitation among women.[37] During the civil war, under the leadership of Inessa Armand until her death in 1920 and of Alexandra Kollontai until her fall from political favour in 1922, Zhenotdel concentrated on winning the support of women for the Red Army and the party. Zhenotdel adopted the tactic of trying to reach those women who were not organised either by trade unions or the party, both housewives and certain categories of workers employed outside factories.[38] During the famine of 1920–21, it focused on relief work.[39] However, the women's department was not simply a Communist version of pre-revolutionary feminist philanthropy. It sought above all to raise women's political consciousness and to make them active participants in the defence of the revolution in their own right, and on a massive scale, in the knowledge that they had the support of the state. At the same time, women were still being drawn into work which was traditionally regarded as in the female sphere. Their low levels of literacy and job skills narrowed their choice of occupation. In response, Zhenotdel had sections attached to every level of the party, to factory committees, soviets and trade unions, so that women could gain practical experience. Thus, although Zhenotdel organised in neighbourhoods, it concentrated on women in their place of work.[40]

Although they came up against condescension, hostility and even outright opposition from many male comrades, Zhenotdel delegates were nevertheless involved in general party work. From its inception, Zhenotdel organisers travelled all over Russia into the villages as well as the towns, educating women in literacy, health and childcare. The women's sections, with delegates of workers, peasants and housewives, met twice a month with a trained party member whose task was to teach them their new legal rights, deepen their understanding, and prepare them to take part fully in building the socialist society. Zhenotdel published simply worded magazines addressed specifically to women. It also set up day-care and eating facilities, and

37. For the work done by the women's department in the 1920s, see Carol Eubanks Hayden, 'The *Zhenotdel* and the Bolshevik Party', *Russian History* (1976), vol. 3, no. 2, pp. 156–73; Richard Stites, '*Zhenotdel*: Bolshevism and Russian Women, 1917–1930', ibid., pp. 174–93.

38. *Kommunistka* (June–July 1920), nos. 1–2, p. 31.

39. Bochkareva, Liubimova, *Svetly put'*, pp. 68–78; A.M. Kollontai, *Rabotnitsa i krest'ianka v Sovetskoi Rossii* (Petrograd, 1921), pp. 6–7; L. Katasheva, *Natasha: A Bolshevik Woman Organiser* (London, 1934).

40. See Elizabeth A. Wood, 'Class and Gender at Loggerheads in the Early Soviet State: Who Should Organize the Female Proletariat and How?', in *Gender and Class in Modern Europe*, ch. 12, p. 298.

organised housewives into consumer and producer co-operatives. The delegates who gained this experience were expected to pass it on to the women whom they represented.[41] However radical Kollontai's writings on the woman question were, the women's department avoided anything controversial, such as talk of the abolition of the family, and concentrated instead on winning the support of ordinary women, rural and urban, for the Communist regime, with its promises not of an abstract equality with men, but of practical help such as social services, education and training, which the party argued would ease, in time, their double burden. When head of Zhenotdel, Kollontai herself acknowledged this tactic as the only sensible one:

> Firstly we had to win their confidence before we could say to them: 'Look, you have children who tie you down. Would it not be a good thing to have creches for the children?' Working women are interested in that kind of thing, whereas they are left cold by Communism. They will put up with us Bolsheviks only if we give them practical help.[42]

Thus the party's focus was on practical work which would draw in ordinary women, such as setting up crèches, communal canteens, departments for safety at work.[43] There was considerable success: by 1923, there were 30,000 women in the Communist party, of whom 62 per cent were from the working class, compared to 8 per cent from the upper class, 14 per cent from the intelligentsia, 11 per cent from the peasantry and 4 per cent from the white-collar sector.[44] Zhenotdel hoped that these women would serve both as role models for, and as propagandists among, other women workers. Barbara Clements, however, points out that more Communist women chose to work in the education department than in the women's department.[45] Rather than simply a rejection of work among women, this might have been a return to the practice of the 1880s of educating women as a necessary step towards their liberation. At any rate, by 1928 the women's department had offices in every region of the Soviet Union.

41. Chirkov, *Reshenie zhenskogo voprosa v SSSR*, pp. 53–67; Smith, *Women in Soviet Russia*, pp. 48–60.
42. Kollontai, *Rabotnitsa i krest'ianka v Sovetskoi Rossii*, p. 32.
43. *Kommunistka* (1923), no. 11, p. 19.
44. *Kommunistka* (1924), no. 4, pp. 8–10.
45. Barbara Evans Clements, 'Baba and Bolshevik: Russian Women and Revolutionary Change', *Soviet Union/Union Sovietique* (1985), vol. 12, part 5, pp. 161–84: 171.

However, in the immediate post-revolutionary period, with the rapidly deteriorating situation caused by the civil war, there was little time to devote to that educational aim, or even to give much thought to what would constitute sexual equality under Communism. As millions of men were recruited and conscripted into the Red Army and state service, more women were needed to staff the factories and government offices, schools and hospitals, day nurseries and public dining halls. By 1920, women constituted 65 per cent of Petrograd's labour force, outwith the military and political sectors; in heavy industry, the pre-war male stronghold, women now made up 46 per cent of the workforce. Yet that higher percentage masked a fall in numbers, which reflected the flight from the cities in search of food: in 1920, there were 434,000 women in heavy industry, which was around half of the 1917 figure (881,000).[46] Writing in 1923, a female textile worker, Fat'ianova, described the severe conditions under which she and her comrades laboured in a Moscow factory during the civil war:

> After the revolution it was only workers who stayed on in the factory. . . . We decided to fight in defence of our factory, which wasn't shut down. We used to work at least three days a week and the rest of the week we would search for fuel for both the factory and our own homes. There was a grove around the factory which we stripped so bare for fuel that it didn't exist at the end of the war.
>
> When a consignment of fuel and food got stuck on the road we would come to its rescue. We would harness ourselves and pull it to the factory gates. . . . The same story was true for the crèche. When it opened it was meant for 75 children. All the equipment and food we regularly had to supply ourselves. At night we would make bedlinen and clothes for the crèche. . . .
>
> You could say that we carried the revolution on our shoulders. And we didn't give in! No matter how hard it was we defended our factory. And since those days, [the factory] has become extremely important to our lives.[47]

Thus civil war left civilians having to cope with the social dislocation which it caused, including food and fuel shortages, refugees, child abandonment and rampant prostitution. The latter two were related, and reflected a general increase in the level of juvenile crime, which had been evident before 1914 but had accelerated under the impact of world war and civil war. Such homeless, abandoned children, known as *besprizorniki*, were numbered in the

46. Chirkov, *Reshenie zhenskogo voprosa v SSSR*, pp. 158, 117.
47. *Vsegda s vami*, pp. 138–9.

millions by the end of the latter conflict.[48] With the Communist preference for communal childcare, there was no incentive to adopt such children; but since the new regime had to expend the bulk of its scarce resources on the military conflict, there was little left for public services. Moreover, there was a struggle between two government departments, the People's Commissariat of Enlightenment (education) and the People's Commissariat of Public Health, for jurisdiction over the problem. Thus, dealing with the children and youth on a practical level (providing them with food and shelter, clothes and medical treatment) was left to the teachers and to Zhenotdel. Hence women's traditional domestic skills were harnessed to deal with an enormous demographic problem which affected the cities in particular, and with which few working people had much sympathy, since they were often the targets of juvenile crime. However, with the authorities wavering between treating *besprizornost* as a social problem or an anti-social crime, many of the children preferred to remain on the streets rather than enter a state institution. In her study of this issue Jennie Stevens quotes a song popular among these homeless children:

> Long forgotten and abandoned
> From early, early years,
> I was left a tiny orphan
> And my lot was grief and tears.
>
> And perhaps they will arrest me
> And shoot me to the ground
> Not a soul will remember
> Where my little grave is found.[49]

Famine exacerbated the social disruption caused by years of military conflict. Moreover, severe food shortage was accompanied by epidemics. Thus in the winter of 1919–20, there was an influenza epidemic followed by a typhus epidemic in central European Russia, which one female physician, V.N. Povalishina, described as a 'nightmare'. In practice, many in the medical profession had opposed the October revolution. In her study of Petrograd during the civil war, Mary McAuley has shown that in contrast to the city's male-dominated profession numbering over 2,000 in 1914, by 1921

48. Jennie A. Stevens, 'Children of the Revolution: Soviet Russia's Homeless Children (*Besprizorniki*) in the 1920s', *Russian History/Histoire Russe* (1982), parts 2–3, pp. 242–64: 246. See also B. Madison, 'Russia's Illegitimate Children Before and After the Revolution', *Slavic Review* (Mar. 1963), vol. xxii, no. 1, pp. 82–95; V. Zenzinov, *Deserted: The Story of the Children Abandoned in Soviet Russia* (London, 1931).

49. Stevens, 'Children of the Revolution', p. 255, and note 57.

there were only 950 physicians, half of whom were women.[50] The situation was worse in the countryside. However, the severe threats to public health which faced the country during the civil war, the fact that medical personnel were accorded greater rations in conditions of severe shortage, where money ceased to exist, and that private practice was frowned upon, were all incentives to enter state service. Povalishina, moreover, was in the tradition of service to the people discussed in Chapter 2. She worked in a rural hospital in the Moscow province. She recalled the experience of the 1920 epidemic, and the difficulties she encountered in dealing with such widespread illnesses in the conditions of civil war. Peasants in her district had to travel long distances to procure bread in the grain-producing areas, only to find on their return that their villages were inundated with people fleeing the famine in the city. She therefore had to cope with a swollen population without even the most basic supplies of medicine, let alone food and fuel. One mother brought a lamp from home so that her daughter might die in a little comfort. In 1920, the number of beds in Povalishina's hospital had to be cut from 50 to ten, and of staff from 34 to 20; they had rations for ten patients, but were treating up to 30. Four nurses died of typhoid. Overall, this hospital, with two doctors (one female, and one male), two feldshers (one female and one male), and a midwife served 22,000 people. With help from the local population, the hospital survived for eighteen months. Nor were shortages simply due to the war. Povalishina complained that the government bureaucracy added to their problems.[51]

This growth of bureaucracy worried many of the leading Communists, including Kollontai. The revolution had promised workers' control of production, but the civil war had led to the re-establishment of managerial authority; the widespread use of specialists from the old order who were offered the incentive of privileges so attractive in times of scarcity; wage incentives which disappointed the hopes for egality and served to undermine working-class solidarity (and reinforced the inferior position of women since incentives usually pertained only in male-dominated industries); the insistence on labour discipline; and the all-pervasive centralisation which was inimical to any kind of shop-floor democracy. Fearing that the revolution was choking in a fog of directives from

50. Mary McAuley, *Bread and Justice: State and Society in Petrograd 1917–1922* (Oxford, 1991), p. 278.

51. V.N. Povalishina, *Tridtsat' let kul'turnoi raboty uchastkovogo vracha v derevne* (Moscow, 1925), pp. 19–20.

above, Kollontai became a leading supporter of the Workers' Opposition in 1920, whose manifesto she wrote. The Workers' Opposition believed that the Communist party was losing touch with the working class in whose name it held power. In its determination to defend the revolution and hold on to power, the Communist party had established, in essence, rule by administrative decree and summary justice. The resulting bureaucracy was characterised by a pervasive and often brutal arrogance. Kollontai felt that the regime's attempt to manipulate discipline and enthusiasm in the struggle for survival was destroying the spontaneity of the working class.

Yet however trenchant her criticism of the bureaucracy, Kollontai's call for workers' control would hardly have helped women in the 1920s, let alone in 1917. The revolution in 1917 had stimulated a widespread movement of workers taking control of their factories through their trade unions, factory committees and soviets. Owners and managers simply disappeared, leaving their employees, they hoped, to realise the indispensability of the former masters. Whereas the authorities came to accept that managers and specialists were indeed necessary for the running of industry in such an emergency as civil war, workers were highly resentful of their return. At the same time, what shop-floor democracy and workers' control meant in practice was by no means obvious; but while most accounts of this period focus on struggles between factory committees, trade unions and the Communist party, what is clear is that women workers played little if any part. Indeed, given their position in both the workforce and the organisations of their class, it was not clear that women workers would benefit from a victory of the Workers' Opposition. As will be discussed below, old attitudes towards women continued to be held by male workers, reflected in a proverb printed in *Rabotnitsa* in 1928: 'a hen will never become a cockerel, a woman will never become a man'.[52]

The death rate during the civil war was higher among fighting men than among women and children, but besides the epidemics and famine, sexual diseases were prevalent among the population at large. Indeed, as pointed out above, many women and children resorted to prostitution, out of desperation caused by having to flee the conflict, losing homes, unemployment or wages too low for subsistence, and abandonment. At the same time, women dominated the urban labour market during the civil war, with increasing numbers

52. *Vsegda s vami*, p. 144. See also Barbara Evans Clements, 'Kollontai's Contribution to the Workers' Opposition', *Russian History* (1975), vol. 11, no. 2, pp. 191–206.

moving into offices, while there was a decline in domestic service. Despite essential wartime manufactures, industry effectively collapsed during the civil war, while the state increasingly took control of the economy. Those with clerical or book-keeping skills clearly benefited by the expansion of state service. Nevertheless, in general women tended to remain in the same sectors as before the revolution: textiles and clothing (now augmented by the manufacture of Red Army uniforms), food and tobacco.

The Communist party had taken power as an urban party representing the working class in a country which was predominantly peasant. The revolution weakened, in some cases fatally, all the previous authorities which had oppressed the peasantry, while the peasant family was greatly strengthened and the traditional way of farming was reinvigorated. Moreover, the civil war often cut off the village from the city, forcing the former to be increasingly self-sufficient, not only in terms of farming but of crafts, while the cities suffered such serious shortages that thousands left in search of food. Men were more likely to leave the cities than women as the former were more likely to have maintained links with the family farm. As Povalishina noted, such incomers were not always welcomed. The same can be said about the representatives of the government who went to the villages on propaganda visits, including the Zhenotdel delegates, whose meetings the vast majority of peasant women shunned throughout the civil war.[53] This may partly have been due to male disapproval of the potential Communist influence on women. Thus peasant men often put pressure on women at soviet or commune meetings, either through curses or ridicule.[54] In 1919 a prominent Communist party leader, Grigorii Zinoviev, compared relations between male and female peasants as a form of serfdom, in which the former assumed that they were a kind of special estate which refused to consider peasant women as equals.[55] Yet it was not simply a case of female passivity in the face of the exertion of patriarchal power. Kollontai had identified the female peasantry as an agent of revolution in the countryside. In practice, however, peasant women themselves remained deeply suspicious of the Communist party, resisting attempts to persuade them to vote in soviet elections.[56] A major reason was fear of Communist ideas about the family and childrearing, and a susceptibility to rumours of 'nationalisation' of

53. See for example *Kommunistka* (1921), nos. 11–12, pp. 40–1.
54. See for example *Kommunistka* (1922), no. 1, pp. 24–5, nos. 8–9, p. 35.
55. G. Zinoviev, *Rabotnitsa, krestianka i Sovetskaia vlast* (Petrograd, 1919), p. 16.
56. See for example *Kommunistka* (1924), no. 4, pp. 14–15.

women and children.[57] Even before the Bolsheviks had seized power, peasant antipathy had been obvious, reflected in the following letter to a party paper directed at the armed forces, recounting the experience of a visit to a small town by a Bolshevik soldier:

> The degree to which Bolsheviks are mistrusted became clear to me through a number of incidents which I witnessed myself. For example, one of my comrades – a sailor from the Guards – arrived in his home village for a break. The villagers found out that he was a Bolshevik, and during the first distribution of soldiers' rations, all the soldiers' wives unanimously demanded that his wife should not receive any. Luckily for that poor woman, the committee did not comply with their demand, but this unfortunate woman is still continuously reproached, while her husband is accused of selling himself to [kaiser] Wilhelm. The second incident is no less interesting. A street-trader, a woman by the name of Rotsiborskaia, ran through the streets declaring with fear in her voice that two Leninites had arrived . . . and in all probability plundering of the shops would soon start. I had difficulty in calming down that frightened woman.[58]

Rotsiborskaia would have been particularly afraid because any money which she earned from specifically female crafts (discussed in Chapter 2) was traditionally regarded as the peasant woman's private property, which rumours of nationalisation threatened. This impression may have been reinforced by the civil war experience of the state forcibly taking grain from unwilling peasants in order to feed the Red Army and the cities. Moreover, peasant women with extended families saw no benefit in doing their traditional household tasks communally, and feared that their children would be lured away from the village by the urban Communists. There was recognition that there was little socialised childcare in the countryside, and instead of state provision, peasant women were encouraged to help themselves by learning how to set up crèches.[59] Thus the Communists had little to offer peasant women in the post-revolutionary period, apart from promises, hope and exhortations. Indeed, the most tangible benefit which the Communist regime offered peasant women was the divorce legislation, which led to the break-up of a minority of households and the irony of the Zhenotdel supporting the rights of village women to private property.[60] However, for the

57. See for example *Kommunistka* (1921), nos. 12–13, p. 67.
58. *Soldat* (1 Oct. 1917), no. 40.
59. A.S. Kurskaia (ed.), *Zhenshchina nachinaet zhit' po-novomu* (Moscow, 1925), p. 36.
60. Schlesinger, *Changing Attitudes in Soviet Russia: The Family in the USSR*, pp. 147–51.

majority of peasants, female and male, divorce was deeply unsettling to the traditional way of life and work, and was yet another alien urban imposition. On the one hand, the instability of the civil war enhanced the value of traditional institutions for peasant women; on the other, it left many among them, notably soldiers' wives and widows, with heavy burdens, particularly if they were the family's main breadwinner.[61] Yet even these women would often not describe themselves as Communists.[62] Hence the concentration by Zhenotdel on practical rather than ideological aspects of the improvement in the conditions of working women. What is clear is that while the majority of peasant women did not actively support the Communists, a minority, made up of those women who might be seen as on the margins of village life (such as single women in charge of households), were more susceptible to the party's appeal. The sometimes hostile and generally unhelpful treatment they received from the villagers, however, would serve as a basis for conflict when their men returned from the front line.[63]

Women and the New Economic Policy

Krupskaia argued that although not every woman could participate in the civil war, each one was needed to play an active part in the construction of the new society.[64] However, it was to be built on a foundation of an economy and a society shattered after seven years of war and a recent devastating famine. The Communists adopted the New Economic Policy (NEP) in March 1921. NEP saw the end of grain requisitioning which had so alienated the villages during the civil war that at the end of 1920 there had been massive peasant risings against the Communist regime in the Tambov province. NEP also brought relaxation of tight restrictions on private enterprise and trading, especially in light industry and services, and labour regulations. NEP was intended to promote the recovery of agriculture and industry and to heal rifts within the Communist party itself. Economic recovery was essential not simply to appease the peasantry and unify the party, but because there had even been resistance,

61. See for example *Kommunistka* (1921), nos. 12–13, pp. 66–7.

62. *Kommunistka* (1923), no. 6, p. 39.

63. Beatrice Farnsworth, 'Village Women Experience the Revolution', in Beatrice Farnsworth, Lynne Viola (eds), *Russian Peasant Women* (Oxford, 1992), ch. 8; this essay is also found in Abott Gleason, Peter Kenez and Richard Stites (eds), *Bolshevik Culture* (Bloomington, Ind., 1985), ch. 14.

64. N.K. Krupskaia, *Izbrannye proizvedeniia* (Moscow, 1988), p. 65.

including strikes caused by severe shortages of food, fuel and consumer goods and appalling working conditions, from the very people whom the Communists claimed to represent, the urban workers.[65] NEP might be seen as lasting until the end of the decade, replaced by Stalin's adoption of the five-year plan for industry and the forced collectivisation of agriculture.

The end of the civil war saw a drop in demand for female labour: by 1921, women made up 35 per cent of factory workers, whereas by 1924 their share of that workforce had dropped to around 25 per cent; three years later that percentage had risen by only 1.4.[66] In terms of the labour force as a whole, the percentage of female workers fell slightly between 1923 (when it stood at 29.5 per cent) and 1927 (28.5 per cent).[67] One interpretation of this fall in female employment is that it simply reflected an end to the wartime emergency, which had artificially inflated the numbers of women workers. What these percentages and figures also reflect is the problem of persistent, high unemployment during the period of the NEP.

What is not so immediately apparent is that unemployment hurt women more than men. In 1922 women made up between 55 and 60 per cent of the unemployed overall, but in some regions that rate was higher: for example, in the region of Tver women constituted 66 per cent of the unemployed, while in the city of Tver they were as much as 69 per cent.[68] In July 1924, women made up 45.3 per cent of the unemployed, and while the absolute percentage of those out of work dropped, that of women actually increased. Workers with high qualifications, the majority of whom were men, were in demand, but even if women were skilled, they would still be laid off first. Though wages for women workers were lower than for men, employers deemed the former more expensive due to the time women took off work because of the demands of household responsibilities.[69] Thus women tended to hold on to a job, however low paid, whereas men were more willing, and had more opportunity, to change employment in search of higher wages.

In addition, Communist protective legislation closed off many jobs to women. This led *Kommunistka*, the theoretical journal aimed

65. See S. Fitzpatrick, A. Dallin and R. Stites (eds), *Russia in the Era of NEP: Explorations in Soviet Society and Culture* (Bloomington, Ind., 1991); Alan Ball, *Russia's Last Capitalists: The Nepmen, 1921–29* (Berkeley, Calif., 1988).

66. *Kommunistka* (Apr. 1924), no. 4, p. 45. See also K.N. Kovalev, *Istoricheskoe razvitie byta zhenshchiny, braka i sem'i* (Moscow, 1931).

67. A.G. Kharchev, *Zhenskii trud v SSSR* (Moscow, 1928), p. 52.

68. Emel'ianova, *Revoliutsiia, partiia, zhenshchina*, p. 128.

69. *Kommunistka* (May 1925), no. 5, pp. 39–42.

at the female working class, to call for labour regulations, particularly those which prevented women from working night shifts (which in practice were frequently flouted), to be revised. It recognised that the regulations were not always observed, and insisted that in their present form they served to discriminate against women, especially those who were pregnant or had young children. Indeed, it was pointed out that there was no list of occupations forbidden to women, but simply an article in the labour regulations which made it impossible for them to find work in certain areas which were considered harmful to a woman's reproductive system.[70] *Kommunistka* disputed the claim that maternity leave cost the employer anything but the inconvenience of finding a replacement for the woman. It acknowledged that employers resented having to give women time to breastfeed their babies, but pointed out that all it amounted to was two half-hour breaks each day for seven months, which was a tiny percentage of time 'lost' at work.[71]

Hence *Kommunistka* insisted that trade unions should have a duty to help women workers improve their qualifications.[72] For every 100 women workers, only 25 per cent were skilled and 21.7 per cent were semi-skilled, whereas 53.3 per cent were unskilled.[73] A survey of 1,300 workers in March 1923 revealed that among qualified workers, only 16.6 per cent were women; and although the percentage of women was considerably higher (36.9) among the semi-qualified, it was even higher (42.6) among the unqualified.[74] Zhenotdel argued that as long as the situation in which the majority of women workers remained without skills continued, the state would face the social problems of high rates of prostitution and of homeless and abandoned children, while sexual equality would remain illusory. Given their low educational levels, how were women to be trained? It was felt that much of it would have to be done in the factories, both at the workbench and in factory schools, during working hours and in a woman's spare time.

Zhenotdel worked with trade unions to register unemployed women at labour exchanges, and help them find new jobs. One way of achieving the latter was to set up co-operatives, not only for crafts such as sewing and lacemaking, but for women who would work in kitchen gardens, as cleaners, and in canteens. Zhenotdel also established hostels for homeless women and children, and canteens for the unemployed. Although Zhenotdel co-operated with

70. *Kommunistka* (Apr. 1925), no. 4, pp. 45–51.   71. Ibid., pp. 47–8.   72. Ibid.
73. Ibid., p. 46.   74. Emel'ianova, *Revoliutsiia, partiia, zhenshchina*, p. 130.

trade unions, the latter also tried to ensure that their members, predominantly men, suffered the fewest job losses, which helps explain the fact that the number of unemployed women grew faster than that of men. In Moscow, Zhenotdel managed to get women onto the commission which decided redundancies, but they remained in a minority.[75]

The revolution, then, had not changed the dominance by men on the factory shop-floor and in the trade unions; indeed it was replicated in the factory committees which had sprung up in 1917. During the civil war, some women outside the main cities of Petrograd and Moscow had tried to set up their own trade unions. Though short-lived, functioning only in 1919 and 1920, and lacking the support of Zhenotdel, these female unions indicated dissatisfaction with the existing representation of workers which was weighted so heavily in favour of men.[76] This was reflected in the small numbers of women who had responsible positions within trade unions, even in industries in which there were significant numbers of female workers. Thus in 1921, only 16.2 per cent of union officials in textiles were female; 19.6 in tailoring; 10.5 per cent in the public sector; 8.7 per cent in chemicals; and 3.5 per cent in food processing.[77]

Indeed, after the civil war female membership of trade unions actually dropped: in 1922, the percentage of women in trade unions stood at 28.8, but within a year it had fallen by 2.4 per cent.[78] The trend, however, was for women to join, though slowly, existing trade unions. In 1923, there were 1,449,000 female trade-union members; in 1925, 1,752,725; and in 1927, 2,569,000.[79] Between 1923 and 1927, the total number of female trade-union members doubled. However, the number of male trade unionists also doubled.[80] Thus at a Moscow textile factory in 1924, women constituted 30 per cent of trade-union membership; by 1927, that had risen to 50 per cent.[81] Yet this was above the average for female membership, and reflected the fact that the highest percentage of female trade-union membership was to be found in the 'female' areas: in 1927, 55.1 per cent of female textile workers were unionised; 54.3 per cent in education; 64.1 per cent in health; 80.7 per cent in restaurants and cafés;

75. Ibid., p. 129.
76. Barbara Evans Clements, 'Working-Class and Peasant Women in the Russian Revolution, 1917–1923', *Signs* (1982), vol. 8, no. 2, pp. 215–35: 231–2.
77. Emel'ianova, *Revoliutsiia, partiia, zhenshchina*, p. 213.
78. *Kommunistka* (Apr. 1925), no. 4, p. 45.
79. Emel'ianova, *Revoliutsiia, partiia, zhenshchina*, p. 212.
80. Rashin, *Zhenskii trud v SSSR*, p. 22.
81. S. Lapitskaia, *Byt rabochikh Trekhgornoi manufactury* (Moscow, 1935), p. 132.

and 59.8 per cent of seamstresses.[82] In 1928, women made up only 26.1 per cent of all trade unionists; by 1931, that had risen to 41.1 per cent.[83] Except among better-educated, single women, domestic commitments meant that, whatever the growth in female membership, women's participation in trade unions continued to lag behind men. At the seventh trade-union congress in December 1926, a woman speaker noted that she was one of only 7 per cent of delegates. Another complained that, when women became literate, employers no longer wanted them. A third pointed to the small proportion of women workers promoted to responsible positions in the railways.[84]

Moreover, as Elizabeth Wood has pointed out in her study of class and gender relations in the 1920s, despite all Zhenotdel's efforts to work with the trade unions, the latter resisted appointing organisers who would specialise in work with women.[85] Their argument was that the interests of male and female workers were essentially the same, so that to differentiate between them would be to divide, and weaken, the labour movement. In practice, the trade unions reflected the interests of the male majority, notably in terms of employment, wages (with the man regarded as the family breadwinner) and training.[86] As Kollontai related, the struggle over this issue was fierce.[87] Nor was it simply a case of the male majority opposing Zhenotdel, since some female trade unionists, such as Anna Riazanova, not only feared 'feminist separatism' but were concerned that women's issues would be a matter for women only, and not be accorded the significance they deserved in the wider labour movement; instead, they would be neglected, and even ignored.[88]

This argument highlighted a dilemma for the Communists: they wanted to involve women in the construction of the new society on an equal basis with men; but they recognised that women had particular interests related to their sex, and particular organisational needs related to their low level of education and political awareness. It was also the case that female and male interests often clashed during NEP, especially over employment issues. Indeed, Diane Koenker has portrayed the shop-floor in Russian industry

82. Kharchev, *Zhenskii trud v SSSR*, p. 23.

83. Kovalev, *Istoricheskoe razvitie byta zhenshchiny, braka i sem'i*, p. 37.

84. Bilshai, *Reshenie zhenskogo voprosa v SSSR*, p. 126; E.H. Carr, *Socialism in One Country, 1924–1926* (Harmondsworth, Middlesex, 1926), vol. 1, pp. 392–3.

85. Wood, 'Class and Gender at Loggerheads in the Early Soviet State', p. 300.

86. *Kommunistka* (Nov. 1920), no. 6, pp. 10–11.

87. A.M. Kollontai, *Trud zhenshchin v evoliutsii khoziaistva* (Moscow, 1923), p. 157.

88. A. Riazanova, *Zhenskii trud* (Moscow, 1923), pp. 283–6.

in the 1920s as a 'gender battleground', in which divisions between female and male workers had increased rather than diminished by the end of the decade.[89] In her study of the printing industry, Koenker has identified three areas of gender conflict on the NEP shop-floor: sexist behaviour, including widespread harassment of female by male workers; efforts of the latter to sabotage any training schemes for women workers, which were underpinned by the assumption that 'skill' was intrinsically a male attribute; and the concept of the 'family wage', behind which lay the image of the male breadwinner.[90] To a certain extent, such hostility had been present before the revolution, reflected in women's complaints of the lack of respect shown to them not only by foremen but by rank and file male workers. Now, however, women's lack of skills and low level of political consciousness were held up as proof of their natural inferiority and as just cause for the refusal of men to train them.

Not surprisingly, the figures for women and men attending Rabfak (the 'workers' faculty', which was essentially an attempt to educate workers in preparation for higher education), and those who graduated and went on to college or university reveal that considerably fewer women than men attended in the mid 1920s; and that, while the drop-out rates were similar for the sexes, there were still far fewer women than men going on to either full- or part-time higher education. In 1925, for example, 303 women were full-time first-year students in Rabfak and 95 were part-time (representing respectively 16 and 13.2 per cent of the total number of students), compared to 1,603 male full-timers (84 per cent) and 625 male part-timers (86.8 per cent). Of those who graduated that year and went on to full-time higher education, 788 were men (85 per cent of the total), 140 women (15 per cent); and of those who went on to evening classes, 73 were men, and only eight were women.[91] Even for men, these figures were low. Yet the much poorer showing of women in Rabfak does not necessarily indicate a lack of interest in acquiring skills. Women proved particularly interested in gaining qualifications in the textile industry. Indeed, the reconstruction of the economy after the civil war began with light industry, including clothing, shoes, food processing and chocolates. During NEP, this

89. Diane P. Koenker, 'Men Against Women on the Shop Floor in Early Soviet Russia: Gender and Class in the Socialist Workplace', *American Historical Review* (Dec. 1995), pp. 1438–64: 1439.

90. Ibid., pp. 1446–7.

91. *Iz istorii formirovaniia sotsialisticheskoi intelligentsii* (Leningrad, 1972), pp. 64–5.

sector, in which female labour predominated, accounted for two-thirds of the gross national product.[92]

Kommunistka had pushed for the raising of women's skills and Zhenotdel had lobbied hard within the party to put pressure on trade unions and factory committees to include women. Yet both the journal and the women's department seemed to feel that they faced two almost insuperable obstacles: the resistance of men and the apathy of women. Thus it was not simply a case of men complaining about women, since female activists were also critical of what they saw as the continuing passivity of the bulk of the female working class. Of course, there was the other side of the coin: men sometimes opposed and prevented their wives becoming active in the labour movement, while the reforms of the marriage laws which had been intended to empower women had provided men with even more room for mistreating their women.[93] Women in unregistered marriages lacked legal protection until 1926. Whether registered or not, the ease of divorce was criticised by women workers as absolving men of responsibility for their sexual behaviour, allowing them to 'trade in' older for younger wives. In the face of low wages and high unemployment in the 1920s, women experienced marriage reform as an additional burden, deepening their sense of insecurity. Unwaged mothers whose husbands abandoned them were particularly vulnerable. Divorce for lower-class women meant poverty. A man's wage was rarely sufficient to support a family. If he established a second family and met his financial obligations to his first, both would have a low standard of living. Not surprisingly, men evaded paying alimony. Nor could the state simply take over the financial responsibilities of raising the children of divorced parents and abandoned mothers. Peasant and working-class women in the 1920s simply did not have the necessary economic independence to become Kollontai's new women.

Thus the working class remained divided along gender lines, in terms of the type of jobs open to women and men, wage scales, skills, and expectations, with women at the bottom of the ladder in all of these. As for those skilled women workers who were also political activists, such as Razumova, the trend was to take them out of the factory and put them into either the expanded public services or into political work, in both cases reinforcing the gendered division

92. Emel'ianova, *Revoliutsiia, partiia, zhenshchina*, p. 133.
93. See for example Wendy Z. Goldman, 'Working-Class Women and the "Withering Away" of the Family: Popular Responses to Family Policy' in Fitzpatrick *et al.* (eds), *Russia in the Era of NEP*, pp. 125–43.

of labour. As we have seen, even skilled women were at high risk of unemployment during NEP. Often decisions on redundancies were made according to a family's need, though the result was that more women than men were laid off if they had a family member working in the same enterprise.[94] Koenker concludes that 'as long as class was defined in masculine terms, as in the workplace, then Soviet women were left with few possibilities for resisting and transforming these attitudes'.[95]

Thus, too, although women's wages had grown in relation to men's since the civil war, the former remained considerably below the male average: in March 1924, the average wages earned by women stood at 64.4 per cent of those earned by men. However, in what were traditionally male industries, women earned significantly less then men: in the metal industry, they earned 49.6 per cent of the average male wage, and in mining, 42.1 per cent. In industries in which women were strongly represented, such as printing and the food industry, they earned a higher percentage of the average male wage (82.6 in the former, 73.6 in the latter).[96] Again, averages obscured the fact that women tended to remain at the lower end of wage scales, which in turn reflected the lower level of skills among the female labour force. Women's wages grew in the 1920s: in 1914, women earned on average 51.1 per cent of men's daily wage; by 1927, that had risen to 64.4 per cent. Yet that percentage was the same as three years earlier, while there had been little substantial change from tsarist times in the difference between female and male wages, since women in the 1920s still generally earned between 50 and 75 per cent of male wages.[97]

Many women, however, now headed families, due to the loss of men in the wars between 1914 and 1920. Indeed, there was a change in the age profile of women workers in the 1920s, with fewer young girls being employed, but women working for longer. Thus in the textile industry, the number of female workers under 20 years of age fell from 25.5 per cent in 1897 to 13.6 per cent in 1926; but the number of women at work in the age range of 40 to 59 doubled in the same period.[98] However, there was a drop in the numbers of women over 60 years of age who were employed, so that despite the

94. Margaret Dewar, *Labour Policy in the USSR, 1917–1928* (London, 1956), p. 139; Bochkareva and Liubimova, *Svetlyi put'*, pp. 135–7.

95. Koenker, 'Men Against Women', p. 1464.

96. Rashin, *Zhenskii trud v SSSR*, pp. 48–9; Yemel'ianova, *Revoliutsiia, partiia, zhenshchina*, p. 135.

97. Ibid. p. 43.   98. Ibid.

considerable numbers working in the previous category, female workers in industry were on average younger than men, which might help explain the higher wages of the latter.

Yet although there were still industries which were regarded as male preserves, job opportunities for women were widening in the later 1920s. Between 1923 and 1926, the numbers of women in heavy industry and transport doubled.[99] Before the revolution, the numbers working on the railways had been tiny; by 1927 there were 82,000 women employed by the railways, making up just under 9 per cent of the total workforce. Around a third were white-collar workers, including telephonists and telegraphists. Of blue-collar railway workers, women made up only 5 per cent. The gap in wages between women and men was greatest among blue-collar workers, where in 1925 the former earned about 70 per cent of the latter's wage; in contrast, in that year, female white-collar workers earned 95 per cent of men's wages.[100] Numbers of women working in the railway sector did not take off until Stalin's push for modernisation in the 1930s. Zinaida P. Troitskaia, who was born in 1913 and whose father had been a railway worker, became the first female assistant engine driver in 1931, going on to become the first fully qualified woman engine driver in 1935.[101]

Still, the major growth area for women workers remained textiles, with considerable growth in food processing, paper and glass manufactures. Certainly, there was expansion in the white-collar sector, but again women remained in the minority, and at the lower end of the scale. For example, they made up just over 16 per cent of both the public sector and postal and communications workers. Moreover, they were tending to congregate in particular areas which were deemed 'women's work'. Thus, in the latter industry, they made up 91.3 per cent of telephonists, and 46.5 per cent of secretarial and clerical workers. In the public sector, 46.5 per cent of accountants were women, of whom only 19 per cent had senior positions. Indeed, 70 per cent of public sector white-collar workers were women.[102] The same was true of education. Women predominated among primary school teachers, whereas in all areas of higher education, with the exception of short courses, they were in a minority. They predominated in courses training primary and music and drama teachers, nurses and accountants. Very few rural women

99. Emel'ianova, *Revoliutsiia, partiia, zhenshchina*, p. 134.
100. Rashin, *Zhenskii trud v SSSR*, p. 5.
101. G. Akopian (ed.), *Zhenshchiny strany sotsializma* (Moscow, 1939), pp. 69–71.
102. Rashin, *Zhenskii trud v SSSR*, p. 23.

took courses in agriculture, but considerable numbers enrolled in courses in handicrafts, reflecting the traditional division of labour among the peasantry. Moreover, once women gained a skill or qualification, they rarely sought to improve on it.[103]

Given their initial low educational level, this is perhaps not surprising. One of the biggest obstacles between the Communists and women was the high rate of illiteracy among the latter, especially peasants. In 1921, it was recorded that three times as many women as men were illiterate in the country as a whole; that 756 out of every 1,000 women in the population were illiterate, the vast majority of whom were peasant; and that among urban women workers, 56 out of every 100 were illiterate.[104] The Communists, particularly through Zhenotdel, expended considerable energy on combating illiteracy. Zhenotdel tried hard to attract peasant women to literacy classes, setting up crèches, or rooms where the children could be kept when their mothers were in class, or sending a teacher to the woman's home if she could not attend the class. Zhenotdel also set up circles for literate peasant women to pass on their skills. There was some success: whereas in 1921 only 244 out of every 1,000 women were literate, by 1924 that figure had almost doubled, to 440.[105] Yet the task was enormous, so that the rising figures for female literacy seemed insignificant, at a time when literacy figures for peasant men, especially those who had served in the Red Army during the civil war, had risen considerably. By the end of 1925, out of every 100 peasant women, only 19 were literate.[106] Thus in 1925 there were still three times as many illiterate women as men, and in small, remote villages almost all the women were illiterate.

Leading Communist educationalists such as Nadezhda Krupskaia believed that the spread of literacy among peasant women would have positive effects for their children as well as for the women themselves. Krupskaia had written in 1899 of the problems of child-rearing in the village. The work expected of a woman, whether in the fields or in cottage industry, was such that she had to leave infants at home, in the care of an older child or an old woman; breast-feeding would be irregular; and it was the practice to pacify babies by rocking the cradle until they lost consciousness.[107] Educating mothers, it was hoped, would result in a more rational way of

103. Ibid.   104. Emel'ianova, *Revoliutsiia, partiia, zhenshchina*, p. 185.
105. Ibid., p. 188.   106. Ibid., p. 189.
107. Krupskaia, *Izbrannye proizvedeniia*, p. 13.

childrearing, free of the old harmful peasant practices such as violently rocking infants, or giving them 'poppy' juice or the *soska*.[108] The latter was described by a French visitor at the end of the eighteenth century as 'a milk poultice, tied up in a long bag, at which the infants, left alone for hours, suck away' and on which they often choked.[109] Other visitors in the late nineteenth and early twentieth centuries confirmed that such practices for pacifying babies were still prevalent.[110] Yet in the 1920s it proved so difficult to attract physicians and qualified midwives to rural areas that, by 1930, almost 90 per cent of peasant women still gave birth either alone or with the help of a local female healer.[111] The country doctor Povalishina was a representative of the nineteenth-century idealism of service to the peasantry, whereas the new regime focused attention on the urban working class. This was reflected in the reluctance of those with medical training to leave the city, or, if they did, to remain long in the countryside. In his study of rural health care Samuel Ramer writes that by the late 1920s the feminisation of the medical profession was well under way, and that many of the women had family ties in the city which they were so unwilling to break that over 70 per cent of unemployed doctors were women who refused to leave the cities in order to take a rural post.[112] Not only were living conditions and salaries poorer in the countryside, but rural physicians still experienced cultural and social isolation, and sometimes encountered peasant hostility.

The Communists accepted that the revolution would only gradually win over peasant women, that only little by little would they begin to 'unlock their chains to the pots and the trough to which they had been shackled for centuries'.[113] In government propaganda, however, a simplistic contrast was drawn between the complete lack of peasant women's rights before the revolution and their happy lot under Communism, reflected in the sad songs sung by peasant brides-to-be in tsarist times and the joyful songs of the village woman who had become literate. The following 'before' and 'after' songs

108. Kurskaia, *Zhenshchina nachinaet zhit'*, p. 38.

109. J. Chappe d'Auteroche, *A Journey into Siberia* (London, 1770), pp. 351–3.

110. Henry Norman, *All the Russias* (London, 1902), p. 43; W.E. Walling, *Russia's Message* (London, 1910), p. 174. See also P.P. Dunne, 'The Enemy is the Baby: Childhood in Imperial Russia', in L. de Mause (ed.), *The History of Childhood* (New York, 1974), pp. 385, 388.

111. Samuel C. Ramer, 'Feldshers and Rural Health Care in the Early Soviet Period', in Susan Gross Solomon and John F. Hutchinson (eds), *Health and Society in Revolutionary Russia* (Bloomington, Ind., 1990), pp. 121–45: 135.

112. Ibid., pp. 136–7.   113. Kurskaia, *Zhenshchina nachinaet zhit'*, p. 25.

were included in a 1925 publication which was part of a series in the 'away with illiteracy' campaign aimed at women:

> Without a thought or a care
> they gave me away;
> my golden age of maidenhood
> has therefore been cut.
> Did they indulge and pamper
> me in my early years,
> cherish my beauty
> away from the sun,
> to spend the rest of my life
> with a husband
> in tears and sorrow,
> unloved and unhappy?
> My relatives tell me
> I'll get used to it in time:
> 'If you marry a sweetheart
> you might have even harder times'.
> It is easy to say that
> when you are so much older
> and compare yourself
> to someone much younger.

After the revolution, however, that miserable passivity could be cast off with the aid of literacy, allowing 'Tatiana' to become a commissar:

> She might have lived the rest of her life like that,
> threshing and cooking and washing
> like other peasant women,
> cursing her bitter lot.
> But new times have arrived
> and on hearing strange words
> her village roots began to crack.
> Breaking century-old chains,
> Tatiana, a common woman,
> became an ispolkom [executive committee] chairwoman.
> Other ordinary women scoff at this,
> saying that she would be better off at home.
> It's obvious these peasants are mistaken,
> and Tatiana is not interested in their gossip.
> Serious Tatiana has no time to listen to them
> when she has so much work in the soviet.
> All day long she fulfils the role of commissar.
> She takes care of rations, of the school.
> Only very late at night

does she rest after a busy day.
It is hard but Tatiana is not a coward,
and she really loves her work now.
There are many Tatianas. Black earth Russia
is managed by strong peasant women.[114]

Much of the literacy campaign's propaganda was based on such songs, poems and short stories composed by peasant women who had recently learned to read and write. They convey genuine expressions of joy at no longer being tied to the kitchen and wonder at being able to communicate with the world outside the village. As we have seen, however, despite all the efforts the numbers of literate peasant women grew only slowly, which retarded their progress in other areas. Writing in 1927, Krupskaia recorded that since the revolution women made up only about a tenth of village soviet membership, in contrast to the still low figure for town soviets of a fifth. Indeed, on the tenth anniversary of the revolution there were only nine chairwomen in village soviets, representing 1.6 of the total.[115] Yet there had been progress: whereas in 1922, only 1 per cent of village soviet members were female, by 1925 the percentage had risen to 9, and by 1927 to 11.8. The corresponding percentages for female membership of town soviets were 9.8 in 1922, 18 in 1925, and 21.4 in 1927.[116] One reason which Krupskaia gave for the gap between urban and rural women's participation in political and social activities was that peasant women were even more important to the village economy. She also argued that the low figures did not accurately reflect just how startling change had nevertheless been, and for proof she pointed to the large participation of peasant women in the recent congress of women workers and peasants in Moscow.[117] Indeed, voting records for elections to the soviets show that the political participation of rural women rose substantially in the 1920s.[118] Certainly, by the mid 1920s hundreds of thousands of peasant women were taking part in projects which were organised by Zhenotdel.[119] Yet it was still the case that by the mid 1920s the revolution had had an impact on the work of relatively few peasant women, and generally on ones who had no influence on the main village community. Nevertheless, however small the inroads

114. Ibid., pp. 23–5.
115. *Zhenshchina-stroitel'nitsa sotsializma* (Tomsk, 1927), p. 115.
116. Krupskaia, *Izbrannye proizvedeniia*, p. 171.   117. Ibid.
118. Dorothy Atkinson, *The End of the Russian Land Commune 1905–1930* (Stanford, Calif., 1983), p. 241.
119. *Zhenshchiny v SSSR* (Moscow, 1975), p. 9.

Zhenotdel made, its work meant that the village was not entirely isolated either from the cities or from Communist influence. Moreover, the Red Army relied on young male peasant recruits. As soldiers, they would acquire, often from female teachers and political workers, basic literacy skills which were now seen to be increasingly useful, as more opportunities for state service opened up to the lower classes.

Perhaps it was the position of women in the upper classes which best showed the levelling effect of the revolution, particularly during the civil war. Professional men and women could barter their services and skills for food and fuel, but often the wives and daughters of wealthy men had to resort to private trading, selling their personal property, and occasionally themselves, at street corners and in markets. A foreign correspondent who was in Moscow in 1929 described the sorry condition into which those in the upper classes, men but especially women with neither skills nor the opportunity to leave Russia, had fallen:

> It is Sunday morning and I have a rendezvous with a lady to visit what had been described to me as 'the most amazing sight in Moscow'. This is the great open-air sale of private goods and chattels in the Smolenski street, which is allowed by the government to be held every Sunday. It is a concession to private individuals who are so utterly broke that they cannot raise money by any other means. When I arrived on the scene I could hardly believe the evidence of my own eyes. Imagine a bitterly cold day with the thermometer registering 20 to 30 degrees of frost, and the ground covered with snow. The trams pass through the centre of the street and with tingling bells drive great lanes through this immense crowd. Furniture and household goods stretching for miles are piled up on both sides of the road, leaving the pavements clear for prospective customers. Outside this mass of junk stand men, women and young girls of all ages, mostly belonging to the upper and middle classes to judge by their looks and original demeanour. Here they stand or squat shivering in the snow for hour after hour in the hope of selling the few remaining articles left in their homes in order to raise a few roubles for the purchase of food.[120]

Yet formerly wealthy families sometimes managed to keep at least one servant. Although domestic service had declined during the civil war, throughout the 1920s there were openings, working for example for the nepmen, those businessmen who benefited from the legalisation of private trade within soviet Russia, as well as among

120. E. Ashmead-Bartlett, *The Riddle of Russia* (London, 1929), p. 207.

professionals and party leaders, and foreign visitors. As before the revolution, the vast majority of servants were female, generally young peasant girls who saw domestic service as their entry into city employment. Domestic service was seen as a remnant of tsarist times, and a reflection of the backwardness both of public services and of industry. Yet as a sympathetic observer, the wife of a foreign correspondent, noted, the lack of labour-saving devices and the lengthy shopping process meant that maintaining a household was such a complicated affair that any woman who wanted to work outside the home needed help in the home. Her own first maid, Frossya, was a young peasant girl:

> She went to evening classes for adults, and in very few years the ignorant village girl became a literate, citified young lady. When she had her own child, she brought it up according to all the modern rules of feeding and hygiene. She would not let her old mother take care of the baby for fear that, in old peasant fashion, she would pacify the child with a rag filled with chewed-up bread.[121]

Frossya clearly benefited from the revolution, though it is not recorded what she did on leaving domestic service. Yet just as before the revolution, domestic service still accounted for a disproportionately high number of prostitutes in the 1920s. Indeed, the impact of the civil war and then of high rates of female unemployment during the 1920s led to an increase in prostitution, which many in the Communist party associated with the continuation of capitalism under NEP. Two main groups were identified in the mid 1920s: those who worked where they lived, and those who travelled, often on the railways. There was a hierarchy among both groups. For example, among the latter there were some who enjoyed first-class accommodation, and others who travelled with the freight. Among the 'settled' prostitutes, some worked on the streets, others were based in restaurants and theatres. The latter were generally better off than the former, in terms of lodgings, clothes and earnings. As before the revolution, there were also occasional prostitutes who were trying to supplement low pay, such as domestic servants, retail and white-collar workers, especially if they had children to support. Since the Communist party had scrapped the tsarist 'yellow ticket' system of registration and closed down the brothels, prostitutes either worked on their own, or set up an illegal brothel-commune, in which they had equal rights and duties. What most distressed the new regime, however, was the prevalence of child prostitution,

121. M. Fischer, *My Lives in Russia* (New York and London, 1944), pp. 47–8.

which was linked to the problem of the deserted and homeless, the *besprizorniki*.[122]

Initially, the Soviet aim was to rehabilitate the *besprizorniki*, but the persistently high rates of juvenile crime led to a switch in focus, to punishment. Elizabeth Waters detects a similar shift in approaches to prostitution in the course of the 1920s, from regarding the prostitute as a victim to seeing her increasingly as integral to the corruption encouraged by NEP.[123] Indeed, Kollontai included in her definition of prostitution those women who had sexual relations with men in positions of power in return for material privileges.[124] There was widespread suspicion that women from the middle and upper classes were not only joining the ranks of high-class prostitutes, but corrupting the male working class by either becoming their mistresses or their wives, sapping their commitment to the revolution by their demands for material comforts.[125] Victor Serge expressed the general disillusionment of so many of the revolutionaries when he wrote of the period between 1926 and 1928:

> The sordid taint of money is visible on everything again. The grocers have sumptuous displays, packed with Crimean fruits and Georgian wines, but a postman earns about 50 roubles a month. Agricultural day-workers and female servants get 15, with their board added, it is true. Party officials receive from 180 to 225 roubles a month, the same as skilled workers. Hordes of beggars and abandoned children; hordes of prostitutes. We have three large gaming-houses in town, where baccarat, roulette and chemin-de-fer are played. The hotels laid on for foreigners and party officials have bars which are complete with tables covered in soiled white linen, dusty palm-trees and alert waiters who know secrets beyond the revolution's ken. What would you like – a dose of 'snow'? At the Europa bar 30 girls show off their paint and cheap rings to men in fur-lined coats and caps who are drinking glasses brimming with alcohol: of these a third are thieves, a third embezzlers, and another third workers and comrades deep in a black mood which, around 3am, breaks out into fights and drawn knives. And then, the other night I heard someone shouting with strange pride: 'I've been a member of the party since 1917!' The year the world shook. Here, on snowy nights before dawn, sledges are halted, drawn by proud thoroughbreds, their drivers bearded just

122. See E. Krom, *Prostitutsiia i mery bor'by s ney* (Smolensk, 1925).

123. Elizabeth Waters, 'Victim or Villain: Prostitution in Post-Revolutionary Russia', ch. 8 in Linda Edmondson (ed.), *Women and Society in Russia and the Soviet Union* (Cambridge, 1982).

124. Kollontai, *Prostitutsiia i mery bor'by s ney*, p. 10.

125. See for example Kollontai's novel, *Free Love* (London, 1932).

like those who served the playboys of Tsarist days. And the manager
of a nationalised factory, the wholesaler in textiles from the Lenin
factory, the assassin hunted by informers who are drinking with him
– all drive off smartly with some daughter of the Volga or Riazan
squeezed up close on the narrow seat, some daughter of famine and
chaos with nothing to sell but her youth, and too much thirst for life
to join the list of suicides that it is my task as editor to check.[126]

The higher rates of unemployment among women than men, and
the increase in divorces in the 1920s, helped explain the continuing high levels of prostitution and the prevalence of sexually trans-
mitted diseases, which in turn fed the anxieties of the Communist
authorities over the assumed threat to the collective of such selfish,
undisciplined behaviour. Besides the new legal rights which proclaimed sexual equality, it seemed that the only women to benefit
from the revolution had been urban working women. Yet even they
found that in the competition for work under NEP, both employers
and trade unions favoured men. Indeed, the latter remained the
bastion of the male working class, determined to protect their jobs
at any cost, including that of female unemployment. Ironically,
once Stalin had defeated his political rivals, his push for the rapid
modernisation of the economy meant not only an end to the unemployment problem, but a massive demand for female labour.

By 1930, the ideal Communist woman was both a full participant
in economic, social and political life, and an efficient homemaker,
since the state lacked the resources to provide the necessary services and the emphasis now would be on heavy industry. Ideology
clearly played a role in shaping that ideal, which few women then
could fulfil, but so too did circumstances and the legacy of a vital,
if diluted, peasant patriarchy. Arguably, the 1917 revolution and
the consequent civil war strengthened the peasantry in terms of its
weight in the economy and society, at the expense of a weakened
industrial and urban stratum. The Bolsheviks inherited a tradition
of authoritarian rule which they justified in continuing and reinforcing on account of the military assault on the new state until
1920, and the hostile international isolation of that decade. It
appeared very much a man's world, constructing a new order from
the ruin of the old while in constant fear of renewed intervention
from all sides. In her assessment of the legacy of the civil war,
Sheila Fitzpatrick suggests that although understandable in the circumstances, the reaction of the Communists in cultivating a macho

126. Serge, *Memoirs of a Revolutionary, 1901–1941*, pp. 198–9.

image and treating the party like a fighting brotherhood in the 1920s ensured that women inhabited a 'kind of second-class citizenship in the Bolshevik party'.[127] That image was very much for the younger generation, but Stalin's adoption of the five-year plan for industry in 1928 and forced collectivisation of agriculture in 1929 recalled the essentially masculine heroic ideals and qualities of the civil war, when they had won against the odds.

127. S. Fitzpatrick, 'The Legacy of the Civil War', in Koenker *et al.* (eds), *Party, State and Society in the Russian Civil War*, pp. 385–98: 393.

Epilogue

In 1930 the Zhenotdel was suddenly abolished, on the grounds that it was no longer necessary. Stalin's plans to modernise the economy and the opposition he faced meant that even the limited resources in terms of personnel and finances devoted to the women's department were seen as a diversion, especially since it commanded the less than wholehearted commitment of the party. Work among women continued after 1930, but it was not seen as essential in itself. Rather, such work was primarily defined in terms of the general tasks of the party and especially the needs of the economy. Stalin's stress was on discipline and order, and while women were expected to be as submissive as men in building the economy, the underlying assumption was that the changes wrought in the material base would transform the position of the former.

Certainly, his plans for industrial growth called for the employment of women on a huge scale. Soviet strategy for achieving sexual equality was based on expanding female employment and job opportunities. Yet throughout the period of Communist rule, there was still a sexual division of labour, women tended to be concentrated in traditional female occupations, the new areas they entered tended to become feminised, and men dominated in those sectors of industry which were more technologically orientated. Though female education by the 1980s had outstripped that of men, women's jobs were, as in the 1920s, generally of lower social status, with lower pay and inferior working conditions. Economic policies since the first five-year plan of 1928 had neglected consumer and service sectors, resulting in shortages and irregularities in supply which made shopping very time-consuming for women, who were still held to be primarily responsible for both housework and childcare.

In Soviet society, great emphasis had been placed on social duties and obligations, which in practice remained defined by gender despite official rhetoric about sexual equality and the high level of female participation in the economy. Indeed, in her study of sex-role socialisation since the 1920s, Lynn Attwood concluded that

212

the aim of women's equality had been used to justify the exploitation of their work potential, while references to nature as well as social duty ensured their continued service in the home and family.[1] Hence, socialism did not transform women's personalities. Instead, it grafted 'new' qualities, which were derived from paid employment and formerly associated with men, such as independence, initiative and self-confidence, on to traditional feminine, nurturing ones, resulting in the creation of 'superwoman and the double burden'.[2] Yet such qualities had never been exclusively masculine, as we have seen.

What seems to have been exclusively feminine was the double burden which in practice was made worse by Gorbachev's efforts in the late 1980s to restructure the economy (known as *perestroika*). *Perestroika* reinforced already existing trends in female employment, including the feminisation of certain areas, notably the service sector, while there was closure of childcare facilities, a much lower rate of recruitment of women than men into the privatised sectors of the economy, and more difficulty for female entrepreneurs than for male in securing financial backing.[3] El'vira Novikova and Zoya Khotkina conducted a survey during the Gorbachev period of office to discover why women in Russia accepted the double burden, and their inequality. They interviewed women in 1985, the year Gorbachev came to power, and again five years later, and found that the earlier responses had been much more optimistic. Gorbachev's policy of openness (*glasnost'*) had allowed a more accurate reflection of the daily lives of women workers to emerge, but had also led to calls for women to return to their 'natural' role in the home, which seems to contradict the actual experience of the majority of Russian women in our period. *Perestroika* had increased the practical difficulties which women faced in combining a job and running a home, especially in an economy not orientated towards consumerism. Novikova and Khotkina found that, objectively, most women wanted to succeed in both roles and saw the combination of family and paid employment as essential, for themselves and not just from economic need; but they had become so ground down by the problems of everyday life, especially under *perestroika*, that by

1. Lynn Attwood, *The New Soviet Man and Woman: Sex-Role Socialisation in the USSR* (Basingstoke, 1990).
2. See Chris Corrin (ed.), *Superwomen and the Double Burden: Women's Experience of Change in Central and Eastern Europe* (London, 1992).
3. See Mary Buckley (ed.), *Perestroika and Soviet Women* (Cambridge 1991), and Linda Edmondson (ed.), *Women and Society in Russia and the Soviet Union* (Cambridge, 1992).

1990 they showed a clear preference for focusing all their energies on the home.

However, the notion of 'choice' for a woman between domesticity and employment was at odds both with their ideal of a combination of the two, and with the sharply deteriorating economy and the high level of divorce and single-parent families. The conclusion to the survey was that in periods of extensive economic development, such as under Stalin in the 1930s, women's involvement in the workforce increases considerably, but in periods of economic difficulties and reforms, such as the New Economic Policy in the 1920s and *perestroika* in the 1980s, women are expelled from the labour force in much larger numbers than men.[4]

After seventy years of carrying the 'double burden' it is hardly surprising that women are exhausted. In much of the literature on Russian women since 1917, but especially in the late 1980s, the impression of their lives is one of constant grind, of no rest and little leisure, of struggling to bring up a child in cramped living conditions. Yet the women are seen not only, or not so much, as victims, but as manipulating their position as selfless 'martyrs', even by Western feminists. Attwood records that Soviet commentators by the 1980s thought that women had gone beyond equality to create a new system of matriarchy, under which men were the oppressed sex.[5] Even the double burden had come to be seen as a heroic self-sacrifice which gave women a form of power: 'woman can do everything; men can do the rest'.[6] Such a proverb, on the face of it, is in sharp contrast to the traditional peasant sayings about the inferiority of women; but implicitly women were seen as gaining only the double burden, only drudgery from their 'liberation'. Still, however much a victim, the Russian woman worker had also become an oppressor: by developing the habit of managing on their own, they had marginalised men, and by seeing the home as their 'kingdom' Russian women had been seen as partly responsible for the continuation of traditional gender roles.[7] Yet they were also combining a number of demanding roles, gaining self-esteem and satisfaction from the flexibility and ingenuity which such a balancing act required.

4. E. Novikova and Z. Khotkina, ' "A Piece of History": The "Soviet" Woman Today', *Journal of Gender Studies* (May 1992), vol. 1, no. 3, pp. 286–302.

5. Attwood, *The New Soviet Man and Woman*, p. 200.

6. Francine de Plessix Gray, *Walking the Tightrope* (London, 1989), p. 47.

7. See Susan Richards, *Epics of Everyday Life: Encounters in a Changing Russia* (London, 1991), p. 127.

Larisa Kuznetsova, who became co-chair of the Union of Russian Women (an organisation within the Communist party) wrote in *Rabotnitsa* in March 1990: 'Does that mean we'll go on talking to the mirror, looking at our reflection and moaning to ourselves about how hard life is and how tired we are? Of course, it's easy to hit a woman when she's already down.'[8] Down but by no means out. However few and isolated, there are women pushing for women's rights, while this examination of Russian women has modified the image of passivity and stoicism, with resilience and initiative. In 1934, A.D. Batova, who worked in the same textile factory in Moscow for over forty years, gave us a glimpse of her life through the intermediary of a Soviet scholar.[9] Batova was portrayed as suffering during the revolution of 1905, but as experiencing improvement in her life after the revolution of 1917, and by implication under Stalin's forced modernisation of the economy. Yet the claims for improvement were modest, since she remained a working woman whose double burden was at best ameliorated by better working conditions and pay, and more respect in the 'workers' state'. However minor that may seem, for the first time, even if indirectly, she was telling her own story, and had an audience to listen and learn from it. The recorder, who in the early 1930s could publish only if the work conformed to the needs of the state, as defined by Stalin, nevertheless implicitly acknowledged that there was continuity as well as change in Batova's life. Placing Batova centre stage gives us a different angle from which to view such poor women's lives. Batova inhabited and manœuvred within a patriarchal system, yet saw herself as a partner to her husband; and however essential her wages were to the well-being of their household, Batova derived satisfaction from working in the factory.

If we consider two female physicians who worked in Russia in the late nineteenth century until after the revolution, Yulia A. Kviatkovskaia and Mariia P. Rashkovich, it is clear that they successfully combined a professional career with intimate friendships and close family ties. For them, there was no contradiction between public service and personal fulfilment.[10] Of course, there were women who sacrificed themselves, whether for society or family, such as Olga, the wife of the peasant-worker Andrei, and the physician

---

8. Larisa Kuznetsova, 'Talking to the Mirror', *Journal of Gender Studies* (May 1991), vol. 1, no. 1, pp. 44–52: 52.

9. I.D. Kor (ed.), *Kak my zhili pri tsare i kak zhivem teper'* (Moscow, 1934), p. 11.

10. *Vospominaniia vrachei Yulia A. Kviatkovskaia i Mariia Pavlovna Rashkovich* (Paris, 1937).

Veretennikova.[11] Yet while they may be seen as stereotypes of the submissive female, whether to a patriarch or an ideal, they were not necessarily typical. First, the peasant woman Olga accepted her husband's beatings at a time when increasing numbers of peasant women were prepared to take their men to court.[12] As a lower-class, non-political (rather than apolitical) woman, Batova seems more typical than Olga; as professional women, Kviatkovskaia and Rashkovich seem more 'rounded' figures than Veretennikova, however much we admire the latter's idealism. As for those women who were professional revolutionaries, the social democrats Vera Karelina and Nadezhda Krupskaia, though from very different social backgrounds, seem more typical than the terrorist Vera Figner: both Karelina and Krupskaia were dedicated to the working class; both married men whose ideals they shared (and did not simply follow); both saw work among women as essential for the revolution; and both were committed to ideals and not just to their men.[13]

There was certainly continuity. Yet there was also considerable change, for example in the social hierarchy, particularly between urban lower- and upper-class women. The peasant woman's situation seemed least affected, yet she too saw developments, however gradual.[14] In the 1920s, the 'Bolshevik feminist' Kollontai had stressed the central importance of paid, or productive, employment for making women independent and personally fulfilled. Yet the mass of Russian women in the period 1880 until 1930, and indeed throughout the Communist regime, had always worked productively. Kollontai's stress was on freeing women from the domination of emotion, but most Russian women put family above personal feelings. Kollontai saw the changing psyche of the 'new woman' personified in the single woman worker who was totally reliant on her own abilities, and who rejected the customary dependence of women, described by Kollontai as one of clinging dependence on the male breadwinner.[15] Yet marriage in this period was very much

11. For Olga see M.I. Pokrovskaia, *Po podvalam, cherdakam i uglovym kvartiram Peterburga* (St. Petersburg, 1903), pp. 64–5. For Veretennikova see 'Zapiski zemskogo vracha', *Novyi mir* (1956), part 3, pp. 205–32.

12. See Beatrice Farnsworth, 'The Litigious Daughter-in-Law: Family Relations in Rural Russia in the Second Half of the Nineteenth Century', pp. 89–106 in Beatrice Farnsworth and Lynne Viola (eds), *Russian Peasant Women* (Oxford, 1992).

13. Vera Karelina, 'Vospominaniia: na zare rabochego dvizheniia v S-Peterburge', *Krasnaia letopis'* (1922), no. 4, pp. 12–21. R.H. McNeal, *Bride of the Revolution: Krupskaia and Lenin* (London, 1973). Vera Figner, *Memoirs of a Revolutionist* (New York, 1927).

14. See Beatrice Farnsworth, 'Rural Women and the Law: Divorce and Property Rights in the 1920s', pp. 167–88 in *Russion Peasant Women*.

15. A.M. Kollontai, *Novaia moral' i rabochii klass* (Moscow, 1918), p. 30.

a partnership of need, however skewed in favour of men. According to Kollontai, women under capitalism were weak and submissive. Yet, as we have seen, Russian women were strong though in a subordinate position. Perhaps the point was not the 'choice' of either work or emotion, family or individuality, since women were used to, and seemed to want to combine, both. Rather, they needed time apart from both to develop fully. E.O. Kabo's research into Moscow working-class life in the late 1920s included a detailed time-study of women and men at work, in the home, at leisure and sleep.[16] There was little of the last two for both sexes, but noticeably for women. What is interesting is that, while both men and women worked full-time, the former spent more time at work and the latter more time travelling to work, possibly because of commitments to children. Women, especially housewives, spent more time on the family allotment than men. Men spent more time on 'free' activities (reading newspapers, playing card games, frequenting taverns, attending further education classes) and on sleeping, and less time on domestic tasks, than women. Housewives had by far the least time for meals, leisure, self-improvement and rest. Seventy years later, little had changed. Vitalina Koval reviewed official statistics for 1989:

> on average the working woman has at her disposal only two hours and 24 minutes of free time (one hour and 56 minutes for those who work on collective farms) in every day. Most women (76.8 per cent) spend this time taking care of their families. On average women spend one hour and 39 minutes a day watching television, listening to the radio, or going to the theatre or movies. They spend 11 minutes a day raising their education level and eight minutes a day with guests or visiting cafés, and bars. As for the education of children, which incidentally falls under the category of 'forms of rest' in official documentation, women are left only 16 minutes a day.[17]

Ironically, the same solution was put forward in the 1980s as in the 1920s: the state should create services to enable women to combine their two roles successfully. However, it was also recognised in the 1980s that, for full equality, women and men must have equal starting positions not only in education and at work, but within the family. Like most of us, Russian women are trying at least to cope with existing conditions, and ultimately to overcome them. The

---

16. E.O. Kabo, *Ocherki rabochego byta* (Moscow, 1928), vol. 1, pp. 202–3.
17. V.V. Koval, 'Women and Work in Russia', pp. 17–33 in Vitalina Koval, *Women in Contemporary Russia* (Oxford, 1995), p. 32.

legacy they have, both tsarist and Communist, is one of endurance. Russian women, however, are much better educated and articulate than they were before the revolution, and indeed in the 1920s; and while they are still missing from positions of power, even more so after the fall of Communism than before, they can still make their voices heard.

Glossary

artel a group of workers engaged in a trade together, pooling their labour and income, and/or sharing living quarters and expenses.

baba a generally pejorative term for an older woman (such as 'old crone'); also grandmother, wet-nurse, midwife.

besprizorniki homeless, abandoned children.

Black Hundreds extremist, violent, anti-Semitic right-wing groups whose origins can be found in the backlash against the revolution of 1905.

Central Industrial Region the area where Russian industry was concentrated, covering the provinces of Moscow, Tver, Vladimir, Iaroslavl, Nizhnii-Novgorod, Kostroma, and parts of Kaluga, Riazan and Tula.

Cheka Extraordinary Commission for Struggle against Counter-Revolution and Sabotage, established in November 1918 as the Bolshevik secret police; renamed in 1922 the GPU (State Political Administration).

chinovnik a bureaucrat.

duma the state Duma was the elected lower house of the Russian parliament, set up after the 1905 revolution, in 1906; municipal dumas were elected town councils.

feldsher a paramedic, medical orderly, doctor's assistant.

glasnost' 'openness', policy associated with the Gorbachev period in office (1985–91).

Golos Rabotnitsy *Voice of the Woman Worker*, Menshevik journal.

gubernia a province.

intelligentsia a term loosely applied to all university-educated people, but especially those critical of the established order, both before and after the revolution of 1917.

ispolkom executive committee.

Kadets Constitutional Democrats, members of the Constitutional Democratic party, a liberal party established in 1905.

Kommunistka *Communist Woman*, journal of the Communist party.

komsomol Communist youth league.

kopeck unit of Russian currency: 100 kopecks to a rouble; roughly translated as 'a penny'.

kulak literally a 'fist'; usually a (relatively) rich peasant.

kvass a fermented drink, made from rye bread.

mir village community; also means 'world' and 'peace'.

muzhik peasant.

narod common or ordinary people; mainly peasant and working class.

perestroika restructuring of the economy in the late 1980s.

Pravda 'truth', Communist party newspaper.

Rabfak 'workers' faculty', or school preparing workers for entry into higher education in the 1920s.

Rabotnitsa *The Woman Worker*, Bolshevik journal.

RSDLP Russian Social Democratic Labour party – a Marxist party established in 1898, which split after 1903 into two main factions, the Bolsheviks and the Mensheviks.

rubakha (pl. *rubakhi*) long overshirt.

soska milk poultice used to feed and pacify babies while the peasant mother worked in the fields.

Soviet council.

SRs (sometimes Essers) Socialist Revolutionaries, members of the Socialist Revolutionary party set up in 1901, which split in 1917 into Right and Left SRs.

yellow ticket the document registering a prostitute, for which she had to surrender her passport to the police.

zemliachestvo regional loyalty or association, often of migrant workers; living and working in a town with people from the same village or province.

zemstvo (pl. *zemstva*) elected assembly of local government dominated by the gentry at provincial (*gubernia*) and district (*uezd*) tablished in 1864, as part of the reforms of Alexander II; provided a number of social services (notably elementary education and public health) to the peasantry.

Zhenotdel the department for women set up by the Communist party in 1919, abolished in 1930.

Bibliography

Rather than simply list all the works cited in the notes, we shall outline a selection of works which would be of interest to readers who wish to delve deeper into the subject of Russian women in this period. Contrary to established practice, we shall concentrate on the secondary sources published in English on the assumption that the majority of our readers will either not have access to, or not be able to read, Russian works. We shall indicate which books provide a guide to primary sources and Russian archives.

This study builds upon and is greatly indebted to Western, particularly American and British, works not only on women's and family history, but also on the social and urban history of Russia in the nineteenth and early twentieth centuries. While there is now a considerable body of work on Russian women, much additional information can be gleaned from the latter: David L. Ransel (ed.), *The Family in Imperial Russia* (Urbana, Ill., 1978); R.E. Johnson, *Peasant and Proletarian: The Working Class in Moscow in the Late Nineteenth Century* (Leicester, 1979); Victoria E. Bonnell (ed.), *The Russian Worker: Life and Labor under the Tsarist Regime* (Berkeley, Calif., 1983); Michael J. Hamm (ed.), *The City in Late Imperial Russia* (Bloomington and Indianapolis, 1986); Daniel R. Brower, *The Russian City between Tradition and Modernity* (Berkeley, Calif., 1990); William J. Chase, *Workers, Society and the Soviet State: Labor and Life in Moscow 1918–1929* (Urbana and Chicago, 1987); Mary McAuley, *Bread and Justice: State and Society in Petrograd, 1917–1922* (Oxford, 1991); Susan Gross Solomon, John F. Hutchinson (eds), *Health and Society in Revolutionary Russia* (Bloomington and Indianapolis, 1990); Ben Ekloff, *Russian Peasant Schools: Officialdom, Village Culture and Popular Pedagogy, 1861–1914* (Berkeley, Calif., 1986). Besides the information yielded in the index of such works, some contain articles which focus specifically on women, such as Barbara Evans Clements on the effects of the civil war on women and family relations in Diane P. Koenker, William G. Rosenberg (eds), *Party, State and Society in the Russian Civil War* (Bloomington and Indianapolis, 1989);

221

Elizabeth A. Wood on class, gender and the organisation of women workers in the 1920s and Eric D. Weitz on gender and politics between 1917 and 1950, in *Gender and Class in Modern Europe* , edited by Laura L. Frader and Sonya O. Rose (Ithaca, NY, 1996); Wendy Goldman on working-class women's responses to the government's family policy in *Russia in the Era of NEP: Explorations in Soviet Society and Culture,* edited by Sheila Fitzpatrick, Alexander Rabinowitch and Richard Stites (Bloomington and Indianapolis, 1991).

While not the first book on Russian women's history, *The Women's Liberation Movement in Russia: Feminism, Nihilism and Bolshevism, 1860– 1930* (Princeton, 1978) by Richard Stites is a seminal text, providing a fascinating as well as a comprehensive analytical survey of the position of Russian women. This social history manages to combine descriptive (and often gripping) narrative with concern for particular individuals and small groups. It also contains an extensive bibliography of primary and secondary sources which is indispensable for anyone wishing to follow up on the many themes raised by Stites. In addition, the new edition of 1990 has an 'Afterword' which discusses works published since the first edition.

Since the late 1970s, a number of scholars have built on *The Women's Liberation Movement in Russia,* both by extending the chronology and focusing on specific topics. In terms of women's work, a pioneering study was Rose Glickman's *Russian Factory Women: Workplace and Society, 1880–1914* (Berkeley, Calif., 1984) which stimulated an interest in 'history from below', in the lives of ordinary working women, both rural and urban. Christine D. Worobec's *Peasant Russia* (Princeton, 1991) offers a great deal of information on the peasant family in the nineteenth century, focusing on the decades after the abolition of serfdom (1861). This study enables us to grasp the centrality of women's role within a patriarchal society. It draws on a variety of primary sources, including court cases, government commissions and folktales and songs. Worobec has included a useful bibliographic essay concerning her primary sources, as well as a very full list of works on Russian history published before and after 1917.

The first book dedicated to the female peasantry was published in 1992: *Russian Peasant Women* (Oxford), edited by Beatrice Farnsworth and Lynne Viola. Again the starting-point is the 1860s. The collection traces both continuity and change in peasant women's lives to the present, casting doubt on the stereotype of the powerless peasant woman. Christine Worobec has also collaborated with Barbara Evans Clements and Barbara Alpern Engel in editing *Russia's*

Women: Accommodation, Resistance, Transformation (Berkeley, Calif., 1991). This wide-ranging collection goes much further back in Russian history, to medieval times, while *Women in Russia and Ukraine*, edited by Rosalind Marsh (Cambridge, 1996) considers the position of women since the seventeenth century. The editor's introduction to the latter, on women's studies as well as women's issues, is especially useful, while the themes covered include work, politics, sexuality, health and reproduction. A much earlier anthology of articles, *Women in Russia* (Stanford, Calif., 1977), edited by Dorothy Atkinson, Alexander Dallin and Gail Lapidus, contains a useful overview of women in pre-revolutionary Russia by one of the editors, Dorothy Atkinson, as well as chapters by Stites (on nineteenth-century revolutionary women) and Glickman (on factory women before the First World War), which prefigure their subsequent book-length studies, mentioned above.

The American scholar Barbara A. Engel has contributed a great deal to the history of women in Russia. From her many publications, we would point to two outstanding monographs: *Mothers and Daughters: Women of the Intelligentsia in Nineteenth-Century Russia* (Cambridge, 1983) and *Between the Fields and the City: Women, Work and Family in Russia, 1861–1914* (Cambridge, 1994). The first considers the relationships between upper-class female radicals and their parents, particularly their mothers, in the nineteenth century as well as the gender dimension to the revolutionary, and specifically the terrorist, movement. The second assesses the impact of social and economic change on peasant women, and the lives those who migrated for work forged in the city. The picture which emerges is one in which peasant women helped shape, and were not simply shaped by, the urban society and economy, though the conclusion, that urbanisation and industrialisation favoured men, is pessimistic. In both books, Engel includes a note on her sources, invaluable for anyone intending to research related topics.

Mothers and Daughters explores the lives of radical upper-class women who dedicated themselves to the service of the people by trying to overthrow the established order. Engel, with C.N. Rosenthal, has also translated and edited memoirs of some of these women, in *Five Sisters: Women against the Tsar* (London, 1976). There is an abridged edition of the memoirs of one of the five, Vera Figner, *Memoirs of a Revolutionist* (New York, 1927). Vera Broido's *Apostles into Terrorists* (London, 1977) considers the activities of women in the revolutionary movement in the 1860s and 1870s. There are also a number of relevant biographical studies: Jay Bergman, *Vera*

Zasulich: A Biography (Stanford, Calif., 1983); Barbara Clements, *Bolshevik Feminist: The Life of Alexandra Kollontai* (Bloomington, Ind., 1979); Beatrice Farnsworth, *Aleksandra Kollontai: Socialism, Feminism and the Bolshevik Revolution* (Stanford, Calif., 1980); Robert H. McNeal, *Bride of the Revolution: Krupskaia and Lenin* (London, 1977); R.C. Elwood, *Inessa Armand: Revolutionary and Feminist* (Cambridge, 1992). Barbara Evans Clements has studied two generations of *Bolshevik Women* (Cambridge, 1997), who joined the party before 1921, tracing their lives through to their old age in the 1950s and 1960s.

The first examination of women who worked for reform of the female condition within the system is *Feminism in Russia 1900–1917* by Linda H. Edmondson (London, 1984), which reveals that in Russia the vote did not become an exclusive preoccupation; indeed, the campaign for female suffrage began in earnest only with the 1905 revolution. It concludes pessimistically that the Bolshevik triumph obliterated the feminist movement in Russia. A work which considers one of the main feminist issues in the nineteenth century is *Women's Struggle for Higher Education in Russia, 1855–1900* by Christine Johanson (Montreal, 1987). Like Edmondson, Johanson points out that the majority of female activists did not join the revolutionary movement, but instead sought, with considerable success, to expand women's educational and employment opportunities. William Wagner has an interesting chapter on women and legal reform, 'The Trojan Mare: Women's Rights and Civil Rights in Late Imperial Russia', in *Civil Rights in Imperial Russia*, edited by Olga Crisp and Linda Edmondson (Oxford, 1989).

For women and the cultural history of Russia, see *Women in Russian Theatre: The Actress in the Silver Age* (that is, from around 1898 to 1917), by Catherine A. Schuler (London, 1996); *Russia, Women and Culture* (Bloomington and Indianapolis, 1996), edited by Helena Goscilo and Beth Holmgren. Two fascinating studies of women and Russian literature are *Terrible Perfection: Women and Russian Literature* (Bloomington and Indianapolis, 1987) by Barbara Heldt, and *Women in Russian Literature, 1780–1863* (London, 1988) by Joe Andrew. Laura Engelstein's *The Keys to Happiness: Sex and the Search for Modernity in Fin-de-Siècle Russia* (Ithaca, NY, 1992), which takes its title from the very popular six-volume melodrama by Anastasiia Verbitskaia published between 1910 and 1913, considers family and sexual relations, prostitution and infanticide, violence of husbands towards wives, the prevalence of and attitudes towards venereal diseases. As Engels does in *Between the Fields and the City,*

Engelstein considers the allure as well as the dangers which the city held for women. Related to the latter is Laurie Bernstein's study of prostitution, *Sonia's Daughters: Prostitutes and their Regulation in Imperial Russia* (Berkeley, Calif., 1995).

The bulk of the contributions to *Women in Russia* and *Russia's Women* concern women in the Soviet period. For a brief introduction to the history of women in Russia from the Bolshevik seizure of power to the collapse of Communism in 1991, see *Daughters of Revolution: A History of Women in the USSR* by Barbara Evans Clements (Arlington Heights, Ill., 1994). A detailed survey of the period is *Women in Soviet Society: Equality, Development and Social Change* (Berkeley, Calif., 1979) by Gail W. Lapidus, while Mary Buckley offers an insightful examination of *Women and Ideology in the Soviet Union* (Hemel Hempstead, Hertfordshire, 1989). Linda Edmondson's anthology, *Women and Society in Russia and the Soviet Union* (Cambridge, 1992), covers Russian history since, roughly, 1870, providing an assessment of women's contribution to Russian culture. Referring back to Barbara Heldt's work on women and Russian literature, one of the contributors to the Edmondson collection, Catriona Kelly, points out that pre-revolutionary popular, in contrast to high, culture, did not impose an ethos of 'terrible perfection' on women. Moreover, women held on to their domestic role, even as their criticisms of male attitudes grew in the late nineteenth and early twentieth centuries. It is refreshing to have the spotlight on lesser-known Russian women, and to have such a variety of social backgrounds and political positions to consider. The general impression, however, is of a striking continuity between the tsarist and the Soviet periods.

Finally, Wendy Z. Goldman's *Women, the State and Revolution: Soviet Family Policy and Social Life, 1917–1936* (Cambridge, 1993) which really begins in 1918, considers the impact of the Bolshevik seizure of power on women. It is a thorough analysis of the position of women in Soviet Russia from the progressive legislation of the first (1918) and second (1926) family codes, to Stalin's conservative 'reform' of 1936. Goldman examines the various attempts to impose a theoretical model of sexual equality from the top down, which depended on uncosted but implicitly expensive state intervention in society, onto a poor, predominantly peasant country, ravaged by war and famine between 1914 and 1921, by an urban party whose leading politicians had spent many years in exile. While women were given the right to control their own bodies through the legalisation of abortion, motherhood was seen as a social duty.

Of course, war, civil war and famine undermined family and community ties, while in the 1920s it was women and children who bore the brunt of the New Economic Policy, in terms of unemployment and discrimination at work as well as cuts in government spending, reflected in the great increase of prostitution and homelessness, especially of children. Goldman's study is a timely reminder in the post-Communist backlash against women's rights, of the ideal as well as the shortcomings of sexual equality championed by the revolution.

In terms of our Russian sources, we depended largely on published works, available either at specialised libraries in England (such as the Bodleian in Oxford and the School of Slavonic and East European Studies at London University), or the Russian State library in Moscow, the Saltykov-Shchedrin library in St. Petersburg, and Tomsk University. The majority of the works, both Russian and English, cited in the notes are available through the inter-library loan service, both within Britain and internationally, mostly from libraries in Russia and the USA.

The Russian Empire, 1914

BERING
SEA

N

EASTERN

SIBERIA

KAMCHATKA

SEA OF
OKHOTSK

R. Kolyma

R. Lena

• Lakutsk

nguska (lower)

SAKHALIN

gara

Lake
Baikal

R. Amur

• Khabarovsk

noiarsk

MANCHURIA

SEA
OF
JAPAN

Irkutsk •

MONGOLIA

Vladivostok •

CHINA

⌐ Manufacturing centres
◼ Heavy industry
+—+ Trans-Siberian Railway
—— Other railways

0   1000 miles

0   1000 km

Index